Assimilating Asians

NEW AMERICANISTS

A series edited by Donald E. Pease

Assimilating Asians

Gendered Strategies of Authorship

in Asian America

Patricia P. Chu

DUKE UNIVERSITY PRESS   Durham and London 2000

Printed in the United States of American on acid-free paper ∞

Typeset in Minion by Tseng Information Systems, Inc.

"*Tripmaster Monkey,* Frank Chin, and the Chinese Heroic Tradition,"

reprinted from *Arizona Quarterly* 53.3 (1997), by permission of

the Regents of The University of Arizona.

Library of Congress Cataloging-in-Publication Data

appear on the last printed page of this book.

FOR HELEN YU-LI CHAO CHU

AND WEN DJANG CHU

Contents

─────

Acknowledgments

In writing this book, I received guidance, solace, inspiration, and stimulation from many friends and colleagues. Molly Hite, Mary Jacobus, Dorothy Mermin, Satya Mohanty, Paul Sawyer, and Harry Shaw provided various seeds for thought at the formative stages of my graduate training, and I hope they will see connections between my work and their superb teaching. Srinivas Aravamudan pointed me toward a needed rethinking of "superstition," Mark Scroggins provided a trustworthy editorial eye, Gayle Wald encouraged me to address the suppressed topic of Asian women in the early chapters, and K. Scott Wong provided feedback and needed background material on the Chinese American chapters. In addition, Marianne Noble, Terry Rowden, and many of the friends acknowledged below read and commented on parts of this book at various stages.

Since my arrival at George Washington University, Maxine Clair, Robert Combs, David Hackett, Ronald Johnson, Jim Maddox, Daniel Moshenberg, Faye Moskowitz, Jon Quitslund, Judith Plotz, Ann Romines, Jane Shore, and Chris Sten have provided invaluable mentoring, strategic support, and friendship. With Edward Caress, Donald Lehman, and Linda Salamon, my department chairs have been responsible for leaves that helped to move this work toward completion. Miriam Dow, William Griffith, Linda Kaufman, Phyllis Palmer, and Ruth Wallace provided tips about leave policies at a crucial time. Constance Kibler and Lucinda Kilby provided additional help and humor in practical office matters. The book was written with the support of the University Facilitating Fund and the Junior Scholar Fund of George Washington University.

Sau-ling Cynthia Wong brought her sharp critical mind and sense of the scholarly terrain to my early thoughts about the book. Norman Bock, Shirley Hune, Elaine H. Kim, Lee C. Lee, Robert G. Lee, Walter Lew, David Leiwei Li, Shirley Geok-lin Lim, Amy Ling, John Liu, Lisa Lowe, Gail Nomura, Franklin Odo, Angela Pao, and Stephen Sumida welcomed me into the field of Asian American studies in their own, much appreciated ways. My debts to the conversation, and scholarship, of these colleagues will be clear to all who read this book. Most of all, Gary Okihiro has inspired me over the years with his generous mentoring, his high standards, his tireless efforts to sustain and enlarge the community of Asian American scholars, and his grace.

My special thanks to Priscilla Wald for taking much time to read this manuscript and provide the conversation I needed to make it into a book. My writing has been immeasurably enlivened and enlarged by her sharp critical insights, and I feel deeply fortunate to have found a creative, demanding reader who is also a warm and generous friend.

At Duke University Press, Reynolds Smith has guided me through the editorial process with geniality and skill; Sharon Parks Torian has provided much practical assistance. In addition, I thank the editors of *Arizona Quarterly* for permission to reprint "*Tripmaster Monkey,* Frank Chin, and the Chinese Heroic Tradition."

My family has been amazingly supportive and understanding of the constraints imposed by my work at a time of great difficulty. I particularly thank Virginia B. Ewing, Otto Chu, Victoria Lee, Lily Chu, and my mother for their courage and humor, and I honor the memory of my father, whose gifts to us all we can hardly describe. Arunakanthi Hettipola has freed me for this work by providing excellent child care. My daughter, Eleanor, has given me a new sense of connection with the stories I read and has transformed my life in other ways. Finally, I thank my dear husband, Lee B. Ewing, for sustaining me and our partnership through graduate school, the birth of our daughter, and the writing of this book, a labor of attention and creation that has lasted many years.

Assimilating Asians

Introduction
"A City of Words"

———

"Don't tell anyone you had an aunt. Your father does not want to hear her name. She has never been born." I have believed that sex was unspeakable and words so strong and fathers so frail that "aunt" would do my father mysterious harm. . . . But there is more to this silence: they want me to participate in her punishment. And I have.

In the twenty years since I heard this story I have not asked for details nor said my aunt's name; I do not know it. . . . The real punishment was not the raid swiftly inflicted by the villagers, but the family's deliberately forgetting her.

My aunt haunts me—her ghost drawn to me because now, after fifty years of neglect, I alone devote pages of paper to her.—Maxine Hong Kingston, *The Woman Warrior*

This is a city of words.

We live here. In the street the shouting is in a language we hardly know. The strangest chorale. We pass by the throngs of mongers, carefully nodding and heeding the signs. Everyone sounds angry and theatrical. Completely out of time. They want you to buy something, or hawk what you have, or else shove off. The constant cry is that you belong here, or you make yourself belong, or you must go.—Chang-rae Lee, *Native Speaker*

Lelia gives each one a sticker. She uses the class list to write their names inside the sunburst-shaped badge. Everybody, she says, has been a good citizen. She will say the name, quickly write on the sticker, and then have me press it to each of their chests as they leave. . . . Now, she calls out each one as best as she can, taking care of every last pitch and accent, and I hear her speaking a dozen lovely and native languages, calling all the difficult names of who we are.—Chang-rae Lee, *Native Speaker*

In Maxine Hong Kingston's family memoirs, *The Woman Warrior* (1975) and *China Men* (1977), Chinese American culture is introduced as a complex legacy of family secrets, a repressed history that haunts the American-born narrator.[1] Although the first volume seems to suggest that the narrator's primary quarrels are with her parents and community, whose methods of socializing her seem too Chinese and out of step with the family's life in America, the grimness of that life is gradually revealed to be rooted in the Asian American past in America, the invisibility of that past to mainstream Americans, and its consequent resistance to narration. When Maxine Hong Kingston broke the silence that had been punishing her aunt in 1975, she shocked American readers into recognizing Chinese Americans as complex subjects, subtly changing the cultural landscape for those to follow, but many of her readers did not immediately understand that hers was an American story.

The Woman Warrior is structured around the narrator-protagonist's struggle to overcome the injunction "don't tell," a warning voiced by her mother but also communicated indirectly by the mainstream American society surrounding her beleaguered ethnic community. (That society assigns young Maxine a "zero" IQ because she does not speak English when she enters school; its immigration officials reflexively reckon Maxine's parents, a classical Chinese scholar and a trained midwife-doctor, as illiterate.) When Kingston as author takes up the charge of telling the mother's stories and imagining the untold story behind her father's cursing in the laundry, she writes of a struggle both specific to her family and community and deeply American—a struggle in which speech and authorship are both symbolic of and instrumental to survival and the search for fullness of being.

Twenty years later, Chang-rae Lee's novel *Native Speaker* (1995) uses the story of a Korean American councilman's political aspirations as a metaphor for the political and cultural status of Asian Americans.[2] It asks whether a Korean immigrant, however diligent, charismatic, and gifted, would be permitted to represent the polyglot city of New York as its mayor. In the presumptuous rise and foreordained fall of the immigrant politician John Kwang, the narrator, Henry Park, witnesses the bitter realization of his own dreams of full membership in the nation, dreams that he, as a second-generation Korean American, has never dared to entertain. In the wake of Kwang's spectacular ruin, Henry's image of America as "a city of words" combines his profound sense of estrangement from its promise with his understanding of the nation as a product of cultural struggle, dire yet beautiful. In this marketplace chorale, the participants' very competition creates an unbidden harmony; the nation, like a novel, is built of competing voices. The metaphor of membership based on voice underwrites the buying and selling; indeed, this novel depicts the public buying and selling of one's voice and ideas as the basis for American subjectivity. Moreover, it interpellates readers into this same struggle. The shimmering unclarity of the pronouns *we, they,* and *you* links readers at first with Henry, regarding the street with posttraumatic caution, and then with a generic observer who moves cautiously, nodding to mask incomplete comprehension and perhaps intimidation. As readers, we cannot know whether Henry's "we" situates him—and us—among immigrants dazed by the cadences of a struggle conducted in English or Americans startled by the immigrants' transformation of their marketplace, for as a second-generation Korean American Henry belongs to both groups and neither. All that is clear is that as readers we share his outsider position by the end of the passage: "You belong here, or you make yourself belong, or you must go." If you don't already belong, you must make yourself belong, and to do that you must remake your self or go.

In a symbolic reconciliation of the drastic social contradictions his tale has exposed, Henry ends his story with the image of himself and his white wife Lelia, a substitute teacher of English as a foreign language, enacting her pupils' Americanization at the end of a school day.[3] Naming and labeling each in his or her own tongue, she hails each as "a good citizen" and sends him or her out into the city with a naming sticker, affirmative of citizenship and subjectivity.[4] Addressing us readers privately, the narrator calls their languages "lovely and native," asserting the Americanness of non-English speakers, but this Americanness is implicitly contingent on their learning English. The novel thus symbolically reaffirms the beliefs that it elsewhere denies—that these pupils of English will one day be assimilated subjects. Yet only Lelia is empowered to recognize the children and speak all their languages, while Henry, her husband, is merely her assistant. In the end, Lelia becomes the person who calls the names; Henry, newly silenced by the mob's rejection of Kwang, joins the "we" who can only be called.

To belong in the city of words, Asian American writers must call for themselves "the difficult names of who we are," must make a place in the American national literature where their stories belong. Because culture —specifically the bildungsroman—is a site for imaginatively transforming readers and protagonists into national subjects by erasing or containing their particular differences, Asian American literature reinscribes those differences in an alternative version of the genre, one in which authorship signifies not only the capacity to speak but the belief that speech—or literary representation—is also a claiming of political and social agency.

Hence, I argue that one of the central ideological tasks accomplished by Asian American literary texts is the construction of Asian American subjects through the transformation of existing narratives about American identity. To accomplish these fundamental tasks, Asian American writers have had to address the dislocations particular to Asian immigration, the average American's unawareness of Asian American history and culture, and the deeply entrenched presumption that Asian Americans are not American. Because these factors affect Asian Americans both materially and in their cultural production, they have also entered the literature thematically. The urgency with which these writers insist on their communities' Americanness is underscored by their repeated invocation of the trope of survival, a trope that transcends particular historical moments and links concerns about the communities' interdependent needs for material, cultural, and spiritual survival. Hence, this literature both foregrounds and seeks to resolve the contradictions of being Asian American in a country that has historically construed the terms *Asian* and *American* as mutually exclusive.

Using literary texts by Asian Americans, I discuss how Asian American plots of subject formation struggle to address the historical contradiction between a democratic rhetoric of inclusion and the realities of exclusion, discrimination, internment, and cultural marginalization. In contesting, subverting, and complicating the predominant models for assimilation (the ethnicity paradigms), Asian American texts do two complementary kinds of ideological work: they claim Americanness for Asian American subjects, and they construct accounts of Asian ethnicity that complicate, even as they support, the primary claim of Americanness by representing Asian Americans as grounded in highly specific ethnic histories in America. While these tasks may well resemble those undertaken in other American texts, I analyze the ways in which this literary tradition engages with a past particular to Asians in America, including the cultural history of orientalism, the legislative history of exclusion, and the internment of Japanese Americans.

In addition, I offer the first extended literary study of the *gendering* of Asian American narratives of assimilation. In my analysis, historical restrictions on Asian women's immigration and the formation of Asian American families, as well as differences in cultural representations of Asian men and women, combine to explain why Asian American subjects of opposite genders position themselves differently, and generate different narratives of self-formation, in addressing the work of assimilation. Though the era of anti-Asian exclusion acts appears to be over, cultural representations of Asian Americans continue to mark them as racialized subjects in ways that are heavily gendered, and Asian American self-representations are accordingly strongly shaped by gender and race.

Most importantly, I will argue that Asian American men and women of letters enter into an American literary tradition in which male and female authorship, heroism, and agency are figured very differently. Thus, when

Asian American male authors see Americanness as contingent on Asian American males' separation from Asian cultures and family responsibilities (embodied by women), and when they use figures of oedipal strife, paternity, and sexual competitiveness to represent their struggles for authorship, they are constructing an explicitly masculinized model of Asian American subjectivity based on established models in American letters. For Asian American women, the culturally assigned roles of materially preserving the family and upholding traditional ways pose multiple problems in their efforts to claim authorship, Americanness, and agency by deploying the same individualist discourses. Among Asian American women, not only do many face the "second shift" of domestic care and labor from dawn to past dusk — and would-be writers typically begin with less of the intellectual capital (material support, freedom from family responsibilities, education, and intellectual fellowship) described by Virginia Woolf as "a room of one's own" — but many women bear the additional psychological burden of being conditioned from an early age to see their ideas and experiences as unfit for narration or unworthy of publication — due not only to class and race but also to gender.[5] In addition, these women writers must respond to stereotypical mainstream representations of Asian women as one-dimensional beings, sexualized racial others whose function is to lend spice to other, more "representative" characters' narratives — when they are not excluded entirely. Such conventions, understood in conjunction with the positioning of women as symbols of landscape, society, and nation rather than active subjects, form a problematic framework for narrating and perceiving Asian American women as subjects, much less exemplary American subjects, in their own right. When women writers turn to the richly evocative, well-developed tradition of the female Anglo-American bildungsroman for alternative narrative models, they encounter a tradition, strongly established in the nineteenth century, of defining women's development in terms of their sexual success or failure. Such a tradition, although contested by many modern writers, including those I will discuss, defines yet another ideologically charged norm that problematizes female attempts to imagine autonomous striving and heroism in female terms. As a result, Asian American women writers cannot readily dramatize their own or their characters' Americanness by mimicking male constructions of Asian American subjects as outlaws, rebellious sons, or founding literary fathers; they are bound to challenge those narrative norms. In symbolically contesting their multiple marginalization from a literature defining American identity, Asian American women writers must develop a more varied and arguably more complex range of narrative strategies than their brothers require. This variety has led to their work being attacked and misunderstood by both white and Asian American readers.

By suggesting that it is both necessary and appropriate for men and women to adopt differing rhetorical strategies in the struggle for survival and acculturation, even in the second and third generations, I hope to illuminate the Asian American gender gap. This gap is most dramatically illustrated in the tensions between the Chinese American writers Frank Chin and Maxine Hong Kingston, and it is implicitly based on the premise that there ought to be a single common narrative of a community's experience, a premise I contest. Kingston remarked twenty years ago that the men's and women's stories in her narrative universe did not go together but that she hoped they someday would. This study explores why that day has been so long in coming and suggests that Asian American narratives of assimilation may transcend gender only when its influence on individual subjects is better understood.

Finally, I emphasize that these are *literary* texts by analyzing them as bildungsromane, novels of subject formation. Viewing the Anglo-American bildungsroman as a genre that depicts and privileges certain subjects as exemplary of the nation, I examine how Asian Americans rewrite the genre to register their vexed and unstable positions in America. In place of traditional narratives of the subject's successful socialization, Asian Americans stage what Christine So has called "an eternal moment of potential assimilation."[6] The present participle of my title, *Assimilating Asians*, marks the centrality of assimilation as a tantalizing but unattainable goal in this literature. With the Asian American re-vision of the bildungsroman as a focal point, I argue that the historical barriers to entry, settlement, and citizenship faced by Asian immigrants help to explain how material concerns about founding and continuing a family in America are transformed in the Asian American imagination into a literature about authorship and genealogy. Finding themselves without a clear place in American society, these writers have made the struggle for authorship, and for the founding of a new literary tradition, central tropes for the more fundamental tasks of claiming and constructing Asian American subjectivity.

My argument presents Asian American subjectivity as a dialectic between two mutually constitutive aspects of ethnicity, the Asian and the American. Mine is not the "dual personality" model in which the Asian American subject is rendered neurotic by the incommensurability of his Asian and American halves.[7] Rather, I see these two aspects of an Asian American's culture and identity as organically connected but requiring different rhetorical gestures. To be Asian *American*, one claims Americanness but reshapes conventional narratives of American subject formation; given national narratives that position Asian Americans as ethnic, racialized outsiders in America, Asian American authors respond by imaginatively inhabiting and transforming such stories. Hence, I argue that Asian American subjectivities in these texts are characterized by the emergence of a critical ethnic intelligence that deploys and interrogates traditional narratives of Americanization. In this literature, I argue, one proves one's Americanness by showing one's ability to question the idea of America, thereby fundamentally altering that idea for everyone else. As *Asian* Americans, these authors also construct representations of Asian ethnicity that are useful for their lives in America, sometimes by scrutinizing and rewriting accounts of Asian ethnicities received from Asian or American sources. These two gestures are examined in the two parts of this study, which focus on the making of Americanization narratives and the texts in which American-born authors redefine a particular Asian culture (Chinese) as a component of Asian American identity.[8] Taken together, the two parts should illustrate that the narrative constructions of American selves and ethnic cultures are organically joined in the project of creating a literature that is both American and transformative of established, implicitly Anglo-American norms.

The Immigrant Analogy

In using literary texts to consider Asian American assimilation, I am claiming both that Asian American differs from European American assimilation and that we can understand this difference by reading literary texts. Therefore, before continuing with my literary claims, I need to contextualize my use of the term *assimilation,* especially in relation to the existing sociological literature. To speak of assimilation or ethnicity is to use terminology marked by several generations of sociological studies modeled on "ethnicity paradigms" for race, paradigms based on the study of European immigrants' entry into and adaptations to American society. Led by Robert E. Park and his colleagues in the influential Chicago school of sociology, ethnicity theorists based their work on an ethnic relations cycle whose stages included contact, competition, conflict, accommodation, and assimilation. Within this theoretical framework, racial conflict, such as that experienced by American blacks in their migration to northern cities in this period, was generally explained as analogous to the experience of European immigrants.[9] This "immigrant analogy," and the ethnicity school's presumptions of progress for all, have been criticized on several counts. First, the model tends to promote complacency about the eventual resolution of deeply rooted racial conflicts. Second, the school's use of the term *assimilation* has been ambiguous and shifting. At times, it has implied an ideal of "Anglo-conformity," which required minority groups to adopt the norms and values of Anglo-Americans without any reciprocal adaptations by the core group; at other times, it has been linked with a mutual "amalgamation" of races and cultures, a social "melting pot" in which both the core and the minority cultures would be transformed into something new.[10] Finally, ethnicity theorists have been criticized for failing to distinguish between the assimilation processes of white ethnic groups and those of groups singled out for exclusion on the basis of race as early as the 1920s, when Park and Burgess published their founding definitions. As sociologists Michael Omi and Howard K. Winant have noted, ethnicity theory typically assumes rather than proves the similarity between white and nonwhite immigrant experiences through use of the immigrant analogy.[11]

Within this tradition, a useful analysis is that of Milton Gordon, who breaks "assimilation" into seven variables, notably distinguishing cultural assimilation or acculturation (the change of cultural patterns to those of the host society) from structural assimilation (large-scale entrance into institutions of the host society on a primary group level).[12] Gordon made the key point that minority groups could achieve cultural assimilation through their own efforts but that their structural assimilation, being controlled by the core group, might well be delayed indefinitely despite their best efforts.[13] Also helpful was the "cultural pluralism" paradigm set forth by Horace Kallen and others. This model of American society as a federation enriched by the distinct cultures of numerous ethnic groups provided a needed corrective to the Anglo-conformist model (now thought of as the melting pot), which equated successful Americanization with the renunciation of minority cultures. More recently, scholars addressing the persistence of ethnicity have persuasively described ethnic cultures as continually evolving to meet new circumstances.[14]

Despite these useful variants, ethnicity theory fundamentally minimizes the importance of "racial formation" as a significant organizing principle in social relationships. Here I use Omi and Winant's term designating racial categories and meanings as part of an evolving discursive network generated by a society's political struggles, one that has material effects on assigned racialized positions in the struggle (68). This point is evident in contemporary neoconservative arguments that deny the determining power of race-based structural inequities and call for minorities to address their problems at the level of individual responsibility.[15] By linking such "bootstraps" models with neoconservative policies based on the premises that race discrimination does not exist, or does not merit structural remedies, Omi and Winant explain the policy implications of the ethnicity paradigm as well as the reasons why a critique of that paradigm is urgently needed. The recognition of race as a significant basis of both discrimination and identity formation for Asian Americans is particularly important because of public perceptions that Asian Americans are upwardly mobile, not significantly affected by racial discrimination, and indifferent or hostile to other racial minorities — or, worse, that they compete with or help to exploit other racial groups. Such assumptions have long been contested by Asian Americanist scholarship.

In writing this study, I recognize the usefulness of ethnicity theorists' work in defining ideas such as assimilation, yet I also question the immigrant analogy. Although I recognize that Eastern and Southern Europeans, as well as Irish and Jewish immigrants, have also been seen and treated as alien races threatening the Anglo-American core of American society, I insist that American constructions of Asian Americans as inherently alien, unassimilable, and threatening to the core of American culture and identity are rooted in earlier, European constructions of Asians as fundamentally different and inferior. Hence, I use literary evidence to contribute to a growing body of work describing Asian Americans as a group defined by a common racial history. For instance, scholars have documented a long cultural history in which first Europeans, and then white (and sometimes black) Americans, saw Asians as radically different from themselves, a history that goes back to the racial constructions attendant upon European colonization and continues to be influenced by American relationships with the various Asian nations;[16] the history of immigration and other laws directed solely against Asians;[17] bars to citizenship based on the legal construction of Asians as "nonwhite";[18] the internment of the Japanese Americans in World War II (S. Chan, *Asian Americans,* 122–40; Takaki, *Strangers,* 379–405); and the persistent construction of Asian Americans as generic Asian scapegoats for larger social inequities in incidents such as the lightly punished murder of Vincent Chin by white auto workers in 1982 and the Los Angeles riots of 1992.[19] These and many other studies lead me to conclude that Asian Americans of different genders, ethnic groups, and class affiliations have sufficient common experiences and interests to justify the reading of "Asian American literature" as a cohesive body of texts emerging from a common history. Like Omi and Winant, I base my work on the premise that race in the United States is an ideological system of meanings constructed socially, as a function of political struggle, with material effects, but unlike them I do not wish to argue that it is more basic and central than such categories as gender and class; rather, it is a separate category that interacts with these but must not be subsumed within them. For me, culture is a central site for that political struggle.

Assimilating Readers and Writers

The reading, writing, and teaching of novels and other literary texts have a particular function in a liberal arts education, which I see as fulfilling a double role. On one hand, I believe that a school does function in part as an "ideological state apparatus" (ISA) for instructing citizens in "the ruling ideology" and preparing subjects of all classes to take their respective places in the system, as the Marxist critic Louis Althusser has suggested. In such a system, one's literary education in particular functions to convey both the official culture's accepted values and its sanctioned forms of subjectivity (155). On the other hand, it is also true that education is an essential tool for those who wish to transform a society and that literary education in particular may provide individuals not only with the tools of cultural literacy and expertise in critical thinking but also with access to narratives of others' struggles to survive in, or resist, oppressive public narratives.

My views of liberal education as serving both conservative and transformative ideologies are particularly focused on the teaching, reading, and writing of literature. Cultural critics have described how the study of English was initially intended to promote identification with English national culture among colonial, working-class, and female students, thereby reducing their motivation to demand improved political rights.[20] In the United States, the study of English and American literature, along with instruction in the language itself and democratic values, has long been seen as essential to the socialization of both immigrant and American-born subjects. Hence, the American literary canon has come to function as a site for debate about the nature and proper boundaries of American identity itself.[21] Since the first step in changing public thinking about these crucial topics must involve the writing of alternative accounts, my story about the writing of Asian American literature as a form of cultural struggle, and the emergence of authorship as a central trope for establishing oneself as an American subject, must be understood as part of a broader struggle for national and personal definition that is shared with other Americans.

In *Constituting Americans: Cultural Anxiety and Narrative Form,* Priscilla Wald contrasts "official narratives" about American national identity with personal ones, concluding that "National narratives actually shape personal narratives by delineating the cultural practices through which personhood is defined."[22] Stories of individual subject formation must fit, or at best challenge, recognized forms, which in turn are negotiated in relation to public accounts defining the nation. If, as Wald suggests, the author's narrative of formation is not recognized by others unless it is cast in a form compatible with established discourses (official narratives), the untold, "repressed" stories form the published narratives' unconscious. In poststructuralist theory, a child cannot understand and express himself or herself as a subject except through language.[23] Analogously, the author's capacity to write and publish a narrative of subject formation—that is, to position himself or herself in relation to the "language" of his or her culture's narrative conventions—determines his or her survival as an "author," a subject known through words.

Asian Americans' stories have also been shaped by official discourses, but their relationship to these discourses has been dominated by a double exclusion: while official narratives defined the very character of the nation in terms exclusive of Asians, Asian Americans themselves were also excluded in various ways from participating in public discourses.[24] In this sense, Asian American stories—both literary narratives of individual subject formation and the historical pasts of the various groups that collectively comprise Asian America—are themselves part of that which has been repressed in writing the "official story" of the nation.[25] Hence, in contrast to Wald's procedure of reading the untold stories behind the published narratives of widely studied authors, I generally read the published narratives of less visible authors as the stories untold, until relatively recently, in the "official story" of American literature. By providing paradigms for reading these narratives, I aim to bring into clearer focus the shared meanings and broader significance of this emerging tradition. However, I also suggest that a kind of repression is involved when a member of a marginalized group seeks to claim membership in American society. To describe this process, I borrow the psychanalytic term *abjection,* which has been expanded from its original use to describe the individual psyche and applied to the ideological production of certain groups as pariahs who, as outsiders, define and guarantee the limits of the core.[26] In my readings of Asian American male writers I argue that these writers abject the Asian feminine as a response to their own abjection as racialized others in the eyes of mainstream Americans.

Like Wald, I choose to read Asian American narratives of formation as literary narratives in order to emphasize how authors' choices are shaped by the discursive fields they enter, the audience they hope to reach, and the genres they adopt and adapt. Because literary texts have their own systems of signification, textual readings attentive to such systems can be richer and more revealing—or at least more accurate—than readings that treat artistic works as transparent ethnographic documents.[27] By considering these texts as conscious artistic creations, we can recognize the subjectivities of their authors. We can speak of the texts not only as fictive or biographical life stories but as strategic interventions in American literary constructions of race, ethnicity, and gender. Such an approach underscores the agency of Asian Americans as authors as well as the importance of authorship as the vehicle and trope for agency in this literature. With this in mind, I argue that the literary genre of the bildungsroman is a central site for Asian American re-visions of American subject formation because it has been accorded a place of honor in literary curricula that are, in turn, used to socialize pupils in approved American values. Although I discuss texts from other genres (memoirs, plays, and short stories), I focus on texts that do the ideological work central to the bildungsroman, which Lowe has helpfully described as a version of assimilation.

The Subjects of Bildung

In *Immigrant Acts: On Asian American Cultural Politics,* Lisa Lowe succinctly characterizes the novel as a site for interpellating readers as national subjects. Invoking Benedict Anderson's work on nationalism, she argues that readers of this genre implicitly identify with an "imagined community" of fellow citizens, a community defined by the reading of a shared national literature. In both England and the United States, literary canons serve as sites where individual differences are subsumed within unifying narratives of national identity and material social differences are symbolically reconciled. Within this canon, the bildungsroman is especially prominent, as it is

> the primary form for narrating the development of the individual from youthful innocence to civilized maturity, the telos of which is the reconciliation of the individual with the social order. The novel of formation has a special status among the works selected for a canon, for it elicits the reader's identification with the bildung narrative of ethical formation, itself a narrative of the individual's relinquishing of particularity and difference through identification with an idealized "national" form of subjectivity.[28]

Thus, the traditional bildungsroman socializes readers by inviting them to identify with protagonists as they strive to become good citizens of their nation, a task that requires them to relinquish their "particularity and difference." This formulation both sums up previous accounts of the genre's ideological function and lays bare a function that was always present but generally undiscussed: *assimilating* subjects. It therefore helps clarify why the bildungsroman is a contested site for Asian American authors seeking both to establish their own and their characters' Americanness and to create a narrative tradition that depicts and validates the Asian American experience on its own terms. However, the genre is inevitably transformed in Asian American literature because the Asian American subject's relation to the social order is so different from that of the genre's original European subjects. As I have suggested, Asian Americans have been precluded from identifying simply as "American subjects" by mainstream discourses constructing them as perennial outsiders.

James Hardin, the editor of *Reflection and Action: Essays on the Bildungsroman,* explains that in German the term *bildung* connotes broad, humanistic "cultivation" and "formation" and refers to an individual's development;

it is also a collective name for the cultural and spiritual values of a specific people or social stratum in a given historical epoch—and, by extension, the achievement of learning about that same body of knowledge and acceptance of the value system it implies (xi–xii).[29] Thus, the bildungsroman chronicles a youth's "formation" as he or she internalizes his or her society's values. The Marxist critic Georg Lukács defines the genre's central theme as "the reconciliation of the problematic individual driven by deeply-felt ideals with concrete social realities" (qtd. and trans. in Hardin, *Reflection*, xvi–vi). Lukács's definition stresses not only the process of socialization but the historical specificity of the "social realities" depicted in the genre; in this sense, it is typical of criticism linking the genre with the classic realist novel.[30]

Within the (ideological) discourses of liberal humanism, the classic realist text interpellates the reader by inviting him or her to identify with a particular perspective, as described by Catherine Belsey in "Constructing the Subject":

> The reader is invited to perceive and judge the "truth" of the text, the coherent, non-contradictory interpretation of the world as it is perceived by an author whose autonomy is the source and evidence of the truth of the interpretation. This model of intersubjective communication, of shared understanding of a text which represents the world, is the guarantee not only of the truth of the text but of the reader's existence as an autonomous and knowing subject in a world of knowing subjects. In this way classic realism constitutes an ideological practice in addressing itself to readers as subjects, interpellating them in order that they freely accept their subjectivity and their subjection. . . .
>
> By these means classic realism offers the reader a position of knowingness which is also a position of identification with the narrative voice. To the extent that the story first constructs, and then depends for its intelligibility, on a set of assumptions shared between narrator and reader, it confirms both the transcendent knowingness of the reader-as-subject and the "obviousness" of the shared truths in question. (52–53)

The classic text interpellates the reader by soliciting his or her identification with an imagined authority who speaks for the society, a Subject who transcends and subsumes individual differences. Poststructuralist theory tells us that the subject who emerges from participation in shifting, conflicting discourses is not autonomous, unified, or stable yet is ideologically conditioned to compose himself or herself as such: hence, the seductiveness and enduring influence of the classic text, which invites the reader to function as a subject by sharing the perspectives of another, idealized Subject.

However, various critics have described the Subject of realist fiction as a construct founded on the exclusion (some would say the abjection) of all sorts of particularizing traits and histories. For instance, the realist novel's dialogic conventions have been shown to define the Subject as an educated person, either male or ungendered, without other class, regional, or religious affiliation, through ideological conventions equating standard English with reliable speech and "marked" speech such as slang with less universal and reliable speakers. The realist novel typically places colonies, former colonies, and people of color outside the central action, while creating structures of reference that presume not only their presence but also (white, middle-class) national subjects' right to govern them and consume the wealth they produce off-site. Not only the subjectivities, the labor, and sometimes the bodies of blacks but also those of working-class people are rendered invisible by English culture generally, and certain people, such as working women, may be used as boundary figures to mark the border between privileged and abject people.[31] In short, the realist novel solicits our identification with an implied Subject who is both nominally unmarked by race, gender, and class and defined by the selective exclusion of particularizing traits. By erasing even the operation of excluding its others, this system of reference exaggerates the universality of a perspective that, when returned to its proper framework, defines by a process of exclusion and division.

Of course, neither the author of realist fiction nor his or her surrogate, the narrator, is the only speaker who represents the Subject of fiction. Like the Lacanian babe in the words, the reader of realist fiction must interpellate himself or herself into multiple positions within a single text, aligning himself or herself with characters' as well as narrators' perspectives. As the child's consciousness unifies the multiple positions he or she takes in language, the novel reader's subjectivity unifies the various subject positions emerging from the text.

In a related vein, a central premise of realist fiction is the identification of exemplary characters with a particular kind of interior life—a complex mental and emotional life signified in fiction by the words of an articulate speaker. According to Nancy Armstrong, this verbally constructed "interiority" became identified with the figure of the "domestic woman" in the eighteenth and nineteenth centuries as part of an ideological shift that conceived of family life as feminized and "private," distinct from a masculinized "public" sphere of economic and political competition. By constructing the domestic woman, the bearer of middle-class virtues, as central to the novel, English fiction settled upon a figure with which a broad range of readers could identify. In theory, anyone could possess fine mental qualities (like the heroines'), whereas few could possess a landed estate with an income of four or five thousand a year (like the aristocratic men whose pride they humbled). Armstrong points to Samuel Richardson's *Pamela* (published in 1740), in which an aristocrat's desire for his servant's body is supplanted by erotic interest in her *words,* as a key text in the culture's rethinking of identity: instead of being identified by outward traits (body, gender, class), Pamela is defined by qualities of mind.[32] In Armstrong's account, this represented a challenge to the former English social order, which defined subjects according to exterior class status; in presenting this challenge, the domestic novel played a key part in a general cultural shift that privileged middle-class mental qualities as exemplary. Because women presided over the newly separated domestic sphere, fictional plots concerning women, sexual desire, and marriage were perceived as unrelated to the class competition provoked and sharpened by the upheavals of industrialization; the "rise" of the novel and its central figure, the "domestic woman," who embodied middle-class virtues, solicited the identification of readers with those virtues because they were constructed as transcending the class divisions evident in the economic and political spheres. In both male- and female-centered novels, males eventually had to adopt the same mental qualities — frugality, diligence, Protestantism, postmarital monogamy, honesty, sincerity, modesty, forthrightness, compassion, and articulateness — which became the approved and definitive qualities of the emerging middle class, the novel's target audience. As these figures emerged in the English novel and its American equivalent, the sentimental novel, they came to embody domesticized virtues that were also perceived as definitive of American character in the nineteenth and twentieth centuries.[33] The Victorian novel's nuclear family would become a model for the middle-class, Protestant, heterosexual, hardworking family that Asian Americans, like so many others, were expected to emulate materially (by submitting to American law and the labor requirements of the economy) and culturally (by internalizing these values and, if they wanted to publish fiction, writing narratives showing that they had internalized these values, this sense of self).

Toward an Asian American Bildungsroman

Though Nancy Armstrong's documentation focuses on England and its class struggles, she and other theorists of the novel aptly describe how the realist novel and its subgenre, the bildungsroman, still shape contemporary bildung plots and codes for defining individual subjectivity as a well as the core Anglo-American values that came to be associated with Americanness.[34] For one thing, Armstrong's virtual renaming of English bildungsroman as the "domestic novel" emphasizes two key points. This genre, unlike that of the epic or historical novel, focused on interiority, voice, thoughts, and emotions, rather than public and heroic acts, as an appropriate subject for fiction. For Asian Americans, individual bildung, defined in private and domestic terms, would become the main material for a core body of literature partly because many Asian Americans found this primary level of their experience written out of the mainstream culture. For writers, mastering the genre's rich and subtle range for representing individual experience would provide a way both to establish a character's or narrator's complex interiority and to demonstrate one's mastery of American culture.[35]

Second, the novel partipated in the culture's ideological separation of private and public spheres by representing class conflicts in seemingly apolitical forms as domestic plots. Not only could cross-class marriages symbolize the needed reconciliation of the upper and middle classes in England in a privatized fictional realm, but the emergent class struggles between factory owners and workers, and disagreements between hard-nosed and soft-hearted ideologues about the proper responses to them, were rewritten as gendered, romantic differences in "industrial novels" in which humane heroines tempered hard-edged capitalists.[36] Whereas males were too precisely marked by class, profession, and faction, the domestic novel produced an idealized woman with whom readers could identify and who could therefore become the heart of a broader imagined community—a nation—that subsumed class differences.

For Asian Americans, this separation of spheres and the possibility of coding political conflict in private, domestic, or sentimental terms would be all the more important because Asian Americans write for audiences that generally know little of Asian American histories and do not necessarily share the writers' perspectives on issues of race and nation. Thus, an Asian American's historical novel about Korean, Filipino, or Japanese nationalism, for instance, would have been more difficult to sell to readers who did not share Asian or Asian American frames of reference. (Consider, for instance, the relative invisibility of Vietnamese works about the Vietnam War.)[37] Similarly, Asian American literature about white racism has generally been less successful than literature that omits such themes, about which authors and audience might not share either a consensus or even a comparable base of experience and information.[38] My claim is not that Asian Americans eschew political or historical novels; it is that in writing such novels the authors must either find a frame of reference accessible and acceptable to "mainstream" Americans or accept a smaller audience and continued invisibility; one such frame is the familiar, ostensibly depoliticized narrative of formation. Asian American writers therefore turn to the bildungsroman for a repertoire of representational conventions that purport to transcend such political differences while providing an idiom for addressing them indirectly. This is why, for instance, we see critiques of racism and class exploitation beautifully clothed in rhetorics of liberalism and individual bildung (emphasizing self-knowledge, self-determination, and the desire for truth and justice) in the works of early, activist writers such as Edith Eaton (1865–1914) and Carlos Bulosan (1911?–56), who lived and wrote in periods when anti-Chinese and anti-Filipino racism was widely accepted and unions were seen as un-American.[39]

Adapting Womens' Plots

The presence of a vital tradition of female bildungsroman in English is particularly helpful to me as a critic and, I believe, to these writers.[40] For instance, a female bildungsroman is typically characterized by tension between female development (connected, intersubjective, concerned with mutual nurturance and intimacy) and male paradigms (which emphasize separation, autonomy, and competition). Some women authors have captured this tension between masculine and feminine norms by composing double-voiced narratives that challenged the narrative conventions of unity in various ways such as encoding a socially rebellious plot within a conventional surface narrative, invoking but revising traditional myths or fairy tales, or linking a plot of development with a plot that unravels it. Other strategies include emphasizing women's development in conjunction with other women or conceiving a "collective protagonist" whose identity is wrapped up with others, to communicate the perception that women define their selves more relationally than men; and recognizing that women's conflicts, while not absolutely different from men's, may be more relentless. Thus, female protagonists may pay a higher price for reconciling tensions between inner concentration and external socialization, sexual expression and restraint, or madness and normality.

Both in women's narratives and in the criticism describing them, the sense of grappling with norms for self-formation that are unsuitable or inimical to one's own possibilities and aims forms a crucial model for my own readings, which pit Asian American values and selfhood (typically conveying greater concern with community and family) against the individualist norms that, as we have seen, are presumed to define human, American, and universal experience, while (as critics argue) they in fact frame the novel in a white, male, Western perspective. On the other hand, a division also exists between the genders in Asian American narrative. As suggested earlier, the men internalize and adapt existing paradigms centering on male subjectivity, including a male tradition that specifically rejects the "domestic" novel and its feminized values, while the women adopt strategies shared by women writers of other races. Yet, writers of both sexes use strategies found in women's writing, no doubt because these are basic strategies for challenging or decentering the Anglo-American presence in the genre. For instance, my reading of Carlos' Bulosan's autobiographical novel is based on the premise of two plots, one a "conventional" plot of development and one a "rebellious" indictment of racism. The invocation and subversion of traditional plots and myths is central to the work of Edith Maude Eaton, Bharati Mukherjee, and Maxine Hong Kingston; and the sense of assimilation as a process that unravels as it seems to progress underlies numerous texts, including those of Chang-rae Lee, John Okada, and Mukherjee.

The tension between individualism and an intersubjective sense of self, which is arguably the central tension of female bildungsroman, is present for all the Asian American writers I discuss. Despite their different ethnicities (Korean, Filipino, Japanese, Chinese, and Indian American), the tension in these works comes from the Asian sense of the self as rooted in family and community and the American sense of the self as an autonomous being, free to move from place to place.[41] As we have seen, feminist critics perceive the same distinction as a gender difference within Anglo-American bildungsroman, with the result that the genre itself is a form for examining (and symbolically reconciling) this tension within women's texts. Part of assimilation, for Asian American writers, is the invention of a bildungsroman that describes a subject who combines independence, mobility and outspokenness with a deep sense of affinity with familial and communal others; as a group, these texts work to affirm that both halves of this equation are American and both are Asian.[42] While others have focused on plots of second-generation separation and independence, however, my study questions the Asian American recasting of marriage plots.

The Missing Plot

Because marriage plots are central to gender construction in traditional bildungsromane, their absence or transformation in Asian American narratives may also be read as the authors' rethinking of gender roles in light of the group's vexed relationships with national identity.[43] In particular, Asian American texts tend to avoid the utopian "well-married hero" plot, in which the male or female subject's moral and social progress is figured in terms of romantic choices that culminate in marriage. In America, marriage is a key site for representing the immigrant's Americanization, "emblematic of the promise of America to replace descent with consent relationships" (Wald, *Constituting*, 279, 348–49, n. 63; Sollors, *Ethnicity*). Implicit in such plots is the use of marriage to signify the individual's reconciliation with the social order. Such marriages, placed at the ends of novels, imply the completion of the protagonist's moral education; in Lowe's terms, which are indebted to Louis Althusser, these marriages signify the successful interpellation of the subject into the nation-state.

Marriage, however, has historically been a site where American legislators and cultural discourses have sought to inscribe the rejection of Asian immigrants as potential citizens. Exclusion-era laws distorted and pressured Asian American family structures by preventing many Asian women from following their countrymen into the United States, miscegenation laws outlawed interracial matches in many states, and cultural representations from that time to the present have signaled hostility to Asians in their problematic representations of Asian-white romantic liaisons. Hence, the conventional, ostensibly race-blind courtship plots that often drove Anglo-American bildungsromane do not obviously fit the real or imagined processes of Asian American subject formation. What, then, replaces marriage as the telos for bildung in this literature? As we shall see, Asian American writers join other Americans in avoiding and criticizing the well-married hero plot, but their alienation from this plot is sharpened by mainstream constructions of them as aliens: their critique is cast in racial terms. Within the codes of the bildungsroman, Asian American protagonists generally can't appear as well-married heroes because marriage would signify their successful integration into the nation, a full assimilation that has not yet occurred either in fact or in the symbolic realm of mainstream culture. Hence, other narratives take the place of the well-married hero paradigm: the "immigrant romance," which recounts the protagonist's search for a white partner to Americanize him or her; the abjection of the Asian mother; the construction of Asian Americans as artist-sons engaged in oedipal struggles; and the figuring of Asian American women as sentimental heroines, brave immigrant foremothers, devoted daughters, and postmodernist authors. In substituting authorship for marriage as a central trope for representing Asian American subject formation, these authors remake the bildungsroman to fit the stories they have to tell.

Myths of Americanization

Given the importance of courtship plots in the bildungsroman, it is not surprising that American ethnic texts sometimes use interethnic or interracial romances to depict the assimilation of ethnic or racial "others" into American society, as ethnicity scholars Werner Sollors and Mary Dearborn have noted.[44] For Asian American authors, interracial romance plots also function as sites for negotiating the formation of ethnic American identities, but the dystopian outcomes that tend to dominate interracial love in this literature suggest fundamental skepticism about the Asian American subject's possibilities for assimilation, skepticism that seems rooted in the historic positioning of Asian Americans as racially marked outsiders. My study, therefore, uses interracial plots in Asian American texts to discuss their interarticulation of race and gender in defining Asian American subjects. Whereas men and women writers both depict interracial romance and its implicit promise of Americanization as deeply problematic, distinctly gendered versions of these narratives emerge, suggesting strongly gendered differences in the complex process of Asian American subject formation.

In addition to appearing as symbols of the American landscape and potential trophies of successful assimilation, white women serve as cultural mediators, instructors, gatekeepers, and sometime adversaries in Asian male immigrants' tales of Americanization. The rhetorical functions of white women and the construction of the immigrant romance form the basis of my examination of the works of early immigrant authors Younghill Kang (1903–72, Korean American) and Carlos Bulosan (1911?–56, Filipino American). The functions served by white women in these texts must be understood in light of the close connections Kang and Bulosan make between authorship, Americanness, and masculinity.

By contrast, Asian women in the men's texts are used to represent aspects of the authors' homeland or ancestral culture that are abjected from the male protagonists, the better to establish their Americanness. By attributing these traits to Asian women and dissociating them from the protagonists, such texts implicitly construct Asian American subjectivity as masculine. Such constructions, which I locate both in Bulosan's work and in the novels of John Okada (1923–71, Japanese American) and Milton Murayama (1923– , Japanese American), are continued in the works of other male authors and ultimately are contested by Asian American women.

Next I consider the implications of Asian American men's marginalization in the works of contemporary writers Frank Chin (1940– , Chinese American) and David Mura (1952– , Japanese American). Both claim Americanness by casting themselves as author-heroes in an implicitly male narrative, one that defines their American character in terms of authorial integrity, oedipal rebellion, and the founding (or "fathering") of a literary tradition. Because both Chin and Mura purport to speak not only for themselves but for their ethnic communities, their masculinization of the key trope of authorship raises serious questions about the position of women as Asian American subjects and authors in an emerging canon, one in which five of these authors—Bulosan, Okada, Murayama, Chin, and Mura—have arguably attained a significant, anchoring presence.

Inevitably, Asian American women have written back. Two writers, in particular, both challenge and revise male narratives and generate counternarratives, refiguring American authorship, family formation, and self-construction in feminist terms. Working against the grain of both white and male immigrant representations of Asian women was a necessity for Edith Maude Eaton, who published under the pseudonym Sui Sin Far (1865–1914, Chinese Eurasian), one of the first Asian American women writers. To situate her work, I draw upon the early-twentieth-century poetry of male Cantonese immigrants (edited and translated by Marlon K. Hom from collections published in 1911 and 1915) to show how these "bachelors," physically isolated from their female relatives in China and required by American society to both Americanize (adapt) and remain Chinese (remain socially and economically segregated), respond by projecting this social contradiction symbolically onto their representations of Chinese women. The need to challenge and revise this discursive practice is evident in Eaton's short stories, which describe the immigrant romance from a feminist perspective, and her autobiographical essay, which claims authorship, Americanness, and ethnicity for Asian American women by reconceiving authorship as an expression of filial devotion, an act of cultural mediation, and an assertion of Asian American female subjectivity.[45]

In *Jasmine*, Bharati Mukherjee (1940– , Indian American) also revises the interracial immigrant romance from the Asian woman's point of view, illustrating why women's assimilation narratives differ from men's. Here, the immigrant woman's Americanization is accomplished with the help of white romantic partners, but in order to win their support the woman must submit to their alienating and sanitizing preconceptions of her, thereby renouncing the very past that renders her unique. Because the novel's apparent celebration of this kind of assimilation is grounded in allusions to the English bildungsroman, it illustrates the hazards of adapting the genre as a model for inscribing Asian American female subjectivities.

For both Eaton and Mukherjee, the bildungsroman's celebration of the virtuous "domestic woman" provides useful narrative models for resisting marginalization by creating accessible, sympathetic images of Asian immigrant women as assimilable Americans. However, neither author entirely escapes the genre's tendency to equate feminist consciousness and agency with first world women and fatalist or passive positions with third world women. It remains, then, for other writers to reconstitute Asian female subjectivity as a positive term in its own right rather than the negative half of the Asian American subject.

Chinese American Ethnicities

Following my description of the narrative constitution of Asian Americans as American subjects, I examine how specific texts challenge and complicate that model of subjectivity. In doing so, I focus on the Asian American preoccupation with reconstructing an Asian American past as a response to Asians' historical exclusion and cultural marginalization from the American mainstream. For such writers, the Asian American past becomes a term that works in various ways to mediate or complicate the task of assimilation. At the same time, the very different pasts being constituted by these writers undermine the conventional notion of Asian America as a single coherent subject. Not only are these pasts divided by differences in nations of origin, but within ethnic groups further distinctions arise as a result of class, region, period and circumstances of immigration, and the authors' ideological agendas. To explore one aspect of this diversity, I turn to three Chinese Americans and their various representations of "China." Focusing on Amy Tan (1952–), Frank Chin (1940–), and Maxine Hong Kingston (1940–), I argue that each author reconstructs *China* and *Chinese ethnicity* as terms that mediate his or her exploration of the problem of assimilation. In this sense, the imagined ancestral past serves rhetorical functions similar to those served by the women examined earlier.

Amy Tan uses Chinese immigrant mothers and modern China as a fictional backdrop to construct Chinese ethnicity in *The Joy Luck Club,* a novel whose multiple narratives construct both mothers and daughters as Asian American subjects. From the mothers' perspective, Tan rewrites the immigrant romance, in which white Americans represent America, by making the immigrant women's *daughters* the primary focus of their desires. In her mother-daughter romance, Chinese American daughters represent America and Americanization for their mothers. From the daughters' perspective, Tan's immigrant mothers serve a range of rhetorical functions whose apparently contradictory nature complexly registers and negotiates the range of contemporary American attitudes toward China. For Tan, as for other Asian American authors, the Chinese mother-woman embodies aspects of Asian ethnicity that she seeks to incorporate into a larger narrative of Asian American identity. The novel's Chinese mothers are presented as mythic, essentialized forces of nature; as witnesses and victims of a backward, oppressive, ahistorical culture; as feminist tricksters and critics of American orientalism; and as the empowering sources for Asian American feminist consciousness. The variety of these mother-daughter positionings conveys the contradictory mainstream attitudes that Chinese American daughters must negotiate in their personal rites of Asian American subject formation, but ultimately, I argue, this text demonstrates Tan's deft internalization of these shifting and evolving attitudes rather than a radical revision.

To locate such a revision, I turn to the longstanding debate between Frank Chin and Maxine Hong Kingston about the appropriate use and meaning of Chinese classics in defining Chinese American culture and subjectivity. For both authors, the Chinese "heroic tradition" fills a symbolic void; each reconstitutes this tradition to stand for an idealized Chinese American masculinity that is otherwise absent from American culture. By mapping the numerous ways in which Kingston's novel brings the heroic tradition into Chinese American culture and engages with her critics, while also reconceiving the very ideas of tradition and authorship, I emphasize both the importance of gender in explaining the authors' differences, and the fluid and instrumental nature of "Chinese" culture in the Chinese American context.[46]

With varying degrees of success, Tan, Chin, and Kingston construct *Chinese ethnicity* as a positive term that mediates their portrayals of Chinese American bildung. Tan's reinvention of the immigrant romance as a mother-daughter romance illustrates the various, conflicting, American perceptions of China and Chinese women that mark her moment of composition and publication. Finally, the Chin-Kingston debate about the Chinese classics demonstrates the evolution of Chinese American cultural nationalism, just as Kingston's brilliant literary performance legitimates her creative manipulations of Chinese texts to celebrate and question, but not to lament, the fluid and evolving culture of Chinese America.

ONE

Myths of Americanization

1

America in the Heart:
Political Desire in Younghill Kang, Carlos Bulosan,
Milton Murayama, and John Okada

Trip seemed a dream, or if real, hidden now by all the obstacles of fate, time, space, and the world. But I did not forget her. Nor what I had come to America to find. And I set out now inspired to seek the romance of America. . . . I became the man who must hunt and hunt for the spiritual home. — Younghill Kang, *East Goes West*

In this white dominated society, it was perhaps natural that white girls seemed attractive personally as well as physically. They were in a sense symbols of the social success I was conditioned to seek, all the more appealing, perhaps, because of the subtly imposed feelings of self-derogation associated with being a member of a racial minority. In the inner recesses of my heart I resisted the seductive attraction of white girls because I feared I was being drawn to them for the wrong reasons. . . . Behind the magnetism there may have been an unhealthy ambition to prove my self-worth by competing with the best of the white bucks and winning the fair hand of some beautiful, blue-eyed blonde crowning evidence of having made it. — Daniel Okimoto, *An American in Disguise*

Exclusion and the Immigrant Romance

The fictional narrator of Younghill Kang's 1937 novel, *East Goes West: The Making of an Oriental Yankee* and the autobiographical narrator of Daniel Okimoto's 1971 memoir, *An American in Disguise,* share several definitive traits: a desire to construct themselves as Americans, an awareness of their status as outsiders due to their race, and an interest in white women as representatives of their ideal of America.[1] In questioning his attitudes toward white women and assimilation, Okimoto demonstrates a more contemporary political consciousness of his vexed position as a Japanese American; Kang, writing much earlier, does not have the same language available to analyze his immigrant hero's fixation on Trip, but his novel makes clear that Trip's importance to Han is heightened by Han's isolation as a Korean in a racist country.

Patricia Ann Sakurai has called the trope of the Asian American man's desire for the white female body "the trophy paradigm." In the case of Okimoto's quotation, the desire for the white woman is explicitly critiqued by Okimoto himself as emblematic of "an unhealthy ambition" not only to cross socioeconomic boundaries but to erase the author's own race and to compensate for the "feelings of self-derogation" that he recognizes have been "subtly imposed" on him as a Japanese American. Sakurai suggests that the trophy paradigm is not a fixed signifier with a constant meaning but a complex signifying practice that emerges intertextually. As these quotations suggest, the trophy paradigm recurs in the writings of men from different ethnic groups and in both immigrant and American-born authors' texts. But I suggest that its recurrence throughout such a broad range of texts is nonetheless symptomatic of a common anxiety among Asian American male authors and that this anxiety is not simply about Asian American manhood but about the construction of such manhood in the form of real and literary fatherhood — in short, a racialized anxiety of authorship in America.

While Sakurai notes the importance of the white female body as a potential trophy for Asian American males in the race to assimilate, critics of American literature have documented the widely dispersed trope of the land itself as a female body to be conquered and subdued.[2] I argue, however, that the white woman often serves another function in the "immigrant romance" of the Asian American male author: whether she is a teacher, muse, critic, or reader, she represents the American cultural establishment with which the Asian American author must negotiate in order to establish both his literary authority and his Asian American subjectivity. To put it another way: the appearance of desirable but elusive white women in Asian American men's texts marks the struggles of Asian American males to establish identities in which Americanness, ethnicity, and masculinity are integrated. Various metanarratives may be applied to interpret these struggles, but the one I propose is that for Asian American male writers the struggle to establish their masculinity is linked to the struggle to establish their literary authority and a literature of their own.

An essential starting point for interpreting the functions of white women in male-centered Asian American texts is Asian American history: one of the master narratives of that history is the narrative of exclusion and its effects on Asian American sexuality. The exclusion narrative can be read as a narrative about the legal enforcement of compulsory sexual segregation—from Asian, white, and other women—for generations of Asian males who were welcomed to the United States as laborers but not as permanent Americans. Because of this thinking, most Asian immigrants were made ineligible for naturalized citizenship through a series of court cases.[3] From 1875 through 1943, the immigration of Asian men was severely restricted and the immigration of Asian women was gradually cut off (Sucheng Chan, 54–56),[4] resulting in the segregation of most immigrant men from their countrywomen, who remained in their homelands. In addition, some states —notably California, where many Asians lived—passed miscegenation laws forbidding marriages between Asian men and American women or construed existing laws (passed with black-white matches in mind) to apply to such unions (Chan, 59–61).[5] Finally, female U.S. citizens who married Asian immigrants ("aliens ineligible for citizenship") from 1922 through 1936 lost their own citizenship (106).[6] Thus, many Asian men were prevented from legitimizing any sexual or romantic unions they were able to initiate.

In Asian American studies, *exclusion* refers specifically to the laws restricting Asian immigration and naturalization but more broadly to the whole range of discriminatory practices designed to prevent Asians from identifying themselves as Americans. These practices included segregation in housing and schooling, the passage of alien land laws that prevented Asians from owning property, mass evictions, and outright violence (Chan, 45–61).

The largest group affected by the exclusion laws was the Chinese community, a de facto bachelor society (though many men were married to wives living in China). Because immigration laws were slightly more liberal where Japanese and Koreans were concerned, there were more Japanese and Korean families, but these ethnic communities still had a surplus of single men. Filipino immigrants to the United States were usually young single men. Therefore, our questions about gendered literary representations of the process of assimilation may reasonably begin with two immigrants who wrote about the experiences of their bachelor communities. Younghill Kang, a Korean aristocrat who arrived in the United States in 1921, published his second book, the autobiographical novel *East Goes West: The Making of An Oriental Yankee,* in 1937.[7] Carlos Bulosan, the son of a Filipino farmer, arrived in the United States in 1930 and published his autobiographical novel, *America Is in the Heart,* in 1946.[8] In each case, representations of desiring Asian men and rejecting white women need to be read through the metanarrative of history but also as part of a distinctly literary signifying practice—a literary representation, not a report, of Asian

American men's social experiences. The need for this double reading—both historical and literary—links these texts, and others, despite the differences posed by their representations of different ethnic groups in different decades.

Younghill Kang was one of a small number of Koreans who emigrated to the U.S. mainland, where he wrote about a small community of Korean exiles, including a scholarly narrator based on himself, in the novel *East Goes West: The Making of an Oriental Yankee*. Chungpa Han, the narrator, arrives in the United States at age eighteen in the early 1920s "just in time before the law against Oriental immigration [the Immigration Act of 1924] was passed" (Kang, 5).[9] In her influential study *Asian American Literature: An Introduction to the Writings and Their Social Context*, Elaine H. Kim attacks American critics who read the book as celebrating the openness of American society. Kim's reading emphasizes Han's experience of exclusion from American society (32–43); indeed, the narrator's strong sense of being a wanderer in permanent exile, his friend Kim's sense of hopelessness (which he often shares), and his feeling of belonging to a dying culture must be seen both in terms of the history of Asian exclusion in the United States and in terms of Japan's occupation and colonization of Korea.[10] Han acknowledges this by referring to the Immigration Act at the outset of the novel, and again at its end, when he is befriended by an American senator who urges him to think of himself as an American:

> He said, "Yes, young man, I can see you have come to America to stay, and I'm proud and glad. Now you must definitely make up your mind to *be* American. Don't say, 'I'm a Korean' when you're asked. Say, 'I'm an American.'"
>
> "But an Oriental has a hard time in America. He is not welcomed much."
>
> "There shouldn't be any buts about it! Believe in America with all your heart. Even if it's sometimes hard, believe in her. . . . I tell you sir, you belong here. You should be one of us."
>
> "But legally I am denied."
>
> Senator Kirby actually pooh-poohed this objection. "There are still ways and means of proving exceptions. And that unfair law perhaps will not always last. Next time I hold government office" (. . . his party had been out for a long time), "write me and I will help you." (383)

By reporting this as a dialogue, Kang the author demonstrates the mixed message Han receives from America. Kirby urges him to consider himself American, first overlooking the laws against Han's presence and naturalization then denying personal responsibility for that law and offering help in some unspecified future. By diplomatically withholding comment on Kirby's final promise, Kang leaves the final assessment of Kirby's promised "help" open to the reader.

By the end of the novel, Han has established an entry-level literary job for himself as the oriental news correspondent of a monthly magazine. But his tenuous position in America is summed up in a dream wherein he is first distracted from entering a paradisiac, clearly Asian garden by the loss of his American money and car keys and then chased into "a dark and cryptlike cellar," along with "some frightened-looking Negroes," by men with knives and clubs. As the (implicitly white) men outside shove flaming torches into the cellar gratings, Han awakes and proclaims unconvincingly that in Buddhist terms the dream augurs "growth and rebirth and a happier reincarnation" (401). Clearly, the dream conveys Han's sense of being doubly alienated; he is too Americanized to return to Korea, yet he cannot gain full entry into America because of the color of his skin.

In this context, the novel's interracial romances serve to extend its dominant theme of homelessness. Of the four Korean men who fall in love with white women, only Richard Chai, a brilliant, charming, and disciplined Korean American medical student, wins his beloved in marriage. George Jum, a playboy enamored of a white dancer, fails to sustain her interest and retires to Hawaii, where he becomes engaged to a Korean American bride. Although his prospects seem idyllic ("So here in Hawaii I will spend my hours in eating, loving, and sleeping"), George seems slightly disappointed at his failure to succeed as a movie actor (399). The happy love story of Chai and his WASP bride, Martha Wright, suggests that attitudes toward Asian men were not wholly rejecting; moreover, George's strategic retreat to the welcoming Korean American community in Hawaii suggests one alternative to the battles of assimilation on the mainland. However, the stories of Kim and Helen and Han and Trip are more important to the novel's central themes of wandering, exile, and homelessness.

Kim, a brilliant but gloomy man of letters, wins the affection of Helen Hancock, a New England lady, but not the approval of her relatives, who separate the two. Later, when Kim learns that Helen has died, he commits suicide. When Han hears of the deaths, he thinks of Kim in literary terms but with an intensity that is best understood in terms of Korea's struggle for survival under Japanese occupation. Han remembers Kim comparing himself to Ulysses, set adrift by an earlier Helen, in a revisionist reading that emphasizes Ulysses's wandering over Paris's sexual passion: "Without Helen, Ulysses would never have been shipwrecked again and again in the black treacherous sea. Always he tried to reach the receding horizon . . . (391)."[11] After linking Kim with famous literary suicides of the East and

West, and with the English Romantic poets as a "child of revolution" (395), Han finally figures Kim as a beloved but hopelessly defaced Korean text: "But the greatest loss to me, Kim's friend, was himself, his brain which bore in its fine involutions our ancient characters deeply and simply incised, familiar to me. And over their classic economy, their primitive chaste elegance, was scrawled the West's handwriting, in incoherent labyrinth, and seamless Hamlet design. To me—to me almost alone—a priceless and awful parchment was in him destroyed. Could it not have been deciphered, conveyed to the world?" (393). In Kim, whose mind is "deeply and simply incised" with "ancient characters" cherished by Han for their "classic economy, their primitive chaste elegance," Han sees a reflection of his own mind and heart, in which Korean culture was once inscribed but has since been obscured by the destructively "incoherent labyrinth" of Western writing. By identifying Western culture with a cryptic labyrinth, an obscure place of entrapment and slaughter, Han links it metaphorically with the "dark and cryptlike cellar" where he finds himself in the final image of the novel. That Helen Hancock herself is not as important as the abstract hope of belonging, and of being mentally at rest, which she represents, is suggested by the fact that Han identifies Kim with Ulysses the exile, not Paris, and Hamlet the displaced prince, not Romeo the thwarted lover. Despite the lack of overt historical references, the political subtext may explain the intensity of Han's grief here: the "priceless parchment," which Han so wishes could have been deciphered and conveyed to the world and which he feels "almost alone" in mourning, seems also to be Korea itself, an occupied country of which most Americans at that time (1921–37) had not yet heard. Although the love story is not an overt national allegory, and the novel is not explicitly political, it is not as devoid of historical consciousness or nationalist feeling as some readers have suggested. For a character who loves literature and culture as much as Han does, and who cannot identify with political or military solutions to his country's plight, this passage expresses the deepest possible sense of mourning for his homeland as well as alienation from this adopted country.

That Kim is a "parchment" also indicates the slight archaism that Han associates with the kind of classical East Asian education Kim and he share. That the double writing of Eastern and Western characters has made Kim unreadable except to a fellow exile suggests something about the difficulty these émigrés encounter in reconstructing themselves as American men of letters in the absence of a living community of peers who know how to "read" them and their writing. That their difficulty is not only one of identity or race, but specific to their class identities as exiled upper-class scholars and to the problem of gaining cultural recognition, is suggested by the fact that Richard Chai, the doctor, gains access to the feminized American body of his (blonde, Phi Beta Kappa, medical secretary) beloved through his expert medical knowledge of the (non–racially marked) human body. As a Korean American, Richard also has a more subtle grasp of the rules of American social interaction, which no doubt contributes to his success in courting the aptly named Miss Wright. George Jum, who falls for a dancer and fails as a Hollywood actor before "settling for" a beautiful Korean American wife, is also locked out of success as an American cultural worker. After expressing his disgust that he can expect only minor parts in Hollywood, he goes to Hawaii, where, he writes, "lazy monkeys can pick up the nuts without working" (399). Though George's self-deprecation is typical of his sense of humor, it may also suggest that his self-image has been affected by his stay in Hollywood, where his body marks him as intrinsically "minor."

In this context, Han's longing for Trip may be read not only as a representation of the historical reality of Asian men's social ostracism in the United States but for its significance as a literary representation. For both Han's conduct of the courtship and his narration of it are mediated through his deep love of literature and his knowledge of the Western classics and the Anglo-American literary tradition. He comes to "know" Trip through the reminiscences of Laura James, a former schoolmate with whom she corresponds; among several friends in this group, Han selects Trip because she is a poet. For Han, steeped in Western and Anglo-American culture, Trip's appeal as a *writing* woman places her in a long line of literary heroines whose merits are linked to the presumption that a literary life signifies both domestic virtues and a complex interior life—precisely the kind of life Kang establishes for Han in order to show both that Kang is a "Yankee" and that, as a synthesizer of Eastern and Western cultures, he is an "oriental Yankee." In this sense, Kang self-consciously constructs both Han and Trip as the kinds of national subjects to be found in the bildungsroman tradition that he explicitly insists Han (and therefore he) has read. However, an ironic distance is established between Kang, the self-conscious author, and his hero through such details as Han's failure to heed the warning Kang provides in a sample of Trip's poetry:

> My beds are feathered with down,
> Lily-white, lettuce sweet,
> With huge puffs of silk and satin and wool
> Warm at neck and feet.
>
> My tables are laden with cheer,
> I am the most comforting cook!
> Come, hang your coat with its world dust outside,
> Come and look.

Look—Yet stand off, stand far off!
Oh, my tired traveller, beware!
All are but words, merely painted,
I give but painted word-fare. (337–38)

Here Kang consciously echoes the elegiac feel of W. B. Yeats's enchantment poems, but the feeling of longing has been translated into a specifically Asian American expression of homelessness and exile. Trip, like America, looks homey and welcoming, but ultimately she will put him off with "painted word-fare"—and not much of that, either.[12] Such a moment emphasizes the author's claims to mastery of the literary tradition. To continue the narrative that establishes him as an oriental Yankee, Han attempts to impress Trip with recitations of Western literature, but instead of valuing him as a literary soul like herself she sees him as an oddity: an Asian man who can mimic her culture. In place of the romantic narrative Han seeks to construct, Trip laughingly invents another, that of being accosted by a white policeman bent on protecting her, a supposedly helpless female, from the dangers of Chinatown. Clearly, the story the policeman is taking seriously, and which Trip is humorously titillated by, is the nineteenth-century American horror-fantasy about innocent white girls being unspeakably corrupted by opium-crazed Chinamen in Chinatown.[13] Alternatively, the policeman might be seen as challenging Trip for loitering too much like a streetwalker (while Han runs an errand), but this again perpetuates the stereotype of Chinatown as ripe with vice. By ridiculing the policeman's uncertain blend of protectiveness and suspicion, Trip demonstrates her own independence and liberalism yet also reinforces the point that to others Han looks more like a "Chinaman" than an American. While gracefully laughing off Han's potential for criminal or predatory activity, Trip is also indirectly suggesting that he lacks sexual charisma.

When Han loses track of Trip's whereabouts, he is disappointed but not really crushed because his ideal of "the romance of America" remains intact and pleasantly vague: "Trip seemed a dream, or if real, hidden now by all the obstacles of fate, time, space, and the world. But I did not forget her. Nor what I had come to America to find. And I set out now inspired to seek the romance of America. . . . I became the man who must hunt and hunt for the spiritual home" (349). Here Han equates the elusive white woman with both his quest for "the spiritual home" and the object of that quest. No wonder Kang has named this character Trip. With its echoes of Fitzgerald, Han's idealization of America as a woman, and the rhetoric of transcendence used to describe her, marks this text very much as a male American text. But Han also equates Trip specifically with his love for Western literature, while Trip associates him with Chinatown. As racialized, comically miscommunicating "lovers," they embody the carefully constructed distances between Asians and whites in this country in the 1920s and 1930s, sounding a note specific to Asian American writing. But, in contrast to Okimoto's desire for "the fair hand" of a blonde beauty, which Patricia Ann Sakurai has identified as an expression of desire for the white female *body,* the more romantic Chungpa Han betrays almost no awareness of Trip's body as such, imaginatively exchanging it for the bodies of literary heroines and hyperbolic metaphors ("a mystic blossom set in the land of beauty forever" [334]). In his romantic, abstract way, he is after her mind. When he learns of the deaths of Helen and Kim, he seeks to compensate for the loss of Kim, that "priceless parchment," by assuring himself that Trip still exists; having found her again, he overlooks clear signs of her reluctance to see him and fantasizes about courting her by fathering a literary offspring, a book, with her or, failing that, by becoming a text for her to read and write about (just as Trip and her poem were exchangeable, earlier, and as we saw, the words of the English domestic heroine become definitive of her "self" in the introduction: "I would make her translate Oriental poems, I would get her interested in that. Or I would pose as material. I would get her mind working with me. And that was a good book, she must see we had to write. Was she still sitting charmed like that in the midst of those papery papers? Oh, let me be her servant forever and put myself in paper's place!" (392–93). In short, Trip embodies Han's desire for success and "a spiritual home" in America. But she also represents an antidote to Han's fear of negation as a scholar and writer of literary texts, the fear that he and all that he cares for, his mastery of Asian and Western knowledge and experience, will be obliterated and forgotten, like Kim. His fiercest desire is to win recognition from his adopted country, both as an author and as a unique and "priceless" text.

Trip, then, is also the audience Han seeks in America, someone who will read, translate, and value the "oriental poems" that comprise his subjectivity. Without such an idealized reader, Han is doomed to the same feelings of insignificance and oblivion that drove his friend Kim to suicide. For this ethnic writer in exile, not to be read is to be dead.

For Carlos, the narrator of Carlos Bulosan's novel *America Is in the Heart,* white American women are also bound up with his struggles to write his way into a Filipino American identity.[14]

The novel traces the education and radicalization of a migrant worker newly arrived from a rural Filipino upbringing. As he grows increasingly involved in efforts to unionize itinerant Filipino workers, he also gives himself a literary education. When his health breaks down, Carlos reduces his activism and sets about writing the workers' stories, which are also his own. The loosely structured novel is repeatedly punctuated by Carlos's declarations of his nigh-bardic calling, the call to give voice to the Filipinos' struggle, not only to survive materially but to become visible and understandable to others—the struggle not to become, as Oscar Campomanes and others have described this generation, the "forgotten Filipinos" (Campomanes, "Filipinos," 53).

In this novel of a writer's apprenticeship, white women play three roles, all ideologically charged. Carlos, the fictive narrator, lives in a tough world of itinerant male workers, who, for some of the reasons suggested earlier, could not put down roots in the United States. (Bulosan arrived in 1930, as a teenager, published *America* in 1946, and died in 1956.)[15] The book is rife not only with episodes in which Filipinos are economically exploited but with episodes of brutal and arbitrary violence against Filipinos. In one scene, a Filipino man and his white wife are refused service at a cafeteria; for trying to buy milk for their baby, the man is brutally beaten (144). Since normal domestic relations cannot exist in this world, women in the narrative tend to feel like guests from another planet, particularly if they are white.

Two of the outstanding white women in the text serve to highlight Carlos's struggles as a member of the working poor and as a union activist. In one episode, a series of Filipino strikes is undermined from within by a white woman, Helen, who attaches herself romantically to key men in the union movement, then vanishes just as the movement at a particular site collapses as a result of her espionage. She explicitly tells Carlos that her motive is racial hatred, and Bulosan as author assigns her a (rumored) violent death in what is perhaps a gratuitous act of authorial vengeance (203). Her opposite is Marian, who meets and succors Carlos after he narrowly escapes a violent death at the hands of white vigilantes. Marian, who is dying, deposits Carlos in hotel rooms, goes out "with friends," and returns with large sums of money, which she gives to Carlos, hoping that this will help him survive and develop as a writer. Although she appears to be working as a prostitute, she is tactfully vague about her activities, and Carlos, who perhaps does not comprehend what she is doing until after she dies, accepts her gifts of affection and material support and depicts her in his narrative as sweet, loving, and generous. The text hints very obliquely that she is a survivor of serial rapes that Carlos witnessed (but couldn't prevent) years earlier (212), and when she dies (only a few pages after her appearance) Carlos learns from a doctor that the cause of death was syphilis.

Together the two women—one a femme fatale (Helen), the other a fallen angel (Marian/Mary Magdelene)—represent two faces of America as seen from Carlos's position as a racialized subject destined to be one of the working poor. The scheming strikebreaker embodies both white racial and middle-class prejudice against the Filipino workers. Marian, who is always portrayed as a young girl, is a fellow victim, although her experiences have left her essential core of goodness and innocence untouched, as they almost are in Carlos himself, but as a woman character who can die and depart from the text Marian is idealized as the embodiment of the "good America," the ideal of a nurturing land that Carlos guards in his heart but can find only intermittently in reality. Both Marian and Helen use their sexuality to achieve their political ends — Helen to oppress, exclude, and undermine; Marian to give life to a struggling writer.

Other white women function as Carlos's muses and literary mentors, introducing him to activist journalism, Western literature, and American authorship. In contrast to Han's fantasy of Trip as the American lover who will also read his work, these characters have real intellectual friendships with Carlos and do help him to develop his literary consciousness. Because Bulosan emphasizes the importance of Carlos's intellectual exchanges with these women, as well as their freedom to come and go in his life, it is clear that they are neither trophies nor idealized readers: they are real friends and mentors, but they are not romantic partners. Carlos's feelings about their sexuality are indicated only indirectly.[16]

Bulosan's 1949 story, "As Long as the Grass Shall Grow," suggests why this might be. The story, told retrospectively by a writer looking back on his first year in the United States, describes his relationship with a young teacher, Helen O'Reilly, in a farming town where he has gone to pick peas with his friends, who themselves have been in America only a year. Although both the boy and the young woman steadfastly cast the relationship in terms of reading lessons, his sexual curiosity about her is signaled discreetly from the beginning of the story: "In the middle of that year when we were picking peas on the hillside, I noticed the school children playing with their teacher in the sun. It was my first time to see her, a young woman of about twenty-five with brown hair and a white dress spotted with blue . . ." (77). The blue and white dress, blending with the sky and sea and harmonizing with the bright colors on the hillside, the green of the peas, and the gray of the mountains both identify the young woman with the landscape and contrast with the drabness of the workers' lives, which consist of farm labor, eating, "scrubbing the dirt off [their] bodies, shooting pool, and playing cards all night."

As the narrator gazes at the children one afternoon, the teacher questions him and offers him evening reading lessons. In this initial exchange, the narrator avoids telling the reader his age at the time but notes that O'Reilly thinks him "too young to be working" (78) and refers to him as a boy. By masking the protagonist's age, the author makes it possible for readers to imagine him as more of a child than a young man. Though she includes his companions in the offer of lessons, her decisive focus on the narrator and his eagerness to learn convey a mutual interest that his companions interpret sexually:

> "Would you like to do some reading under me?"
>
> "I'd love to, ma'am," I said softly. I looked at my companions from the corners of my eyes because they would ridicule me if they knew that I wanted some education. I never saw any reading material at our bunkhouse except the semi-nude pictures of women in movie magazines . . .
>
> She drove away in her car, and when she was gone, I went on working quietly. But my companions taunted me. Some of them even implied certain dark things that made me stop picking peas and look at them with a challenge in my eyes. (77)

When O'Reilly arrives to teach the youth that evening, he "steals glances" at her, intrigued rather than put off by the plain masculine clothing she has donned. His friends busy themselves with other activities, but some remain at home playing poker as if conspiring to grant the two an appropriate level of privacy. When the tutoring concludes at ten o'clock, the student walks his teacher to the road; later, he recalls her professed love of walking in the moonlight.

As the lessons continue and are joined by the other youths, the narrative suggests both the eroticism inherent in the teacher-student relationship and the efforts of the teacher and pupils to maintain the proper distance without admitting that they are doing so. The students, wishing to give O'Reilly a dress, are advised by an older man that this would be considered improper; O'Reilly translates their monetary gift into a more professional gabardine suit. When the narrator writes a poem, O'Reilly says it is too early for him to write poetry but encourages him by introducing him to the Song of Solomon. The narrator tiptoes around the strong eroticism of the selection by praising the "rich language, the beautiful imagery, and the depth of the old man's passion for the girl and the vineyard" and she by praising it as great poetry. Besides, as the narrator reminds us, it's in the Bible. Yet clearly both are moved by their shared experience of this poetry, for the teacher says: "I would like you to remember it. There was a time when men loved deeply and were not afraid to love." The narrator vows in return: "*Some day I will come back in memory to this place and time and write about you, Miss O'Reilly. How gratifying it will be to come back to you with a book in my hands about all that we are feeling here tonight!*" (81, emphasis in original). As in the case of Chungpa Han, this narrator's dream of a literary offspring substitutes for a more direct expression of erotic desire for the woman who represents America and Americanization.

Despite the respectful, respectable conduct of teacher and pupils, the reading lessons are considered transgressive and regulated as sexually improper by other townspeople. First "some organization in town" complains about the teacher's meeting the students at their bunkhouse; then she is forbidden by the school board to give them evening lessons in the school building. When the lessons are moved to the teacher's boardinghouse, the students arrive in stealth; yet a man comes to O'Reilly's door, evidently to tell her to stop them. Finally, the narrator is beaten and a threatening note delivered to the students' bunkhouse, warning them to stop the lessons. Miss O'Reilly is hospitalized after some undescribed mishap, loses her teaching position, and leaves town after a bittersweet farewell to her pupils. Through the veil of the narrator's naive and incomplete perceptions, it is unclear what is most objectionable: the youths' regular contact with her or her instruction of them. Though the overt objection seems to be against the perceived sexual exposure of Helen O'Reilly to these suggestible ruffians, the submerged agenda is clearly one of racial domination. Workers who learn to read and think will be less cheap and malleable and will compete economically as well as sexually with native-born Americans. The story implies that it is white men who keep interfering with the lessons and that their primary concern is the continued isolation of the labor force, not O'Reilly's wishes or welfare. Not only is she prevented from teaching her pupils, but she is subjected to increasingly severe sanctions, which appear to include verbal and physical harassment, incarceration, ostracism, and the loss of her job.

Although the narrator confesses "I never saw her again," the ending is not an unmitigated tragedy, partly because its resolution has been foreshadowed at this story's beginning, when the narrator, first seeing the schoolchildren, is reminded of the loss of another friend when he was ten:

We had gone to the fields across the river that afternoon to fly our kites because it was summertime and the breeze was just strong enough to carry our playthings to high altitudes. Suddenly, in the midst of our sport, a ferocious carabao broke loose from its peg and came plunging wildly after us, trapping my friend and goring him to death. That night when I went to see him, and realized that he was truly dead, I ran out of the house and hid in the backyard where the moonlight was like a silver column in the guava trees. I stood sobbing under a guava, smelling the sweetness of the papaya blossoms in the air. Then suddenly nightingales burst into a glorious song. I stopped crying and listened to them. Gradually I became vaguely comforted and could accept the fact that my friend would not come back to life again. I gathered an armful of papaya blossoms and went back to the house and spread them over the coffin. I returned to the guava grove and listened to the nightingales sing all night long. (77–78)

The young boys' innocent aspirations, symbolized by the kites' ascent, are destroyed by the random violence of the carabao. In his first experience of irrevocable loss, the narrator is consoled by the continuing sweetness of the natural surroundings, and the ineffable message of the nightingales. In the same way, neither the boy's aspirations to learning nor his tender respect for his teacher are uprooted by the men's violence; in place of nightingales, the youth is succored by an older man, who affirms the worth of his aspirations ("I could have told you these things before, but I saw that you were truly interested in educating yourself. I admired your courage and ambition" [83]) and essentially insists that evil is not restricted to whites, nor whites to evil.

Earlier, the narrator has mentally promised to return to O'Reilly in memory and write about "all that we are feeling here tonight!" O'Reilly makes a similar covenant to "go on teaching people like you to understand things as long as the grass shall grow" (84). The existence of the story signals that the narrator has kept his half of their covenant; the closure of the story signals his sense that O'Reilly has fulfilled her half as well, a fulfillment symbolized by her apotheosis in the American landscape, now the adult narrator's "home," with which she has been identified from the start: "One morning I found I had been away from home for twenty years. But where is home? I saw the grass of another spring growing on the hills and in the fields. And the thought came to me that I had had Miss O'Reilly with me all the time, there in the broad fields and verdant hills of America, my home" (84). Radical readers might quarrel with Bulosan's decision to contain the subtext of the townspeople's racism through the older man's warning against reverse racism (83) and the web of nature imagery signaling renewal and consolation, but clearly the presence of an impersonal system of racism is the framing context for O'Reilly's teaching, which the narrator retrospectively recognizes as a form of political resistance for which the young teacher, having risked her career and personal reputation, is harshly disciplined. In this case, the racists are again figured as white men, town fathers who seek to restrict the Filipino youths' access both to "their" woman and to literacy, the crucial tool for Americanization and advancement, in a racialized revision of the old Freudian myth of the father who hoards all the women, and presumably the various forms of wealth and status associated with "ownership" of and access to them, for himself (Freud, *Totem and Taboo*, 140–46). O'Reilly is not chattel, and she stands not so much for the possibility of sexual reproduction as the possibility of intellectual, economic, and political competitiveness and enfranchisement in the distant future. However, all these possibilities are coded sexually in the repressed longing of the narrator's rhetoric as well as in the townspeople's disciplinary acts. Hence, the whites appear to object to O'Reilly's fraternization on the basis of sexual impropriety because that is a more accepted form of taboo than intellectual impropriety: the democratic rhetoric of the nation — under which O'Reilly is hired to teach the children of the working poor in the first place — cannot justify restricting her from extending this mission to the workers themselves. This is why the town fathers forbid O'Reilly to use certain *spaces* at night, emphasizing the presumed sexual impropriety, before directly forbidding her to teach the youths, and why the beating and the threatening note — direct denials of democratic ideals — are anonymous.

That sexual relations are also more controversial than intellectual congress to Bulosan's implied readership is suggested by the very care with which his narrator contains his expressions of sexual admiration for O'Reilly and the suppression of the narrator's age at the time he met and studied with her. A similar containment of sexual interest can be found in Bulosan's novel *America Is in the Heart,* in which only Mexican, Indian, and low-class white women appear as sexual partners in the narrator's life story, leaving a safe distance between Carlos and the middle-class white women who are his intellectual friends. In Carey McWilliams's introduction to *America,* Bulosan's own sexuality is similarly contained by rhetoric that acknowledges the mutual attraction between Bulosan and white women, but it describes him as as "an astounding child-man": "Hypersensitive, gentle, wildly imaginative, he had the bright eyes, ready smile, and innocent laughter of a precocious child. Incidentally, those 'Caucasian women' were always as interested in him as he undoubtedly was in them. Most of them were large enough to have held him in their laps with ease but they adored him as much as he adored them" (xviii). Bulosan's desexualized status in the introduction, and the status of his protagonists in *America* and "As Long" as perennial "little brown brothers," may also shed light on the melancholy of Younghill Kang's characters, Kim and Han, young men raised in Korea, where they would have been married by age twenty and have belonged to their country's most elite class if it were not for the Japanese occupation.

In each of these examples, political disenfranchisement and anxieties about literary and intellectual exclusion from American society are represented through the narrator-protagonists' vexed relationships with white women. For Han, the Korean scholar in exile, Trip represents not only his dream of finding a "spiritual home" in America but also his particular need for the appreciation and understanding of an American readership, needs that no doubt mirrored the author's own professional anxieties. For *America*'s narrator, Carlos, white women undermine or aid his drives to survive, help his fellow workers through activism, and become the spokesman for his community through an assumption of professional authorship. For the narrator in "As Long," taboos against interracial contact between the sexes mirror other, more serious taboos. Within the story, the taboo against social contact serves as a pretext for the more serious taboo against learning and the ambition to Americanize and compete as equals; within the rhetoric of the story, the narrator's careful management of his own earlier desire for the teacher's presence reflects his yet more careful presentation of the forbidden topic of racism.

Both Kang's and Bulosan's novels are animated by contradictions between the democratic rhetoric of America and the reality of anti-Asian exclusion. Kang's novel, as well as Bulosan's novel and short story, record the many ways in which cultural and sexual marginalization are closely linked with political and economic exclusion for the Korean and Filipino communities in America. For these writers, interracial sexual desire is a literary sign for the subject's desire for broader acceptance, and a voice, in America. Bulosan's work makes it particularly clear that, for Pinoys (migrant Filipino workers in the United States), the mainstream's taboos against interracial marriage, sex, fraternization, and desire itself are intimately linked with taboos against challenging racism and class exploitation directly (through union work or strident publications) or indirectly (through efforts to assimilate and enter the American middle class). In both texts, these two types of activity are most likely to provoke disciplinary violence.

Gendering Asianness: Filial Nostalgia, Abjection, and Amnesia

Let us say that Asian American male writers are engaged in acts of self-construction that are closely intertwined with other projects: the project of constructing an American identity and the twin projects of founding families and founding a literary tradition, which are connected by the tropes of authoring as fathering and self-authoring as self-fathering. Within these projects, the white woman operates as an object of desire that is linked to the desire to found a new American self, a new American literature, a new American family. White women function not only as trophies attesting to Asian American men's achievement of economic success or even of Americanness but as teachers, agents of socialization, and literary mediators: muses, critics, and readers.

In serving these functions, the white women stand for an "other" linked not only with authorship and entry into the American middle class but with escape from the ethnic family, the ethnic community, and the duties and burdens of the Asian and Asian American past. We might ask why Asian women, so often the objects of Euro-American male desire, are not more central to the Asian American male imagination than I have indicated so far. The answer is, I think, that they are but not primarily as objects of desire. For Asian American writers, male and female, Asian and Asian immigrant women are closely linked with the preservation and transmission of Asian culture to their American children. For immigrant writers, the Asian mother may represent the nightmare of poverty and constriction left behind in the homeland. For American-born writers, the Asian or immigrant mother may bear the burden of voicing and attempting to enforce the American-born youth's filial obligations or, more broadly, his or her family responsibilities. For American-born male writers in particular, the familiar drama of separating oneself from one's parents to establish adulthood is additionally colored not only with the work of mother-son separation and male gendering but with the deeply problematic work of creating an adult male self who is more "American" than the immigrant parent.

Among Asian American writers, versions of the Asian or immigrant mother who is seen by the Asian American son as personifying the ancestral homeland can be found in such texts as Frank Chin's *The Year of the Dragon*, Gus Lee's *China Boy* and *Honor and Duty,* Chang-rae Lee's *Native Speaker*, and John Okada's *No-No Boy*. Among the early immigrant writers, however, Carlos Bulosan's evocation of the mother in *America Is in the Heart* is one of the more sustained and arguably complex representations. Although there is much here that could be read specifically in terms of Bulosan's background as the son of a Filipino farmer and as a working-class, socialist author, the reading that follows is meant to highlight the kind of ideological work that Bulosan's text has in common with other texts by Asian American males and to offer hypotheses about how an Asian immigrant author represents women of his own community. By examining Bulosan's portrayal of his mother in the context of his carefully wrought representation of his homeland, we can see how the Asian mother represents an ethnic ideal that exists outside of history and narrative time; her static remoteness serves as a foil, a ground by which to measure the change and progress of the uprooted Asian American male protagonist.

Although my earlier discussion emphasized that this text has been read as a fictionalized autobiography, I find that the book's representations of the narrator's childhood are so charged with feeling that, in discussing how the narrator's memory and imagination work, I seem to be in the presence of very powerful emotions: these passages feel like artful and arduous literary transformations of an actual person's memories, yet at least one event central to my discussion is clearly fictionalized. Since we do not know which childhood stories are true of the biographical Bulosan family, I'll henceforth distinguish among Carlos, (the boy in the novel); the adult narrator, whom I'll treat as a person with a complex memory and psychology; and Bulosan the author. Though the repressions and recollections I'll ascribe to the narrator may well resemble those of Bulosan, I want to avoid drawing some kinds of conclusions about Bulosan based on this novel, yet I will also refer at times to the author's literary choices.

Part one of *America Is in the Heart* depicts Carlos's childhood and adolescence in the Philippines in which the selfless nobility and simplicity of his parents are set against a narrative of family financial ruin that is carefully coded by the narrator as a consequence of colonialist and capitalist forces. That is, the family suffers first because it buys into the American ideal of universal public education, but the Americans have not made this education *truly free* for Filipinos. Hence, the family sells and mortgages its land in order to educate one son in a gamble that doesn't pay off. Second, the father is unable to defend his claims to the land within the banking and legal system, which is clearly set up to defend the interests of other classes at the expense of his. Both parents, but particularly the mother, are depicted as noble, selfless, and uncomplaining, although their meager capacity to support themselves and their family is gradually diminished by the loss of their land and the departures of their sons. In part one, the narrator quickly and lovingly depicts his mother in a few incidents that illustrate her love of beauty, compassion, diligence, persistence, and forbearance in the face of hardship and provocation (32–39). Later, in America, he signals his and his brothers' continued cherishing of her memory in two incidents. In one, her name becomes the password he needs to reclaim kinship with his estranged brother Amado (123); later, a letter composed to a sick American boy's mother becomes imbued with the nostalgic yearning he has never expressed in any letter to his own mother (247).

Carlos's little sisters are equally idealized and are recalled with a fraternal tenderness exemplified by the memory of his last conversation with his sister Francisca, who gives him her savings with the request that he study in America, return to the Philippines, and teach her and their sister Marcela to read. "That is all I want from you," she concludes. "We will be working hard with mother while you are gone." "There was a big lump in my throat," he recalls. "A little girl giving me five pesos so that I could go to school in America! It was her whole year's savings" (88). The request is particularly poignant because within the novel the beloved brother never returns.

In this scene, the lyric paragraphs that follow perform a double function. As the final images of Bulosan's family, they inscribe it in an idealized pastoral landscape, and they link these images with the snare motif, which connects the pure mother and sisters with the sexualized women of color who appear elsewhere throughout the novel: "My sisters clung to my hands, looking at me with pleading eyes. There was a meadow lark somewhere in the sunlit field, and it was singing rapturously. Not far way a peasant girl was singing a *kundiman,* or love song, and a young man answered with a song as sweet and innocent. Nearby a little boy was playing with a quail that he had snared with horsehair in the unharvested *mongo* field. In a metallic instant, I remembered how Luciano and I had snared birds" (89). The scene ends with the image of the mother, who "in the aching surge of a moment . . . put her face in her hands and sobbed loudly between fits of agonized laughter" (89), silently enacting both her own grief and the deeply divided emotions of young Carlos, who already knows that the possibilities for his mother's future are cruelly constricted and who secretly looks forward to a better life elsewhere.

Meanwhile, the almost operatic sound-images of the lark "singing rapturously," the peasant lovers' duet, and the boy with the snared quail link this moment of passionately compressed memory (imbued as it is with the adult narrator's nostalgic sense of its transience) with the earlier episode of the parrot and the quail. During Carlos's childhood, his brother Luciano teaches him to catch parrots by luring them with a caged quail. When the first parrot lands on the roof of the quail's cage, "singing rapturously" to the quail, it is caught in Luciano's horsehair snares. Carlos calls it "a very brave bird," and Luciano explains: "It is in love with the quail. When you are in love you are brave. You are not afraid of death" (53). The parrot and its successors are then sold to finance Luciano's new business.

The use of the ordinary quail to snare the rare, valuable parrots is Bulosan's metaphor for the threat and reality of women's sexual entrapment of men, particularly educated young men, rare birds among the Filipino peasants. Again and again, in Bulosan's story, promising young men find their careers disrupted by the threat of marriage to uneducated girls, a prospect that in the absence of birth control or stable employment means a certain fall into the net of expanding responsibility and shrinking opportunity in which Carlos's parents are already enmeshed. The snare motif begins with Carlos's brother Macario, whose high school education has been financed by the family's risky sale and mortgage of their meager farmland. Just as Macario has begun the teaching job that will enable him to pay the family debts and salvage their land, a strange girl appears. When Macario declines to marry her, she drives him from town by getting him fired. By repeating this action at Macario's second job in another town, she forces him to leave the Philippines. Similarly, Carlos and his cousin are driven from home, after an evening of sexy but innocent dancing, when their dance partners insist on marrying them the next day. Months later, when Carlos's high scores on a national intelligence exam become public knowledge, he is besieged with girls seeking to mend and cook for him; one girl, Veronica, falsely accuses him of fathering her illegitimate child, precipitating Carlos's flight from the Philippines.

Though Carlos does get away, his flight from the snare of enforced marriage compels him to leave his parents prematurely. Two of his brothers who do marry are also thereby compelled to transfer their financial and other support from their parents to growing families of their own. Leon, the eldest, must sell his portion of the family land and move elsewhere because of the neighbors' prejudice against his stalwart but nonvirginal bride; he's last seen in a family tableau with his nameless wife and children as Carlos passes through by bus on his way to America (8–9). This relatively neutral tableau, which ends the first chapter of part one, is reprised and revised at the end of part one in Carlos's last visit with Luciano, the contriver of the snares, who explicitly warns Carlos not to get caught, as he has been, in the snare of marriage:

> I went to Binalonan to say good-bye to Luciano. His wife had just given birth to another baby. I knew that he would have a child every year. I knew that in ten years he would be so burdened with responsibilities that he would want to lie down and die. I was glad I was free of the life he was living. When I had finally settled myself in the bus, I looked down and saw my brother's pitiful eyes.
>
> "Don't come back to Binalonan, Allos!" he said. "Even if you have to steal and kill, don't come back to this damned town. Don't ever come back, please, little brother!" He was running furiously alongside the bus and waving his hands desperately with the importance of what he had to say. "Don't come back as I have done. See what happened to me?" He let my hand go and suddenly stopped running. (89)

For Carlos and the other young men, marriage to "a mud-smelling peasant girl" (as Carlos's cousin puts it [78]) means the foreclosure of their futures. No matter how much they love their parents and siblings, they must be wiser than the lovestruck parrots or they'll miss the bus. Thus, females represent the boundaries of the boy's narrative of immigration and (incomplete) assimilation; when serving this function, they cannot enter the narrative as active participants.

Bulosan did write a short story about the fate of an emigrant's sisters using the same names (Marcela and Francisca), but the conclusion suggests that he imagined their hardships as so completely oppressive as to be unbearable to live with or to write or read about at length. In "Homecoming," an impoverished young man (Mariano) does go back to see his family after a seventeen-year absence in America and finds one sister unhappily employed at an unpleasant, subtly degrading, domestic job and the other taking in laundry at home (Bulosan, *Becoming,* 90–96). Neither can marry due to poverty. The story concludes with Mariano, just arrived, slipping out at night and fixing the image of the house in his memory because "he knew he would never see it again."

Perhaps *America*'s narrator is able to remember his mother and sisters so lyrically because he is physically removed from them and their constricted options. Within the confines of the novel, one might imagine the little sisters growing up either to replicate their mother's life of struggle or to become demanding, unreasonable girls like the husband hunters who drive Macario, Carlos, and their cousin to America.[17] Much later, an educated Filipina in America explains the behavior of her countrywomen in terms of their material prospects; although the term *Pinoy* refers specifically to male migrant workers in America, she seems to be describing women.

> "The Pinoys can't use their education, either. That is why Pinoys have only one objective—to marry someone with economic security. But the parents are partly to blame: they teach their daughters to be greedy. So Pinoys in general are arrogant and stupid and lacking in humor."
> I nodded silently. (271)

Given the absence of other Filipinas in the text's portrayal of life in the United States, the ambivalence of this account is telling. Bulosan seems to have imported this character (who shortly vanishes from the story) just to voice negative views of his countrywomen. As a good socialist, Bulosan recognizes the material basis for perceived personality defects in peasant and working-class Filipinas, but clearly that theoretical recognition is not enough to overcome the antipathy he seems to have acquired for them. The woman's use of the term *Pinoy* in her analysis of the Filipina personality is also telling, for Bulosan's text records evidence of the gender-specific oppression faced by Filipinas (and other women of color) even as it lacks a separate vocabulary and a conceptual language for discussing it. Thus, in contrast to the lucid and specific accounts of his father's loss of land and the exploitation and resistance of (male) Pinoys, (i.e., class- and race-based analysis), Bulosan both sees and fails to see the oppression of women of color in his text. Since his socialist education has not given him a separate discourse for framing women's experience, he tends to fall back upon moralized sentiment, inarticulateness, or moral shoulder shrugging, such as in the question "What kind of girl was she?" (181), which refers to a fickle Mexican woman who has accepted a brutal beating as an expression of love.

For instance, Carlos's last sight in Manila is a nighttime peek at "a young girl on a bamboo floor with a naked man," a prostitute whose services are offered to him by a new acquaintance, a university student named Juan. When Carlos flees the scene of this offer, Juan joins him, belatedly expressing sympathy for the prostitute:

> "There are many girls like her in Manila," he said sadly. "They come from the provinces hoping to find work in the city. But look where they have landed!" He laughed bitterly.
> I began to run furiously away from him. When I reached my boarding house the men looked at me. I put my arms around a post and tried to ease the wild beating of my heart. I wanted to cry. Suddenly, I started beating the post with my fists. (93)

Juan's account is a traditional "fallen woman" story: the girl who leaves home to seek her fortune, as Carlos is doing, will be undone by her sex. Unlike Juan, the lawyer's son, the boy Carlos cannot use language to distance himself from the girl's plight. Idealistic and sexually inexperienced, with his sister's five pesos still freshly deposited in his cloth belt, Carlos can only run, weep, and pound the posts. Unable to improve his sisters' prospects by remaining at home, Carlos has had to fly the coop, but secretly he knows it is better to be a son. For to be a Filipina peasant, in Bulosan's imagination, is both to be part of an economic and ideological snare—marriage—and to be ensnared from birth by one's sex, class, and race, albeit in ways that remain latent, not fully analyzed, in the text. In Carlos's silent flight from the scene of prostitution, Bulosan as author directs our attention toward the emotional development of Carlos as the future spokesman for his people but away from the kind of specific analysis devoted to his father's loss of land. Though clearly cognizant of the women's oppressed position, Bulosan lacks the analytical tools to balance his feelings of sadness and horror. Hence, the text cannot dissociate these women from the author's own fears of entrapment in poverty and silence.

For the boy Carlos, hardship lies ahead, but with it will come all the attendant compensations of the "quest" plot: physical mobility, the prospects of change and improvement, literacy and the powers it brings, and even the hope of transforming his adopted country.[18] By contrast, the mother and sisters, along with the married husbands and fathers, are barred from this ultimately progressive narrative and relegated to the nonnarratable subconscious of the text. They embody that which the immigrant author must forget and repress, must contain within narrative, in order to construct his American self. Though oppressed by historical forces (as the text emphasizes), they are rendered as static symbols of home, affection, poverty, hopelessness. They form the ground for Bulosan's progressive narrative of Asian American subject formation, but they cannot participate as subjects of that narrative. Even the father's dystopian narrative—that of the lost struggle to save his land from lawyers and moneylenders—is exhausted by the time Carlos leaves. The subsequent formation of the narrator as the Asian American author who represents his émigré community—both by writing and by constructing Carlos's life as a composite of Pinoy experiences—depends on Bulosan's successful separation and his ability *not* to dwell on the suffering at home, about which he can do little and which he implicitly decides he can only ameliorate and manage symbolically, through his acts of remembrance mediated through literary narrative tools such as the pastoral mode of representation, the snare motif, and the trope of the fallen woman.

The beautifully wrought narrative of Carlos's childhood is, then, the trace of the narrator's labors to reconcile contradictory feelings: on one hand, an anguished desire to flee, and on the other the desire to guard his emotional connection to his family and homeland. As we've seen, this ambivalence results in a splitting of the women of the narrator's class into two modes of representation: the nostalgic idealization of the mother and sisters is underwritten by their separation from the darker images of the "ensnaring" Filipina girls, the silent sisters-in-law, and the faceless, voiceless prostitute. The textual proximity of the prostitute scene to Carlos's last view of his homeland also hints at a possible allegorical reading of the exploited woman as a symbol for that homeland, itself a "fallen woman" exploited by colonial powers. Although such a reading is not explicitly developed by the author, the presence of the prostitute as an abjected "other," repressed from the narrator's memories of home, lends an additional dimension to the idealized portraits of the mother and sisters. Given the starkness of his family's social position and Bulosan's ideological commitment to criticizing the exploitation of his class, the affection and the feeling of pastoral beauty and innocence that imbue the narrator's memories of home can only be achieved through this literary abjection.

Here, I use the term *abjection* to refer to that which is cast out in order to define the limits of the subject; that is, the abjected "other" is created to help the subject define what he or she is not. Judith Butler, in *Bodies That Matter*, has usefully described abjection as part of the process by which the subject is constituted, in the context of theorizing how subjects are constructed by identifying within discourses pertaining to sexual identity—"an exclusionary matrix"—that enforce some identifications while excluding or "abjecting" others:

> This exclusionary matrix by which subjects are formed thus requires the simultaneous production of a domain of abject beings, those who are not yet "subjects," but who form the constitutive outside to the domain of the subject. . . . In this sense, then, the subject is constituted

through the force of exclusion and abjection, one which produces a constitutive outside to the subject, an abjected outside, which is, after all, "inside" the subject as its own founding repudiation.

The forming of a subject requires an identification with the normative phantasm of "sex," and this identification takes place through a repudiation which produces a domain of abjection, a repudiation without which the subject cannot emerge. This is a repudiation which creates the valence of "abjection" and its status for the subject as a threatening spectre. (3)

Because abjection is part of the process that defines the subject, the "abjected outside" is "inside" the subject as "a threatening spectre" whose exclusion cannot be recognized directly. Butler, it seems, is introducing a meditation on the abjection of nonheterosexual persons ("abject beings") as well as nonheterosexual aspects of the subject-in-formation ("an abjected outside, which is, after all, 'inside' the subject").

Similarly, cultural critic Anne McClintock suggests that the paradox of abjection is central to modern industrial imperialism: "Under imperialism, I argue, certain groups are expelled and obliged to inhabit the impossible edges of modernity: the slum, the ghetto, . . . and so on. Abject peoples are those whom industrial imperialism rejects but cannot do without: slaves, prostitutes, the colonized, domestic workers, . . . and so on. Certain threshold zones become abject zones and are policed with vigor . . ."[19] McClintock's "situated psychoanalysis" seeks to explain the link between individual abjections (such as the case of a white South African man who disavows identification with the black nurse who raised him) and social abjections (such as the forced removal of black women to "barren bantustans"). The political and psychological dimensions are different, but linked, and must be understood as interrelated. Similarly, several kinds of psychic exclusions help to constitute Carlos/Bulosan as an Asian American subject. First, the identity of the Filipino peasant who is oppressed by colonial and capitalist forces and whose agency is severely circumscribed by poverty and lack of education is epitomized by the mother (among other figures), who is idealized but placed at a spatial and temporal distance from Bulosan as subject; the contrast between his situation and hers defines his subjectivity. This contrast is further heightened by the text's gendering of the two halves. As symbol of the homeland and silent object of nostalgic memory, the mother is gendered feminine and is abjected. By contrast, the son is constructed as the American immigrant, the author, the subject who remembers, and is gendered as masculine. In addition, the mother, as an emblem of purity, family love, and values not tainted by the economic sphere, is imaginatively constituted by being contrasted with, and dissociated from, the abjected female others who *are* tainted by the economic sphere, those who seek to sell their sexuality, from the aggressive husband hunters to the prostitute.

If nostalgia and abjection are two tools by means of which the narrator as immigrant subject adequately distances himself from the painful memory of his mother and motherland, another is amnesia. Late in the novel, after he has begun to establish his work in America, the trajectory of his life as a Filipino son is recapitulated and wishfully revised in a dream sequence that comes to him as he sleeps aboard another bus. Returned oneirically to his Binalonan boyhood, he watches his mother serve dinner to his brothers and sisters, secretly starving herself because there isn't enough food for all. Realizing this, he stops eating and goes outside, rewarded by a look from his mother. Looking back through a window, he is gratified to see his mother join the others in their meal. This dream is immediately followed by another in which he runs away from home because he cannot bear the knowledge of his family's poverty, although he declares his home to be the loving site of "all that [is] good and true" (781). After days of wandering, he is returned home by a kindly policeman who first feeds him and tells him of a man from Binalonan who became "a maker of songs in America." Upon his return, the boy is embraced warmly by his family, now in the midst of another meal. "We have *enough* food now, son," says his mother in one of her very few lines of dialogue. As Carlos begins to eat, he remembers the police chief, "he who was so kind, gentle, and good," and associates him with the newly discovered idea of America: "Were all people *from* America like him? Were all people *in* America like him?" (283). As the narrator awakens and disembarks from his bus, he realizes that these dreams are intact forgotten memories. "How could I forget one of the most significant events in my childhood?" he asks. "How could I have forgotten a tragedy that was to condition so much of my future life?" (282–83).

The dream, which appears only after the narrator has acquired the emotional distance and technique required to contain and express his memories in literary language, recapitulates so much: the misery that first drove him away; the family's emotional warmth; the planting of the idea of America as a kinder, gentler place; the hope of authorship; and, best of all, the wish for a loving return that will magically result in the family having "*enough* food." The italicized *enough* suggests the eruption of English into the mother's dialect, marking "enough" as a concept the dreaming son associates with America. It seems that the narrator has forgotten this memory of blended love and anguish in order to be able to live with his continued absence from home until a period in his life when he is capable of imagining his mother saying "We have *enough* food now, son."

I have used Bulosan's text as a case study to hypothesize why Asian women are not portrayed as exemplary Asian American *subjects* by male authors and why they tend not to be constructed as objects of the male Asian American subject's politicized erotic desire. If white women represent aspects of the male subjects' negotiations with white America in the arduous task of constructing an Asian American subjectivity, Asian women often represent the ancestral homeland and are managed by the authorial imagination as tropes for that homeland. In Bulosan's case, however, I have argued that the analytical tools he uses to criticize American racism and class exploitation in the Philippines and the United States are conspicuously unhelpful to him in intellectually coming to terms with what he had seen of Filipinas at home or of Filipina, Indian, and Mexican women in America. Relying instead on sentimental literary modes for representing women, he ends up depicting such types as the saintly mother, the predatory husband hunters, and the fallen prostitute. By projecting positive and negative emotions about his childhood and homeland onto characters who appear unconnected, the narrator is able to preserve the idealization of his mother/homeland, to recognize yet distance himself from an unspoken perception of the homeland as needy and engulfing, and to reconcile his own needs for psychological separation *and* connection with this past. While beautifully crafted, these literary modes of representation place the female characters outside the plots that mark Carlos the protagonist and Bulosan the author as Asian American subjects. To the extent that they are entrapped in the feminine romance plot of sexual failure (which includes marriage when doomed by poverty), the women are barred from the quest plot, which defines subjectivity in terms of authorial striving and achievement. To the extent that they represent the mute suffering of those who must be left behind (however fondly remembered) in the quest for Americanness, they embody an alternate reality whose abjection helps to define the limits of the Asian American author as subject.

In reading this particular text, I find that I have interpolated a negativity, an ambivalence toward the maternal and the homeland, which seems to fight the author's manifest intent to convey his love and reverence for both. In introducing the critical terms *nostalgia, abjection,* and *amnesia,* I do not mean to criticize Bulosan as an unfilial son or emotionally disingenuous author — I think he is the opposite of these — but to hypothesize that other Asian American writers may also be deploying these rhetorical stances in order to manage or contain unruly emotions toward the Asian mother and the homeland with which she is often identified.

An additional dimension may be added, however, by considering the functions of nostalgia, abjection, gender, and amnesia within discourses of nationalism. As Anne McClintock notes, the temporal disjunction in narratives of nationalism (in which the nation is imagined as both rooted in tradition and endlessly transformed by progressive forces) is often represented as a gender difference: "Women are represented as the atavistic and authentic body of national tradition (inert, backward-looking and natural), embodying nationalism's conservative principle of continuity. Men, by contrast, represent the progressive agent of national modernity (forward-thrusting, potent and historic), embodying nationalism's progressive, or revolutionary principle of discontinuity. Nationalism's anomalous relation to time is thus managed as a natural relation to gender" (358–59). Bulosan's use of this trope is complicated, typically for an Asian American author, by his multiple positioning in discourses of progress and nationalism; among other factors, he wrote both as a Filipino American and as a Filipino nationalist. As a male, we can see him restricting the Filipina mother to the role of representing an idealized national past, and claiming progressiveness and revolutionary force for himself, both as a Filipino American and as a labor organizer in the United States. (In this book, the revolutionary voice tends to be positioned as a voice for working-class Americans rather than Filipino nationalists, as in the manifesto on pp. 188–89.) In also identifying male family members with the idealized homeland, he seems to be struggling with American discourses that construct the Phillipines and its people as the feminized, backward term in the narrative of American national (imperial) progress.

Similarly, I noted in the introduction that Ernest Renan and Homi K. Bhabha consider amnesia (willed forgetfulness about the violence that attends the founding and continued protection of nations) essential both to the writing of official narratives of the nation and to the interpellation of individual subjects in those narratives (Renan, "Nation," 22; Bhabha, "DissemiNation," 311). Carlos's need to forget this hardship is an individual consequence of the United States' need to forget (or remain ignorant of) its colonial history in the Philippines, just as the author's need to "remember" and write of this incident is emblematic of the Asian American need to "re-mind" Americans, including themselves, of the Asian American past.[20] That the runaway incident is "re-membered," to quote Bhabha's pun, can be seen by consulting another version of this story, which appears in "Passage into Life," a sequence of vignettes drawn from Bulosan's papers recently published in the posthumous collection *On Becoming Filipino: Selected Writings of Carlos Bulosan* (ed. San Juan, 47–59). In "Passage," young "Allos" is driven to flight by a scene of intrafamilial violence; by substituting hunger coupled with familial love in the published version, Bulosan the author reshapes the memory, or the earlier draft, to counter colonial stereotypes of Filipino primitiveness ("they can't govern themselves") with the sympathetic images of a hardworking, loving Filipino family struggling with hardship — drawing on classic novel imagery to reinforce the American readership's sense of Filipinos as fitting the national narrative.

Internment Era Abjections

Not all Asian American immigrant authors view their homeland through the kind of distancing narrative stance used by Bulosan (who had not seen the Philippines for many years when he wrote *America Is in the Heart*). It's probable that the tendency to portray Asian women as motherly others embodying the homeland is most pronounced in the work of American-born authors, for whom immigrant parents usually do provide their primary link to a little-known ancestral country. However, there is also an American counterpart to the idealized, absent Asian mother: the controlling, ever-present, Asian immigrant mother whose narrative function apparently is to retard the American socialization of the Asian American children by attempting to make them conform to inappropriate ideas of Asianness.

As we will see, Nina Baym has argued that male American authors and critics tend to identify American society, which is figured as corrupting and entrammeling, with controlling mother figures; the converse of the "mother as enforcer of social norms" is the image of America as "virgin land," nurturing mother, and alluring mate.[21] Baym argues that the socialization of American children is primarily accomplished by women and that women not involved in socializing young people are less visible to them; hence, the literary trope of the woman who enforces and embodies the constraints of society may be particularly common to male American authors due to their early experiences ("Melodramas," 71–73).

In men's Asian American texts, one specific version of this trope is the Asian immigrant mother as the proponent of problematically construed Asian values or as a person whose claims to the American-born son's care and loyalty somehow threaten his capacity to establish his autonomy, masculinity, and American subjectivity, categories that tend to be conflated by the type of male author I am about to examine. Versions of the needy, vulnerable, or demanding Asian mother (overseas or in the United States) occur in numerous male- and female-authored texts (including Frank Chin's *Chickencoop Chinaman,* David Henry Hwang's *Family Devotions,* Sky Lee's *Disappearing Moon Cafe,* Faye Myenne Ng's *Bone,* Bapsi Sidhwa's *An American Brat,* and many others). Among these, Milton Murayama's *All I Asking for Is My Body* and John Okada's *No-No Boy* are often taught in Asian American and ethnic studies courses that privilege the Japanese American male protagonists' struggles to claim American identity (before, during, and after the crisis of World War II, when Japanese Americans were interned on the mainland and placed under martial law in Hawaii) as exemplary of Asian American historical subjectivity during two key historical moments. Yet, to my knowledge the fundamental role of the mothers in the formation of the sons' subjectivities has not yet been fully clarified.

All I Asking for Is My Body (1975) dramatizes Kiyoshi Oyama's coming of age in Hawaii from 1932 to 1943, referring also to events that go back as far as 1902. In the novel, the Oyama family is bound to accept exploitive working conditions on a Hawaiian sugar plantation in order to pay off a debt incurred by the father's father (Grandfather Oyama) through a combination of imprudence, subsistence wages, and bad fortune. Through the voice of the eldest *nisei* (American born) son, Toshio, Murayama makes clear that the Japanese plantation workers' practice of sending their sons into the fields from age thirteen onward can never result in solvency due to the low-wage, high-expense financial environment controlled by the plantation; instead, the plantation encourages the *issei* (immigrant Japanese) to perpetuate their inherited ideologies of endurance (*gaman*), stoicism (*enryo*), and filial piety because this results in the reproduction of a new generation of manageable laborers. The family's mother, Mrs. Oyama, becomes the primary advocate for an interpretation of filial piety that requires her sons' indefinite submission to plantation labor, even when Tosh explains that, after he's worked full-time and given his parents all his wages for years, the debt hasn't been reduced by a penny. Although both parents support the grandfather's no-win interpretation of filial piety, it is the mother who is shown relentlessly nagging the sons with Confucian dogma to keep them from running away or repudiating the debt, while male elders, such as the father and the sons' teachers, are able to be more detached, reflective, and cagey about the problem of applying Confucian standards to life in Hawaii. (For instance, Mr. Oyama is able to prevent his community's savings from being frozen in the panic after Pearl Harbor but also to make an FBI investigator understand that his action in this matter doesn't signal disloyalty to the U.S. government [86]).

Though Murayama's narrator, Kiyoshi, the second son, expresses sympathy for his mother's views and respect for her lifetime of sacrifice, the text clearly privileges the nisei sons as the exemplary Asian American subjects (the daughters are passive observers of the ideological struggle) and uses the mother to voice the inflexible "Asian" ideology, which the sons must challenge in order to establish their Americanness.[22]

John Okada's *No-No Boy* also uses an Asian immigrant mother to embody a version of Japanese ethnicity that the American-born son, Ichiro Yamada, must question and discard in order to construct himself as an Asian American subject. During the war, the U.S. government asked internees to sign a loyalty oath, which included the following questions:

27. Are you willing to serve in the armed forces of the United States on combat duty wherever ordered?
28. Will you swear unqualified allegiance to the United States of

America and faithfully defend the United States from any or all attack by foreign or domestic forces, and forswear any form of allegiance or obedience to the Japanese emperor, [or] to any other foreign government, power, or organization? (Michi Weglyn, *Years,* 136; qtd. in Sumida, "Moral Dilemmas," 225)

Ichiro is a character who, having answered in the negative to both these questions, has been dubbed a "no-no boy" and jailed as a draft resister. Although the novel recognizes that some nisei declined to serve out of a desire to protest the internment, it depicts Ichiro as having refused the draft primarily as an expression of solidarity with his mother, whose view of herself and her family as entirely Japanese now galls him. The novel opens with his return to Seattle after the war, where he must face not only the general anti-Japanese feeling of mainstream Americans but the disapproval of some Japanese Americans because he apparently has compromised the community's efforts to prove its Americanness.

While Ichiro's process of identity construction is far more problematic and incomplete than that of the Oyama brothers, Okada's equation of Mrs. Yamada with a toxic version of Japanese ethnicity is notably harsher than Murayama's critical yet compassionate portrayal of the wrongheaded Mrs. Oyama. In Mrs. Yamada, Japanese motherhood is equated with a fiercely dogmatic, pro-Japanese nationalism and a detachment from feeling and reality that marks her as literally insane. Her death, an apparent suicide, frees Ichiro to begin to reconstitute his ideal of Japanese American identity, in which Japanese ethnicity complements identification with America, an ideal he links with the children's hero Momataro and an idealized but now lost childhood (Okada, *No-No Boy,* 15–16).

If we read the text simply as demonizing Japanese ethnicity and maternity at once, by projecting a hateful Japanese nationalism onto the only significant issei mother in the story, it might seem overtly anti-Japanese and misogynist. In such a reading (which has been provided more fully by Gayle Fujita Sato), we might note that Ichiro's memories of a happy home life in his Momataro monologue don't seem to be supported by memories of his mother as loving, nurturing, or otherwise attractive. We might also contrast Ichiro's broken family with the close-knit family of his admired friend, the veteran Kenji Kanno. In the Yamada family, the sons do not speak with each other and behave with resentful hatred toward the parents. The father is alcoholic, and the mother is insane. The text often suggests that the dissolution of this family is somehow the fault of the mother. Ichiro blames her not only for egging him on to become a no-no boy and for her militant loyalty to Japan but for expressing disapproval of American culture (once smashing a record player he'd borrowed); for serving only Japanese American food; for living like a permanent visitor (refusing to buy decent furniture); for usurping his father's authority in the family; and, most fundamentally, for refusing to recognize that her sons are American. In contrast to the too-Japanese Yamadas, the Kannos communicate well, behave lovingly and considerately toward one another, eat roast chicken and lemon meringue pie, watch baseball, and have no mother. Are motherlessness and cultural assimilation (symbolized by the abandonment of Japanese American food) being valorized, then, by Okada?

Stephen H. Sumida has suggested what is in essence a recuperative reading that "rescues" the text from its moments of apparent celebration of total assimilation; this reading suggests that the book is ambivalent and multivoiced about this issue.[23] As he points out, the novel is most sophisticated when we assume that (although he is not the actual narrator) Ichiro is meant to function like an unreliable narrator at the story's outset, when his feelings against his parents and his own political choices as a no-no boy are most virulent, because these feelings represent the distorted perspective of a young man just returned from internment and imprisonment who must now face scapegoating by the Japanese American community (due to the perception that he compromised their loyalty) and the mainstream community (due to undifferentiated anti-Japanese feelings). In this reading, passages that appear to condemn the retention of signs of Japanese ethnicity must be placed within the larger action of the novel, in which Ichiro's primary friendships and loyalties are to the Japanese American community, in which he refuses to evade the resentment of the community by leaving town for a good job with a liberal white employer, and in which he ultimately decides to stay with his fragile father while seeking answers to his still unanswered larger questions. When placed within the context of Ichiro's clear desire to situate himself within a strong Japanese American community (and his nostalgia for such a community in the Momatoro monologue), the novel's puzzling rhetoric of longing for Japanese American assimilation (most notably Kenji's monologue, 163–64) must be read as ironic and as a peculiarly expressed, utopian wish for the end of race hatred in America. Even the Kanno family's closeness and its "successful" Americanization must be interpreted in the context of Kenji's lingering death due to a wartime injury. Though admired by his community as a patriotic hero, Kenji is one of the most sardonic critics of Japanese American assimilation fantasies: he most clearly and bitterly understands that neither his service nor his imminent death has purchased his community's acceptance by black and white Americans (163).

Sumida's hints ask us to overlook the plethora of evidence linking Mrs. Yamada with the novel's apparent acceptance of the "dual identity" model of Japanese American psychology and to focus instead on the complex, unfinished ideological work that forms the central action of the novel: Ichiro has to try out various accounts of Japanese American identity, including all the problematic ones, in his search for a viable way to understand his and his community's experiences. At the end of the novel, this work is still unfinished because Ichiro, his community, and his country have so much more to do and because the author, who published this novel of political critique and dissent in 1957, was writing before the Japanese American or mainstream communities were ready to hear what he had to say. (The University of Washington's current edition comes with front and back matter describing the editors' discovery of this forgotten masterpiece and its profound rejection by the audiences of its time.) The account that Ichiro needs in order to feel justified in his actions, and which is strangely missing from his consciousness, is one that positions the no-no boys as questioning the constitutionality of the American government's actions in the best American tradition of civil disobedience. Although Okada must have been aware that at least some no-no boys regarded themselves as heroic, truly American, political dissenters even in prison (Sumida, "Moral Dilemmas," 233, n. 9), he has chosen to portray Ichiro as lacking this view of his own actions. As a result, both he and his mother suffer from the view that equates consent with Americanness and dissent with loyalty to Japan; hence Ichiro, and at times the novel, seem to believe that he can only be American by disavowing his mother, who represents both loyalty to Japan and vindictive, irrational thought processes.

What does need further examination, however, is Okada's portrayal of Mrs. Yamada, which seems to suggest that loyalty to Japan, even for an issei forbidden by American law to become an American citizen, would necessarily be nationalistic, anti-American, irrational, and unfeeling as well as unwomanly *and* unmanly. Because of the novel's status as an impassioned representation of the postinternment era, critics have been largely silent about this problematic portrayal except for Gayle Fujita Sato's incisive argument that Mrs. Yamada becomes the embodiment of "bad" Japaneseness.[24] Sato is right, I think, to interpret this characterization as a political failure: her essay suggests, as I have, that Okada conflates anti-Japanese and anti-feminist feeling. While I read Sato's feminist critique with a certain relief ("Someone else thinks the emperor has no clothes!"), my understanding of the novel as not anti-Japanese in any simple way compels me to wonder whether the novel's antifeminism can be so simple, either.

My reading concurs with Sato's assessment that Ichiro's Asian American subjectivity is grounded in the apparent rejection of negative Japanese traits projected onto the Asian immigrant mother, but I suggest that the concept of abjection may help to clarify the extent to which Okada renegotiates the "dual personality" problem through his portrayal of Mrs. Yamada rather than merely replicating it, as Sato argues. If her abjection is the basis for Ichiro's identification with America, I suggest that this founding act of abjection originates not with Ichiro or Okada but with the mainstream culture in which both struggled to articulate their subjectivity. That is, Mrs. Yamada's madness takes the specific form of seeking to constitute her and her family as wholly Japanese, an identification grounded in a bitter rejection (indeed, an abjection) of the country that has rejected *her*. This dis-ease corresponds uncannily with the mainstream culture's wartime abjection of the Japanese American community as essentially Japanese and un-American: she is just the sort of nationalist, anti-American, Japanese nut who was conjured up by the American press and military to justify placing Japanese Americans into camps, symbolically outside the borders of "America," a white nation. As Judith Butler has put it, the "exclusionary matrix by which subjects are formed thus requires the simultaneous production of a domain of abject beings, who are not yet "subjects," but who form the constitutive outside to the domain of the subject" (*Bodies*, 3). If Okada had depicted the development of Mrs. Yamada's madness, we might ask how she came to accept the demonic role assigned her, as a Japanese American, by the American government and press. But Okada never really establishes her as a subject before placing her in this politically abjected position; by definition, he cannot inhabit the consciousness of the character he is using to define otherness (this may be why Butler characterizes abjection as creating both "a domain of abject beings" and "zones of uninhabitability" [3]). Instead, Okada seems at first to replicate the mainstream abjection of Japanese Americans by dividing Japanese American subjectivity into Japanese and American halves and positioning Mrs. Yamada as the alien other, whose abjection helps to redefine her sons as "real" Americans. By placing Mrs. Yamada's intolerable traits within a single character— an Asian mother figure—who then commits suicide, Okada symbolically purges the Japanese American psyche of these unwanted traits so that Ichiro and others in his community can psychically and politically reconstruct their Japanese American subjectivities free of this disturbing, unassimilable element.[25]

Ultimately, however, Okada does *not* simply replicate white America's division of Japanese American subjectivity into incommensurate Japanese and American halves (the "dual personality" model) but conceives the ideal Japanese American subject as one who identifies with both America and his ethnic community. This reconstructed Japanese American subject under construction need not be deracinated: the text supports a reading in which Ichiro seeks to construct himself as a Japanese American who identifies with both his country and his ethnic community. Nonetheless, when placed within the context of other male-authored texts, the use of the issei *mother* to represent the abjected Japanese traits seems fundamental to such texts rather than accidental. For instance, the issei father (Mr. Yamada) can participate in the Japanese national tasks of mourning and reconstruction by sending money and goods to suffering Japanese relatives only after Mrs. Yamada's death. The narrator describes these acts as signs of Mr. Yamada's reversion to "natural" feeling, as if he had been "unnatural" as long as he harbored sympathy for Mrs. Yamada's nationalism and permitted her to usurp his patriarchal authority. But since his care packages are also a private version of the U.S. government's postwar reconstruction of Japan as its Asian counterpart, we may read this "naturalness" as symbolic of Okada's perception that Japanese and American perspectives "naturally" go together in Japanese American subjects — especially male ones — once the war is won and the Asian mother dead and buried.

Kenji and Ichiro are befriended by an articulate, supportive nisei woman, Emi, whose husband keeps reenlisting in the U.S. Army in a vain attempt to erase his older brother's angry gesture of moving to Japan in protest of the internment. In some ways, Emi is an exemplary Japanese American subject. An able explicator of Japanese American identity who also combines ethnic and American identifications, she combines criticism of the U.S. government (in the form of arguments justifying Ichiro's past choices) with a rhetoric of reconciliation (mutual forgiveness between the subject and the state) in her efforts to help Ichiro come to terms with his situation. However, Okada's use of Emi reinforces the text's focus on the male perspective. Like Kenji, Mr. Carrick, and Freddy, Emi functions primarily to elucidate Ichiro's potential subject position, but, unlike these characters, Emi has no story of her own. She exists only to support and discuss the choices and careers of male niseis. Emi's past is defined in terms of her husband, her brother-in-law, and Kenji, her future in terms of Ichiro.

In short, Murayama's and Okada's texts exemplify the pattern of taking the American-born son as the exemplary subject who defines his "Americanness" in terms of his capacity to construct an ethnicized American identity negotiated in relation to authorized ideologies voiced either by immigrant elders or by white American authorities. In their texts, Asian immigrant mothers become purveyors of received ideas about proper Asian conduct. They are dogmatic and less capable of critical reasoning than their male relatives. The one female character who is productively engaged with Asian American ideological questions, Emi, is diminished in authority and autonomy by such dated gendering practices as situating her in terms of parallel men's stories; emphasizing her sexual appeal and availability to men; and having her burst into tears or apologize, signaling submissiveness, whenever she forcefully disagrees with Ichiro. At the same time, Emi is also a very unusual figure in Asian American male texts: an Asian American woman who is not only sympathetic to her male peers and sexually attracted to them but who also helps them in their formatory task of negotiating American ideologies of identity. (It is common for immigrant mothers in this literature to help their male relatives to survive *materially* but to be unable to help *discursively* in the battle for American subjectivity, which is depicted as a male field of struggle.) In short, these texts fail to conceive Asian American women as full-fledged subjects, instructors, or allies in the intellectual battle to found Asian American subjectivity even as they represent white women as the natural performers of these functions in the Asian American male's struggle.

To the extent that these texts present the Asian American mother as the would-be enforcer of misapplied "Asian" values (contrasted with the weaker but more reasonable, more adaptable fathers) that threaten the autonomy, Americanness, and masculinity of their American-born sons, Murayama and Okada develop an Asian American version of Baym's paradigm, the women who represent the "constricting, entrammeling society," from which the heroes must escape in order to establish their autonomous, masculine Americanness and their fitness for literary canonization as exemplary "American" heroes. Perhaps because the father-mother-son triad fits a family structure very familiar to American readers, readers have been slow to analyze the "Asianization" and abjection of the Asian American mother figure in these and other key texts (such as Frank Chin's plays). For the same reasons, Murayama and Okada's texts have been embraced fairly uncritically for their historic merits in capturing Japanese American experience in the periods just before and after World War II.

To put it another way, Kang, Bulosan, Okada, and Murayama may be taken as suggestive examples of a demi-canon in which male Asian American authors construct narratives of male Americanization in the first and second generations in settings ranging from the 1920s through the years just after World War II. While acknowledging their important differences in class, ethnicity, period of immigration, generation, and genre, my reading suggests that these writers use common fictional tropes and narrative conventions to represent constructions of male Asian American subjectivity or, more precisely, constructions of Asian American subjectivity as normatively male. For the immigrant writers Kang and Bulosan, the construction of American subjectivity is intimately linked with the project of constructing the subject as an author. Given the severe economic and social marginalization of these authors' ethnic communities, authorship also meant visibility before the American middle class and honorary entry into it. For

Kang's scholarly hero, authorship substitutes for his loss in America of elite status. For Bulosan's fictional alter ego, authorship offers a symbolic means of addressing the problem of caring for his family and defending his fellow workers; *America* suggests that, although Bulosan enjoyed some of the psychological benefits of the middle-class profession of authorship (such as better understanding of his circumstances, a sense of greater control over his fate, a renewed sense of mission and self-respect, and public recognition), he never gives up his initial identifications with peasants and farmworkers. Authorship is particularly important to the protagonists of these novels because they arrive in the United States at moments when it is difficult for Asian immigrant men to marry and found families there. Authorship therefore serves as a symbolic means of self-fathering and fathering literary, if not actual, progeny while also intervening in the public discourses that publicly justify their marginalization, the discourses that form the orientalist side of the exclusion narrative.

In their portrayals of white women as mediators of the Asian male's entry into American society via the claiming of authorship, Kang and Bulosan anticipate the concerns of the 1970s cohort of Asian American writer-critics, represented in this study by Frank Chin, and the later cohort of authors informed by the 1970s authors, a diverse group for whom I take David Mura as one example. Finally, I take Bulosan's ambivalent constructions of Filipinas as suggestive of a group of rhetorical strategies employed by first- and second-generation writers to represent and contain ambivalence toward their homeland and family obligations. This ambivalence is redoubled in the casting of immigrant mothers as advocates of "Asian" ideologies (actually problematic ideologies constructed in response to American circumstances), which must be overcome or escaped by American-born sons in order to establish their autonomy, manhood, and Americanness in texts by American-born authors Okada and Murayama.

Intertextually, these texts are united by their positioning of male subjects as exemplary of Asian America, defined by their capacity to interrogate and deploy American discourses: Kang and Bulosan, by constructing themselves and their protagonists as authors; and all four authors, by constructing their male protagonists as critical interrogators of American democratic rhetoric. In their texts, white women appear as aides (and obstacles) to the development of that critical capacity; Asian American women either appear iconically (as silent embodiments of the past who don't participate directly in the son's discursive apprenticeship), or as inept interpreters of ideology, slow learners who keep repeating the old Asian saws and cannot take the new American reality into their minds. Okada's Emi, one of the few male-created Asian American women characters who also appears to take part in this task of producing an innovative discourse of Asian American sub-jectivity, is recuperated into Okada's male-centered text by virtue of her service on multiple levels to the concerns of her male counterparts. Those concerns have been most dramatically presented in the critical work of the *Aiiieeeee* editors and the argumentative language of Frank Chin, to whom we will now turn.

2

Authoring Subjects:
Frank Chin and David Mura

Frank Chin, Nina Baym, and the
Gendering of the Canon

Perhaps the most insistent and influential story told about the struggles of Asian American males for authorship is that told by Frank Chin and his coeditors, Jeffrey Paul Chan, Lawson Fusao Inada, and Shawn Wong, starting around 1973, when they published their first Asian American anthology, *Aiiieeeee! An Anthology of Asian American Writers.* Because this story has been reprinted in subsequent essays signed by Chin alone, I will refer to these ideas as his, although they were initially jointly published. Over these two decades, Chin's essays and interviews have developed a myth that links concerns about Asian American authorship, Americanness, and ethnic identity with concerns about masculinity, cultural preservation, and survival on both the material and cultural levels.[1] By comparing Chin's critical work with Nina Baym's analysis of canon formation within American literature, I will demonstrate that Chin's essays also adumbrate (but don't articulate directly) a concern with filiation, descent, and genealogical continuance, which is another central nexus of concerns—and an eminently American one—within Asian American writing.[2]

Chin's argument, which has become one of the shaping paradigms for Asian American cultural studies, was an extension of the exclusion story into the cultural arena. In what I'll call Chin's extinction thesis, he argued that the underlying idea of America as a white nation, and Americans as whites, had been translated into the cultural exclusion of colored peoples from positions of unmarked, or universal, subjectivity in American culture. Thus, Asian Americans were expected to identify with Asian cultures even if born and raised in the United States. They were never perceived as American, and they found their particular experiences as Asian Americans devalued or erased from cultural productions.

A significant corollary of this point (the emasculation thesis) was that Asian American men were not only materially and politically marginalized but culturally emasculated as well, both as characters in cultural productions and as authors, creators, or interpreters of such productions. Before the term *model minority* came into vogue, Chin identified the thinking of people who identify Asian Americans as Asian, oriental, and exotic, and hence as friendly, amenable, and submissive, as "racist love," a thinly disguised form of American orientalism.[3] Racist love was a forerunner of the current "model minority" paradigm, which depicts Asian Americans as exemplary minorities because they ostensibly achieve success without demanding fundamental changes in American society.

Chin's second major point, which I'll call the authenticity thesis, was that Asian American authors who catered to white perceptions of Asian Americans as fundamentally foreign, and their culture as kinky and exotic, were guilty of "faking" Asian culture. In the two decades between the publication of the first *Aiiieeeee!* anthology and the second (the dates of the critical introductions are 1973 and 1991, respectively), the definitions of *fake* and *real* Asian American culture shifted. *Faking* at first meant offering traditional Chinese culture as in any way representative of Chinese American consciousness, but later, after Chin came to embrace the images of Chinese masculinity he found in the Chinese "heroic tradition," he singled out for attack authors who constructed their own versions of traditional Chinese stories or who made up Chinese customs wholesale.[4] Under the guise of defending "real" Chinese American culture and experience from slanderous falsification, Chin singled out for his strongest attacks writers who portrayed Chinese or Chinese American men as ineffectual, perverse, oppressive to women, confused about their identities, or sympathetic to the idea that Western or American culture was distinct from and superior to Eastern or East Asian culture or character. Among Japanese Americans, Chin attacked post–World War II writers who, traumatized by the internment, wrote about the problems of reconciling their Japanese heritage with their American identity. Chin was (appropriately) offended by their acceptance of the mainstream view that Asianness and Americanness constituted dichotomous poles. In his 1991 essay "Come All Ye Asian American Writers, the Real and the Fake," Chin lambasted Maxine Hong Kingston, David Henry Hwang, and Amy Tan for fabricating accounts of Chinese culture and subjectivity that were written "to the specifications of the Christian stereotype of Asia being as opposite morally from the West as it is geographically." Chin described the stereotype this way:

This is the stereotype of Asia, Asians, and Asian Americans.

The first yellows came to America with no intention of settling. They were sojourners. They intended to stay in America just long enough to make a fortune, then return to China or Japan to live high on the hog.

Chinese and Japanese culture are so misogynistic they don't deserve to survive. The men are intelligent, brilliant, and perverse — either pervertedly evil, like Fu Manchu, whose strange idea of torturing white men is to send them to be with his beautiful nympho daughter. Even the bad yellows are, thus, subcutaneous white supremacists.

Asian culture is anti-individualistic, mystic, passive, collective, and morally and ethically opposite to Western culture . . . (8–9)

To discuss the second half of Chin's "Come All" essay, I need to refer to the internment of the Japanese Americans. Earlier, I recapitulated the Asian American exclusion narrative as a context for the immigrant writers Carlos Bulosan and Younghill Kang. In doing so, I delayed mention of a central episode related to the broader phenomenon of exclusion (but not immigration restrictions per se) that also affected American citizens of Asian descent: the internment of 112,000 people of Japanese descent (both immigrants and American citizens) during World War II (S. Chan, *Asian Americans,* 45; I use Chan's estimate for the number of internees). As others have demonstrated, the unwarranted suspension of this community's civil rights was clearly based on the same exclusionist thinking that led legislators first to prevent Japanese settlers (issei) from owning land or becoming naturalized citizens and then to construct them and their American-born children (nisei) as incorrigibly alien and un-American. In Sucheng Chan's concise account of this period (123–39), the "once a Jap, always a Jap" rationale for the internment is demonstrated by General John De Witt's statement calling for the community's removal from the West Coast on racial grounds: "The Japanese were 'an enemy race,' declared the document, whose 'racial affinities [were] not severed by migration' and whose 'racial strains' remained 'undiluted' even among members of the second and third generations. Therefore, because the army had no ready means to separate out the disloyal from the loyal, all persons of Japanese ancestry, regardless of their citizenship status, must be removed from the coast" (125).

Frank Chin, surveying Japanese American writing in 1991, also took aim at post–World War II writers such as Daniel Okimoto, who used the term *dual personality* to describe the postinternment division of the Japanese American sensibility and for accepting a simplistic, historically uninformed, and essentialist explanation for the supposed lack of Japanese American resistance to the internment.

For the Sansei, the stereotype and the dual personality take the form of an ugly, nagging, personal question: Why did their parents—the American-born Nisei, the second-generation Nikkei—accept and endure the obvious constitutional wrongs of the evacuation and internment without protest or resistance? Okimoto's painful answer is: Too much passive Japanese culture. Japanese culture is the culture of the pathological victim, born in camp to parents whose entire generation was too chicken to stand up for these rights in court. (Chin, "Come All," 51–52)

In Chin's subsequent discussion, Japanese Americans are divided into collaborators with the American government on one hand and heroic draft and internment resisters on the other; the practitioners of civil disobedience are portrayed as heroic outlaws and loyal Americans—because they insist on questioning the constitutionality of their community's detention—who must contend with a majority of Japanese Americans who have been taught in the camps to view Japanese as culturally passive, weak, and inferior and have accepted the view that Japanese Americans should submit to the internment, serve in the armed forces, distance themselves from their ethnic culture, move away from Japanese communities, and intermarry with whites in order to "prove" their Americanness to an obviously racist white majority. The resisters Chin compares with the bandits of the Chinese novel *The Water Margin* and the forty-seven ronin (leaderless samurai) of the Japanese play, *Chusingura*.

What emerges from Chin's Manichean account of Chinese and Japanese American culture and history is his desire to construct Chinese and Japanese Americans as independent people of ethical and psychological integrity and ethnic pride; his linking of these traits with a heterosexual, masculine code of conduct derived from this personal interpretation of certain Chinese and Japanese texts; and his willingness to caricature and demonize writers whose work does not accord with his vision. Although Chin does praise some women and attack some men, he seems to identify "real" accounts of Chinese and Japanese history and culture strongly with affirmations of ethnic male heroism, decency, heterosexuality, and authorship. Chin's central ideas—the extinction, emasculation, and authenticity theses—seem strikingly to accord with another myth equating American manhood and authorship, that identified by Nina Baym as definitive of canonical American novels. She calls it the "melodrama of beset manhood"; I'll call it the author-hero myth.[5]

In her essay, "Melodramas of Beset Manhood: How Theories of American Fiction Exclude Women Authors," Baym cites influential critical books ranging from 1941 through 1974 to discuss canon formation in the 1970s, when feminist scholars' efforts toward recanonizing American women writers paralleled the efforts of the *Aiiieeeee!* editors and other Asian American cultural critics to write Asian Americans into the American canon.[6] Given the congruence between Chin's canonization criteria and those Baym describes, it's clear that Baym has described the mainstream culture in which Chin and his cohort received their formal literary training.

In brief, Baym argues that from the beginning of American literary criticism the criterion for quality in American literature has been "Americanness" rather than formal excellence because those seeking to validate the independence and uniqueness of American literature also sought politically to break the shackles of English cultural domination, including English standards for formal literary excellence. Thus, American texts were assessed for their use as documents defining the nation's cultural essence. Citing Lionel Trilling as one example, Baym argues that American critics ended up favoring male, middle-class WASPs who felt slightly alienated from the mainstream by virtue of their literary profession. Then, in Leslie Fiedler's influential account of American fiction, this "consensus criticism of the consensus" was construed to exclude women by identifying them with the consensus being attacked, "the flagrantly bad bestseller" against which "our best fictionists," all males, had to struggle for "their integrity and their livelihoods" (Baym, "Melodramas," 69). Fiedler belittled women writers as hacks producing "melodramas of beset womanhood," which he dismissed as obviously unable to convey anything essential about the American character. In retaliation, Baym describes the central myth of Americanness favored by male critics as a "melodrama of beset manhood": "This melodrama is presented in a fiction which, as we will later see, can be taken as representative of the author's literary experience, his struggle for integrity and livelihood against flagrantly bad bestsellers written by women. Personally beset in a way that epitomizes the tensions of our culture, the male author produces his melodramatic testimony to our culture's essence — so the theory goes" (70).

According to Baym, the quintessential American author constructed by these critics produced a story whose content reflected the circumstances of his own career, a tale that went like this: "The myth narrates a confrontation of the American individual, the pure American self divorced from specific social circumstances, with the promise offered by the idea of America. This promise is the deeply romantic one that in this new land, untrammeled by history and social accident, a person will be able to achieve complete self-definition . . ." (71). The romantic component of the myth, which led critics to devalue texts emphasizing the individual's social circumstances, became a means for devaluing texts about the specifics of female or minority experiences. Self-definition would be achieved, however, in opposition to the destructive forces of society, and the struggler's prime refuge from these forces would be the American wilderness, which "offers to the individual [a] medium on which he may inscribe, unhindered, his own destiny and his own nature" (71). In fiction and criticism by men, both the "encroaching, constricting, destroying society" and the nurturing wilderness were portrayed as female, creating a mythic structure problematic for women writers and therefore eschewed or reimagined by them. However, women's departures from or variations on the male norm were devalued or disregarded by male critics.

Baym then argues that the heroes of these myths were replicating the heroic task critics saw as the authors': "Fundamentally, the idea is that the artist writing a story of this essential American kind is engaging in a task very much like the one performed by this mythic hero. In effect, the artist writing his narrative is imitating the mythic encounter of hero and possibility in the safe confines of his study, or, reversing the temporal order, one might see that mythic encounter of hero and possibility as a projection of the artist's situation" (76). In short, the mythic hero was a stand-in for the heroic, struggling author. Hence, the myth of heroism, which was so uncongenial to women protagonists, also became a vehicle for excluding most women writers.

Finally, Baym demonstrates that a Bloomian twist on the equation of the quintessential American hero with the quintessential American author is the conflation of authorship and authority with paternity. Her example is a thesis offered by Eric Sundquist, which is based on the idea that novels about artists are in fact about the authors themselves: "Writing a narrative about oneself may represent an extremity of Oedipal usurpation or identification, a bizarre act of self fathering. . . . American authors have been particularly obsessed with fathering a tradition of their own, with becoming their "own sires". . . . The struggle . . . is central to the crisis of representation, and hence of style, that allows American authors to find in their own fantasies those of a nation and to make of these fantasies a compelling and instructive literature" (Sundquist, xix; qtd. in Baym, "Melodramas," 77–78). In short, Baym argues that American literature has been shaped by critics to conform to an exemplary myth which defines the quintessential American as a man who struggles against a feminized and feminizing society by fleeing to the American wilderness, a blank but also feminized page upon which he may inscribe his own vision of self and society; this myth doubles as a prototype for a myth of authorship itself that implicitly defines the quintessential American author as a similarly struggling hero.

Baym's analysis of gender bias in the formation of the American literary canon provides a telling context for assessing Chin's account of Asian

American literary history. First published in 1981, Baym's account discusses influential critics of the 1940s, 1950s, and 1960s who defined the standards of American literary excellence assumed by Chin, who attended college in the 1960s. Chin, beginning his project of Asian American canon formation in the early 1970s, models his criteria after those established for the American canon: he fashions a central myth as definitive of the culture, and he marks this myth in terms of gender. Second, the myth Chin constructs and obsessively repeats is the story of a lone hero, or preferably a band of brothers, battling the forces of a corrupting society. He structures his essay "Come All" by fitting all the cases that concern him into this myth, which is thereby repeated in various forms a dozen times. The first and most important iteration is represented by the image of the one Chinaman playing flamenco guitar (an artist of the ethnic "real" in Chin's unique cultural universe) versus a conspiracy of white supremacists and writers of the "fake," the emasculating Asian American stereotype; among Chinese American writers, most proponents of the fake are Chinese American women, the most important ones being Kingston and Tan (who make up, adapt, and steal Chinese and other myths and who also attack Asian misogyny) and Hwang (who has created a treacherous, feminized, homosexual Chinese male character). Chin then repeats his myth four more times as he recounts famous episodes from *Three Kingdoms, Journey to the West, Water Margin,* and a Chinese American text, *An English-Chinese Phrasebook,* which he identifies as core texts in a Chinese American heroic canon. Next he recasts his myth in terms of Japanese American history, as he opposes Mike Masaoka and the Japanese American Citizens League (JACL). He portrays both Masaoka and the JACL leadership as overly accepting of the government's racist policies and contrasts them with those he identifies as heroic dissenters: James Omura, the Heart Mountain draft resisters, and the subsequent writers of "the real" account of the internment experience, Peter Suzuki, Michi Weglyn, and John Okada.[7]

These examples seem clearly to resonate with Baym's account of the indirect exclusion of women from American literature. In "Come All," the sellout authors are women and a man who write about gender issues as well as racial ones rather than construing Asian American males strictly as outlaws beset by American racism. The Chinese ur-heroes are male outlaws (except for a few token women, as we shall see). Kuan Yin, a central female figure in *Journey to the West* who exemplifies a Buddhist ethos of mercy, redemption, and detachment rather than rebellion and heroism, is not mentioned, and the defining proof of Japanese American authenticity is draft resistance.

In short, the examples used in "Come All" to define Asian American reality are all variants of a central story, traceable to the literary culture described by Baym, in which the *Aiiieeeee* editors and their allies, writers of the real, combat "that mob of scribbling women," gender benders and assimilationists (Kingston, Tan, Hwang, Okimoto, Masaoka, and others). Thus, fictional battles represent authorial battles, authorial battles represent cultural ones, and the *Aiiieeeee* critics are also the heroes of Chin's myth of Asian American literature.

Finally, it seems that for Chin, as well as for critics like Sundquist and Bloom, to write or to author is to "father oneself" as well as one's children. The concern with creating a text and creating a canon are inextricably linked to concerns about creating a descent line of one's own, in this case an Asian American line. The cultural fathers the *Aiiieeeee* critics must slay are, first, the white creators of the detested Asian stereotypes and, second, their alleged Asian or Asian American counterparts, from Pardee Lowe to Amy Tan.

Now that we understand the Chinese opera of beset manhood, how important is it (as my students always ask me)? In fact, it describes a substantial number of texts by Asian American male writers and even indirectly informs many texts by Asian American women writers. This may be because many writers are grappling with the same issues; because, as Americans, they have been educated with the same cultural narratives, which in turn shape their own literary creations; or because these are the texts that have been selected for validation by publishers, reviewers, critics, and teachers trained to view American literature through the criteria Baym has described.

Chinese American Self-Fathering: Frank Chin's Early Plays

Not surprisingly, the myth of the Asian American artist-hero struggling for survival — the Chin version of American critics' canon-defining artist-heros — dominates Chin's own creative output. The protagonist may be a loner or may have one, two, or three close friends who serve as allies in his war for survival, but in Chin's work he is always struggling to come to grips with a working-class, Cantonese, Chinatown background (a "Chinaman" background) about which both the heroes and the texts evidence a mixture of pride and shame. Three texts that were written in the same periods as the *Aiiieeeee* essays and focus closely on problems of authorship, masculinity, and fathering for the "Chinaman" author are the early plays *The Chickencoop Chinaman* (premiered in 1972) and *The Year of the Dragon* (premiered in 1974) and the novel *Donald Duk* (1991).

In these texts, marrying, courting, or possessing white mates is equated with assimilation into the white majority culture, with upward class mobility and with leaving, denying, and betraying Chinatown culture and identity. An analysis of the early plays makes clear the roots of Chin's ideological aims in the accessible *Donald Duk;* from the beginning, he seeks to construct a version of Chinese American artistry and heroism in which ideal attributes of middle-class WASP culture—economic security, independence, confidence, and faith in the future—can be claimed without renouncing one's Chinatown roots.

The Chickencoop Chinaman is structured primarily around the theme of the Chinese American hero's search for a father, or more broadly for a positive male cultural identity. In the prologue, the protagonist, Tam, figuratively fathers himself by describing his creation as a verbal and volitional act rather than a physical birth—thereby disavowing that Chinamen have mothers:

> Chinamen are made, not born, my dear. Out of junk-imports, lies, railroad scrap iron, dirty jokes, broken bottles, cigar smoke, Cosquilla Indian blood, wino spit, and lots of milk of amnesia.

> My dear, in the beginning there was the word! Then there was me! And the Word was CHINAMAN. And there was me . . . (6)

The maternal principle thus erased from the text is linked with Chinese identity and culture by the "Hong Kong Dream Girl," who wishes Tam would acknowledge his "Cantonese heritage" and his "mother tongue," only to have these denied by him. (He also dismisses the Dream Girl, a stereotypical icon of Chinese femininity who appears as a majorette, by leering at her.)[8]

Tam has identified himself as an ethnic verbal construct made of cultural debris, cultural forgetfulness (milk of amnesia), and language. Having carefully "forgotten" his mother, he reveals in the course of the play that "Chinamen do make lousy fathers. I know. I have one" (23), but his only memories of a specific father figure are those of an elderly old man whom he has befriended, whom he calls a "crazy old dishwasher," and who he says is not his father. When Tam refuses to respond emotionally to a fatherless boy, Robby (saying "I'm not your buddy. I'm an old dude who tells kids jokes, bosses 'em around gruffly, roughhouses 'em, has a swell time, and forgets 'em, cuz that's what adults do" [18]), he seems to be describing not only himself but the fathering he has received. A bit later, he says he wants his own children to forget him, apparently because he feels they'll be better off identifying with their middle-class white stepfather (27).

In lieu of a Chinese father or hero, Tam seeks white and black heroes. He recalls how in childhood he fantasized that the Lone Ranger was secretly

Asian, but the Ranger appears in this play only to disillusion him by mouthing racist stereotypes:

You China boys been lucky up to now takin' it easy, preservin' your culture.

. . . some culture! Look at this shirt! A hero like me needs fast service. I said light starch, and look at this! This is what I tamed the West for? You better do something about preservin' your culture, boys, and light starch! (35)

The black boxer Jack Ovaltine Dancer seems a more promising ethnic American hero, and Tam seeks to perpetuate the story of Jack's heroism by interviewing his putative father and trainer, Charley Popcorn, for a film about the former champ's great relationship with his father. Tam suffers a setback, however, when Charley Popcorn proves not to be Jack's father and seems suspicious of Tam, whose Asian face is at odds with the "black" voice he heard on the phone. Evidently, Jack Dancer has already out-authored Tam by doing his own self-fathering. Not only has he reinvented his former trainer as the ethnic father of his dreams, complete with imaginary whiplash scars to authenticate his blackness, but he has published the story in a book.

An apparently white woman (Lee) and her former husband, a middle-class Chinese American (Tom), serve to explicate the play's views on assimilation and class mobility. Tam and his Japanese-American friend, Kenji, speak of white women as costly trophies. Having just met Lee, Tam says, "They say a man with an old lady with big tits is ambitious. The bigger the tits on his lady, the greater the ambition." Kenji adds that tall, blonde, buxom women are "the scariest kind" (28). Surprisingly, Lee does not protest this rating system; indeed, she seems tacitly complicit with it. With no apparent income, profession, or community, she appears to be looking for a husband, as well as a father for her son Robby, in a search for self-definition. Moreover, she claims to be pregnant, but as she is not visibly so (either in the text or the production photos provided), it's unclear whether she is really with child or merely seeking to manipulate some man into marrying her and fathering her (actual and potential) children. Just as Tam seeks to clarify his identity in relation to a strong male other and is working his way through Chinese-American, white, and black father-heroes, Lee has tried Chinese-American, black, and white husbands without establishing the self-defining marriage she seeks. The similarity between Lee's interracial drifting and his own prompts Tam to identify her—apparently accurately—as partly Chinese and passing as white.

When her former husband, Tom, appears, Tam accuses him of constructing Lee as white as a way of erasing his own ethnicity: "You wanted to be 'accepted' by whites so much you created one to accept you" (59). Tam and the stage directions label Tom as "middle class" in dress and manner, setting up a dichotomy in which Tam's manners, which Lee and Charley Popcorn think are black, are defended as more authentic for "Chinamen" than Tom's. Middle-class Chinese Americans are by Chin's definition not Chinamen no matter what they actually do or think. In the play, Tom's more convention-ally WASP-like demeanor (less belligerent, enacting objectivity and detach-ment) and his acceptance of the model minority paradigm are criticized; the implication is that, in Tam's opinion at least, Tom is a Chinese American Uncle Tom.

The theme of the missing father-hero, the text's ambivalence toward interracial matches and upward mobility, and Tam's lack of literary, pater-nal, and sexual confidence are linked in multiple ways. The middle-class white father to whom Tam seems to have ceded his children has been said to be "a better writer" than Tam by Tam's absent mother. Tam and Tom (alter egos) compare stories about whose ethnic self-constructions represent greater progress: Tam's streetwise, alienated, "black" voice or the relatively staid-sounding memoir of middle-class achievement and self-acceptance Tom is writing, for which the punning title, *Soul on Rice*, sounds improb-ably funky (it is the black-identified Tam, not the white-identified Tom, who should be quoting Eldridge Cleaver's *Soul on Ice*). For Tam, the boxing film is meant to reestablish his artistic and mythmaking credentials and demon-strate these talents to his estranged children. And the film, whose existence seems contingent on Tam's ability to locate or construct the proper father for Jack Dancer, is paralleled by the child Lee claims to be carrying, a child whose transformation from words to flesh also seems contingent upon the task of finding and constructing a proper father.

The play closes with a tentative affirmation of the possibilities of father-ing, self-fathering, and authoring so polemically explored. Kenji volunteers to father, or to be a father to, Lee's forthcoming baby, and Tam determines to proceed with his film, yet leave intact Jack Dancer's public myth of filia-tion to a powerful father, by making a strictly professional fight film that neither affirms nor discredits the boxer's myth of ethnic origins.

The Year of the Dragon could be construed as one more version of the classic male author's "struggle for integrity and livelihood against flagrantly bad bestsellers written by women." The struggling male would be Fred Eng, who at forty has published only one short story; the best-selling woman author is his sister Sissy (clearly not a name connoting heroism in Chin's lexicon), author of the best-selling Mama Fu Fu cookbooks. As Sau-ling Wong has noted, Fred's term *food pornography* conveys Chin's condemnation of enterprises like Sissy's, which pander to mainstream tastes for ethnic variety without challenging the consumers' assumptions about the centrality of Euro-American culture and identity (Wong, *Reading,* 55–61). Despite Fred and Sissy's mutual affection, he resists her offer to work for her burgeoning cookbook-centered business and makes clear his contempt for it.

Sissy also represents the white, middle-class version of the "feminized and feminizing society" against which beset male authors must struggle for survival. Sissy has joined the white, middle-class mainstream by going to college, moving to Boston, marrying a WASP man interested in Chinese culture, and assuming the traditional role of "ambassador of goodwill" (Elaine Kim's phrase) or explicator of "Chinese" culture to the white majority through her cookbooks. By opposing Fred and Sissy, Chin imagines the quintessential Chinese American author—the author of the "real," the Chinaman—as male, working-class, and obscure; as a writer who is female, middle class, and commercially successful, Sissy represents the bad bestseller, food pornography, the "fake," the sissy.

However, real and fake cultural productions are not aligned strictly by gender in this play. Fred's central struggle is not with Sissy but with his father, Pa. The intensity of that struggle (which kills Pa literally and Fred in spirit) signifies that Chin's extinction thesis doesn't fully account for the internal drive of his work. In his critical work, Chin seeks to construct a pure version of Chinese American manhood and integrity, yet his plays say clearly that he feels no such thing exists. We saw how *Chickencoop Chinaman* traces the author-surrogate's fruitless search for a paternal figure, an original ancestor, to anchor and authorize his efforts to "author" himself, his film, and his children. *The Year of the Dragon* provides such a father but portrays him as culturally, emotionally, and ethically bankrupt. Not only is Pa Eng, seemingly the definitive Chinaman, personally unattractive (sexist, authoritarian, self-absorbed, manipulative, verbally and culturally inept, and irresponsible) and a destructive father; he is also a food pornographer, a purveyor of the detested "fake." Not only does Pa support himself with a tour and travel agency that panders to orientalist stereotypes of Chinatown; he has required Fred to drop out of college, run the business, and conduct the tours, thereby stunting his son's literary career and personal independence. The play identifies the tours with food pornography in no uncertain terms: Fred's complicity as a food pornographer is even explicitly sexualized by his practice of sleeping with white women tourists, who presumably consider him part of the tour. Fred seems to have substituted sex for his former practice of writing when the tours were done, which made him feel "all right" (137). He struts and brags about his promiscuity

("my own private game preserve"), but in terms of the twin goals of authoring and fathering he is destroying his future by throwing away his sexual
energy, as well as his verbal wit, on the seduction of tourists.

If we compare this play with Chin's critical essays, the play's portrayals
of artistic resistance and collusion and the process of cultural extinction are
more psychologically complex and hence more persuasive. Sissy's assimila-
tionist choices are neither praised nor fully condemned; there is a certain
cartoonishness to the play's insistence that Sissy has married Ross *only* because she needs a white, middle-class man to affirm her worth and that
his status needs are somehow satisfied by marrying a Chinese American
woman. However, the play makes a persuasive case for Sissy's need to leave
the world of this particular Chinatown family in order to construct a viable
identity as an intelligent, adult woman. If the model for "authentic" Chinatown manhood, Pa, is unappealing, the model for Chinatown womanhood,
Ma, is one of juvenile dependency. Married to Pa since the age of fifteen,
Ma in her fifties has the emotional maturity of an adolescent. The play does
not suggest that she has any interior mental life, other than the mechanical
recitation of old songs and youthful romantic fantasies, or any significant
capacity for negotiating with others in or outside of the family. Since she
is the only image of Chinatown womanhood offered within the play, Fred's
criticism of Sissy's decision to construct or "author" her own identity differently, as a middle-class writer, is tempered with sympathy and affection.

Chin's metanarrative also mirrors Baym's in its construction of a war between the author-hero and the destructive society outside him. In Baym's
account of American literature, the author is male, the society feminized.
In Chin's, the author is Asian American, the society predominantly white,
with factors like gender and class taking important but secondary roles. This
racialized culture war is a central theme of *Year of the Dragon* and exerts
great pressure on each character, but the central conflicts are intrafamilial.
Dramatically, the central conflict is between Pa and Fred. Fred wants Pa to
acknowledge him as a writer, son, and independent subject (as opposed to a
vassal and an extension of Pa's own needs) and to signal his intersubjective
recognition of Fred by giving permission for Fred's stepmother and brother
to leave Chinatown permanently. Pa wants to deny everyone else's subjectivity and require that they all stay in Chinatown to keep him company,
even after he dies. This father-son struggle, however, is actually the cause
and dramatic manifestation of Fred's fundamental problem, the inability to
claim and validate his own subjectivity.

Pa dies without affirming Fred as a separate subject, a lack of affirmation signaled by his contempt for Fred's request, his appropriation of Fred's
labor as his own (he thinks he has supported Fred, not vice versa, although
he doesn't actually work), his refusal to acknowledge Fred publicly within

Chinatown, and his contempt for Fred's fiction. Therefore, Fred lacks the internalized sense of wholeness and self-worth he needs in order to overcome the invisibility, the sense of erasure, he has experienced in his personal and literary career outside of Chinatown. Fred's fantasy of being recognized by a powerful father and becoming his heir can never be realized, not only because his father is too self-absorbed to recognize *anyone* else as a subject but because this father is never truly powerful, and never in touch with what Chin would consider an untainted ethnic culture. Pa Eng is always the dying father of broken English, Charlie Chan jokes, and Eng's Tour-n-Travel. Moreover, the father is portrayed as having no heart, no interiority, himself. All he has is public faces, a series of postures: mayor, paterfamilias, tour guide. These are the roles he ostensibly bequeaths at the moment of his death, when he offers to acknowledge Fred as his "number one son" at a Chinatown gathering, but actually he is offering a lifetime of service to his memory: running Pa's business, supporting his wives, and raising his other son. Fred must refuse these because as a writer what he seeks and requires is something Pa doesn't have and can't grant: recognition of an interior life that transcends these roles.

In short, Chin's two plays are richer than his critical account in their representations of the artist-hero's struggle for integrity. In the essays, the Chinese outlaw fighting a corrupt government becomes the archetype for the Chinese American artist-hero fighting racism in the mainstream audience and media. In the plays, this Manichean dichotomy breaks down in interesting ways. The plays acknowledge that for a Chinese American artist there is no pure, originary culture. They suggest how Chinese Americans may seek to create their own heroes from black, white, or Chinese models (the Lone Ranger, Ovaltine Jack Dancer, or the Word of the Chickencoop Chinaman); the would-be ethnic artist, in defining his self, may co-opt or be co-opted by white stereotypes, as in the cases of Eng's Tour-n-Travel and Mama Fu Fu, which have different effects on Fred and Sissy, as we shall see. And they record how the negative effects of white racism may be internalized and how the battle described as external in the Chin essays may become an interior, intrasubjective struggle.

How does interracial love interact in this play with the processes of assimilation, finding one's voice as a writer, and defining oneself? Fred's and Sissy's views about interracial liaisons, writing, and self-definition are the obverse of each other. Fred believes that interracial *sex* may be instrumental (a source of status and physical pleasure) but irrelevant to self-definition. *Writing* should not be used in this cynical fashion because it's the one means by which an Asian American can enact the American romance of the "the pure American self divorced from specific circumstances" who, "untrammeled by history and social accident, . . . will be able to achieve complete self-definition" (Baym, "Melodramas," 71). Only through writing does Fred hope to define and affirm his own interiority and fulfill the American artist-hero myth.

Sissy, by contrast, sees her writing as instrumental, neither intrinsically valuable nor self-definitive. Therefore, she feels no ambivalence about producing salable word products, drawing on her ethnic knowledge as one of many writing tools, in order to support other objectives such as supporting her family, enabling them to leave Chinatown (a slum), establishing a middle-class way of life, and supporting Fred's very different literary aspirations. On the other hand, Sissy views her interracial marriage to Ross as a site where her subjectivity is truly constructed and affirmed by Ross's love, which both affirms Sissy's background and transcends it ("I . . . I appreciate everything. . . . I don't think this is the time for normal Oriental hospitality and restraint. I love her. I married her. You can accept us as part of the family or you can . . ." [184]). Although she realizes that to others she may seem to be "just another yellow girl on a white man's arm," she does not see her marriage primarily in terms of external status considerations but as the means by which she transcends such considerations and achieves the "deeply romantic" promise that "in this new land" — Boston for Sissy — "untrammeled by history and social accident," she "will be able to achieve complete self-definition" (Baym 71): "Out there we'll be able to forget we're Chinamen, just forget all this and just be people," Chin has her say, perhaps honoring her as one of the guys by having her call herself a Chinaman (Chin 110).

Yet the play makes clear the paradoxes of Sissy's exit strategies. As her brother Johnny points out, she implicitly considers WASP, middle-class subjects unmarked or normative and "Chinamen" as pejoratively marked. She wants to "forget all this," but she chooses a husband who loves her as a Chinese American (84) and enters her public career as a Chinese American (Mama Fu Fu). Although Chin's critical work might point toward an extremely critical reading of Ross as a well-intentioned orientalist and Sissy as opportunistically benefiting from her collusion with, or manipulation of, racial and sexual stereotypes, I suggest that another reading is more appropriate.

As we can see in the examples of Fred (failed writer, tour guide, unacknowledged number one son, and "God's gift to sluts"), Johnny (younger brother, juvenile delinquent), and Ma (perennial child bride), the options for Sissy within the Eng family—and, by implication, Chinatown—are mentally and spiritually destructive. Given this representation of Chinatown, she's right to leave. But Sissy doesn't seek to deny her family or erase her race or past. She comes back to try to bring her family out with her, offering to give Fred a job and a share in her business and to raise Johnny.

Sissy's choice of Ross and the cookbook business represent her desire to retain a sense of herself as Chinese American, albeit in terms of her own making. If she chooses to make these constructions in dialogue with a white husband and audience, it may be because, as we have seen, she cannot be an independent or self-defining subject within her family due to Pa's tyranny and self-absorption, her mother's weakness, and Fred's incessant, self-pitying chatter. But I would characterize her career as a subaltern negotiation (in Gayatri Spivak's sense) rather than a collusion because she is moving strategically to fulfill her aims—self-fulfillment and the rescue of her family—and because these aims are ethical and reasonable.[9] Nor can she be faulted for "selling out" her culture, misrepresenting it in some crucial and politically damaging way, because, as the play tells us, her culture, the fake culture of Eng's Tour-n-Travel and the real culture of the Eng family melodrama, is always already an improvisation, a hybrid, a social construct.

Sansei Self-Fathering: David Mura's Memoirs

David Mura's poetry and memoirs strive most explicitly to address the relationships between interracial sexual desire, the problems of assimilation or ethnic identity construction, and the struggles of the author-hero in Asian American guise. In his two memoirs, *Turning Japanese* and *Where the Body Meets Memory*, and selected poems, Mura constructs himself as a version of the American author-hero, one alienated from the mainstream, like Chin, by his race. Mura's particular contribution to this colloquy lies in the directness with which he seeks to relate the issues of interracial desire, assimilation, and the aftereffects of internment within his own life. Briefly, Mura's memoirs, supplemented by his biographical and historical poems, form a kind of conversion narrative in which racial tensions heighten the stakes of a self-destructive adolescence and young manhood in which David acts out rage and depression through a life of promiscuity linked with the consumption of pornography (seasoned with alcohol and drugs). As he detaches himself from these addictions, marries, and begins a career as a poet, Mura's writing functions, like a course of therapy, to construct a healing narrative, but the narrative he constructs traces the inception of his troubles, including his preoccupation with white women, to his marginalized status as a Japanese American male.

The line of causality Mura proposes is this: once upon a time, before the war, his parents, intelligent, handsome, hard-working nisei, existed in a community in which their ethnicity did not bar them from feeling and acting American and their sexuality was affirmed by their healthy relationships within the Japanese American community. After the wartime traumas of internment, dispossession, and direct expressions of race hatred, they responded to the paradoxes of their status—as citizens who could be interned without reason or notice, yet could also be drafted to serve their country—by doing everything they could to assimilate into a WASP, upper-middle-class lifestyle. In their case, however, assimilation involved amnesia and denial—a lack of reflection or remembrance of the internment experience, denial of the impact of racism on their lives during and after the war, silence about what it meant to be nisei parents in postwar America, and, finally, silence toward David's unhappiness (in his mother's case) and discipline or disapproval (in his father's) whenever their son departed from the Puritan work ethic and code of conduct they had embraced.

By placing Mura's life story into dialogue with the fictional or fictionalized ones of Bulosan, Kang, and Chin (whose artist-protagonists were surrogates for themselves), it becomes possible to see a common thread: the dread of extinction, both literal and literary, and choices in life and literature that are responses to that fear. In fact, Mura describes several different responses to that fear, his parents' and his own.

David's parents, Tom and Terry Mura, respond by enduring, conforming, and assimilating. David's mother, a nisei interned at age ten, is characterized by David as using amnesia, repression, and denial to survive and distance herself from this past:

> Years later, you will not remember the train ride to the camp or the doll that you held as you entered its gates. You will not remember the sobs that pierced through the barracks that first night and, night after night, kept coming back. . . . You will not speak the names of Esther Suzuki or Keiko Nakashima, your best friends, or recall the tensions between your father and mother. . . . You will not remember your Japanese or your favorite dress. You will learn easily and quickly that to survive you must forget. (*Body,* 34)

Mrs. Mura is characterized as impeccably tasteful, perennially beautiful and fit, but emotionally remote (227–28). The decor of her house, "immaculately white, the rooms uncluttered, spacious, and filled with light" (45), signifies both a Japanese aesthetic and a passion for assimilating into the tasteful, upper-middle-class lifestyle of their midwestern suburb. David describes how she has forgotten a family quarrel he asks about, throws away her letters to his father, and evades questions about her first meeting with him. "Why would you want to read my letters?" she says, or "This isn't the time to go into that" (44). Remembering his mother's aborted subscription to a classical record club, David contrasts her with Emma Bovary, another housewife who reached for "a finer sensibility beyond her realm" but, unlike his mother, "wreaked suffering and tragedy on those about her and on herself" because she was blinded by longing:

My mother does not lack common sense. She is not one to be carried away.

I, on the other hand, have often let myself be carried away, have embraced my longings with a ferocity that is belied by my composed and quiet demeanor. I am the passion my mother kept at bay, someone who has known unchecked obsession. . . . I have constantly had to learn the lesson over and over that my mother already knew—there are limits, the world will knock you back, sometimes declination and modesty are all we can afford, you just can't change the world. (45)

Thus, David indirectly acknowledges that his mother's silence might be a strategy for survival, but by placing himself, his mother, and Emma Bovary in the same moral universe he signals that for all his imaginative labors he hasn't internalized how much harsher life was for his parents, how severely restricted their options were compared to his.[10] By identifying his dangerous, extravagant longings (obsessions) with those of Emma Bovary, David both departs from the usual tropes selected by Asian American men for claiming American subjectivity and illustrates the centrality of the domestic, middle-class woman as the privileged subject of the novel, a topic we will take up more fully later.

David's father has also chosen to assimilate by turning a blind eye to American racism and by distancing himself from the narratives of the past, including past grievances, that so obsess David. In one of the turning points of David's life story, he asks his parents to come to a session with him and his therapists. Prompted by one of them, Mr. Mura recounts his side of the story: the lifetime of sacrifices he made to support the family and attain success. As the narrative proceeds, David sees physical traces of a submerged subtext and of his father's clearly habitual choice to keep this other story repressed:

Slowly, fractionally, as my father mapped his climb . . . his voice started to tighten, a small quiver moving up his neck to his cheeks, a brief sliver of red venting in his eyes . . .

Then, as if an alarm had gone off, he pulled his head back, away from some unseen fire, and shrugged. "No, no, that was just what you were supposed to do. It wasn't anything at all." (227)

This is indeed one of those moments when the body meets memory. Although the repressed narrative is not fully identified at the time, its existence triggers David's gradual acceptance of his father.

Other anecdotes suggest that one emotion Mr. Mura repressed over the years was rage and that this rage found expression in disciplining David for falling short of his expectations. In addition, David sees racism as a significant reality repressed from his father's consciousness. In David's writing, Mr. Mura admits racism's theoretical existence but seeks to contain its potential emotional impact through the euphemistic, conciliatory narratives in which he has come to believe. For instance, in the poem "Gardens We Have Left," David recalls a habitual remark of his father's implying that life in the camps was an improvement over his prior existence:

> What is it father
> says of the camps? "In L.A. each day I'd sweat
> and shove a mower for my father
>
> across the lawns in Beverly Hills. During the war,
> after school, I played baseball."
> (*Colors*, 96–97; cf. *Memory*, 6, *Japanese*, 326)

By implying that he preferred baseball in the camps, Mr. Mura glosses over his father's loss of his nursery business and reasserts his own normalizing Americanness. Years later, he explains to a Japanese interviewer that the camps were a wartime aberration now recognized as a mistake by "many" Americans: " 'It was unfortunate for many people, but for our family it wasn't so bad.' Of course, his father took financial losses, [Mr. Mura] said, but the camps opened up opportunities for the Nisei in other parts of the country" (*Japanese*, 326). Mr. Mura denies that racism is more harmful to Americans of color and considers it something that can be overcome with the right thinking, the proper metanarrative: "I personally don't feel it. . . . In reality, everybody faces a little discrimination, no matter if you're white, black, or yellow, but if you're very sensitive to it all the time, you may feel you're discriminated against when you're not. If you think you'll be treated equally, you'll be treated equally" (326). David calls this "the ostrich approach," but in light of the therapy scene we could read it sympathetically as Mr. Mura's sincere perceptions from the vantage point of a secure upper-middle-class retirement, as a deliberate euphemism motivated by an admirable ethic of self-denial, of not wanting to emphasize or privilege one's own troubles. Or we might suppose that Mr. Mura, a loyal American *and* a professional publicist, wishes in this particular interview to present America favorably before a critical Japanese audience (the interviewer and his listeners). Even David's ostrich metaphor implies the relatively sympathetic perception that his parents' assimilation was a form of protective camouflage (albeit an ineffective one, David might well say), an attempt to escape the line of fire after the traumas of the war.

Years later, David offers a more incisive metaphor for assimilation, which in turn implies a harsher verdict of his parents' willed blindness. In an interview with Bill Moyers, he recounts the story of Japanese Americans in segregated Arkansas who, when boarding buses, were invited by whites to sit in front and by blacks to sit in back (David's uncle, like Tom Mura, was one such nisei). Taking the bus as a metaphor for American society, David explains the conditions upon which Asian Americans could pass, could claim honorary white status in the front of the bus: "You could sit in the front as long as you pretended that you didn't know what was going on in back. And you could never, never *drive* the bus." Isn't this why David's parents, who lived through the internment era and its aftermath, deny racism?

Toward the end of *Where the Body Meets Memory,* David and his wife, Susan Sencer, recount the cost of assimilation from David's point of view using an oedipal narrative about cultural inheritance. One of the things that angers David, that drives him to be so critical of his parents and to tell stories that emphasize and sometimes exaggerate the force of racism in their lives, is his desire to rebel against what he sees as their low expectations in life. Despite their material success and security, David sees his father as accepting the position of a compliant bastard son to "the white fathers," one so eager for basic acceptance that he doesn't even expect the throne. David, by contrast, is more like a Shakespearean bastard, angry at being disqualified from the succession to which he feels entitled and angry at his father for offering him only this second-class status. As David speculates, "you," the bastardlike Asian American son, become enraged by this position: "You know you're as good as the legitimate heir, it's simply an accident of birth that keeps you from the throne. You want recognition from your father—in this case, not a real father, but the white fathers— and yet you hate *him* because he can never give you recognition, he can never truly acknowledge you or allow you to have what you think you deserve" (emphasis mine). Though it's not acknowledged, this account seems indebted to post-Freudian psychoanalytic theories about infant socialization. As part of these processes, infants learn to differentiate real fathers or mothers from "phallic" parents who possess a fantasized degree of power and freedom represented metaphorically by the phallus. The theorists' abstraction of this power from the biological penis to the metaphoric phallus indicates their recognition that actual fathers, as well as actual mothers, also lack the absolute power and freedom desired in the infant's fantasy life. In these accounts, the unreasonable offspring may then blame either parent for lacking or withholding the all-powerful phallus.

Mura and Sencer, however, discuss how Mura's self-analysis had to go beyond his work with traditional, race-blind therapists to incorporate the impact of race on his psychic life. By extrapolating from such psychoanalysis, they seek to describe the formation of David's—and perhaps other minor subjects'—racialized psyches. Unlike psychoanalytic accounts, this is not a "universal" account of infant socialization but a historically specific account of David's socialization as an Asian American man, the struggle between himself and his parents to define appropriate expectations for someone of his race, gender, and class. In this quotation, the break in David's syntax—where "him" seems to refer to the real father but is actually preceded by "the white fathers"—mimes the psychic confusion described: you, the son, want the ethnic father to give you, as recognition, the freedoms and privileges that in fact can only be bestowed by the white fathers; holding him responsible for that which they withhold, you blame him for their omissions.

While this account may not justify David's harmful or wasteful acts, it persuasively describes his psychic life; its resonance for stories other than David's may be suggested by the way it brings together his life story and those of the angry, American-born artist-sons in Chin's *The Chickencoop Chinaman* and *The Year of the Dragon*. As we saw earlier, Chin's Chinese American author-heroes seek to counteract their isolation and fear of extinction by winning the recognition of powerful fathers, but their attempts are doomed to fail because they do not really understand which fathers' recognition they seek and because the "real" fathers—in this case, the ethnic ones—cannot fulfill the role of the all-powerful "imaginary" ones, who, of course, are white. The same filial indignation, or perceptions of paternal powerlessness, may be found in the works of Milton Murayama, John Okada, Chang-rae Lee, Gus Lee, and other American-born writers of Asian descent.

Both David Mura and Fred Eng, the artist-hero of Chin's *The Year of the Dragon,* seek paternal recognition not only as sons but as writers. As we saw, Pa Eng both disparaged Fred's writing and failed to recognize him properly as a son, a failure punished (symbolically) by the father's death. In David's autobiographical narrative, however, the search for paternal recognition is more complex and more happily resolved. In *Turning Japanese,* David recounts how his father tried to get him to study law instead of literature, even though David wrote to him saying that law would destroy "something vital" in him. A year later, he found discarded poems and short stories that his father had written as a young man along with rejection slips from the *New Yorker* and the *Atlantic*. "As I look at the pieces, I wonder about his opposition to my writing. Perhaps he felt he had given up his dream, had started a family and been forced to seek other work, and he wanted to save me the same disappointment," writes David (*Japanese*, 318). Here is the submerged narrative whose trace David perceives, years later, in the parental therapy scene: "No, no, that was just what you were supposed to do. It wasn't anything at all" (*Memory*, 227). Although at the time he does not consciously know what it is, the fact that this scene marks the beginning of the dissipation of David's oedipal rage fits with what I presume is his later understanding of his father as well as his father's recognition of David as someone like himself but (and this is especially generous) more successful. Tom Mura even spells this out over dinner, in Japan, during David's Guggenheim year abroad:

> "You know, when I die or when I retire, they're just going to get someone else to take my place at Blue Shield. In a way, it will be as if I was never there."
>
> He pauses, sits up a bit, and looks up at me. "But only you can write your poems." (*Japanese,* 318)

In terms of the bastard story, the "throne" for David doesn't refer so much to the possibility of greater wealth or political power but to something closer to David's heart, the literary life. Because, as we shall see, literary writing was crucial to David's efforts to avoid metaphoric extinction by "authoring" himself, such a compromise might well symbolize denying David the possibility of literary progeny and a future literary lineage. Mr. Mura's gift of paternal recognition even includes a reference to the stakes of the game: publicity leaves no durable literary legacy. At Blue Shield, it will be as if Mr. Mura had never been. David's poetry, by contrast, will leave a permanent and valued trace. By giving credit so graciously to David, Mr. Mura leaves implicit his own investments, as a father, in David's success.[11]

The metaphor of the bastard also conveys David's personal sense of entitlement; both as analyst and patient, he seems unaware that it isn't only bastard sons, but younger sons and daughters, who will not inherit the throne. Now, daughters of any race may feel as worthy as sons; they may resent the mothers who seem to be telling them otherwise because the mothers, like David's father, seem to be telling them to be satisfied with less and because they subliminally hold their mothers responsible for the accident of female birth. In a sense, writers like Chin and Mura, expressing frustration at their "disinheritance" from American manhood, are still seeking to avoid the second-class status of women. A crude paraphrase of the underlying emotion might be: "We're mad as hell that everybody thinks we should make the kinds of compromises women do, and because we are afraid of sharing their second-class status we'll make sure our writing emphasizes our manhood." In Chin's case, as we have seen, there is a tremendous rhetorical investment in abjecting—psychically ejecting and denying—the feminine and the effeminate (the homosexual), not only from his own creative works but from Asian American literature. In Mura's case, as we shall see, there are other ways.

David's anger, his rejection of the bastard's position, is linked with the fear of extinction both directly and indirectly. Thinking aloud with his wife, David says that he revolted first against his father and then against white fathers because he felt submission would be "deadly." "I would not have been able to survive," he tells Susie. "I'd have to kill something inside myself. Not let it grow" (*Memory*, 260). Related to this sense of deadness is David's experience as a summer employee at his father's workplace, Blue Cross Blue Shield, where he had to hide his poetry books under his desk. David says, "I knew I'd die of boredom working for some corporation as a lawyer." While the dread of "death by boredom" is a more secure, middle-class problem than the threats to basic physical existence recorded by Bulosan, Kang, and other early writers, the fear of the self's extinction is linked in all these texts with the author's struggle to construct and defend an ethnic self.

Near the end of *Memory*, David recounts the story of a man described by Algerian psychoanalyst Frantz Fanon, a patient who seeks to explain all his psychological problems in terms of his difficulties as a black man in colonized Algeria. The patient, Jean Veneuse, accepts the color line and the inferiority of blacks it implies but sleeps with white women in an attempt to erase his inferiority complex because "Somehow crossing the color line sexually will prove himself as good as a white man" (232). David's response to this account is recognition: "I'd elevated whiteness, I'd inculcated its standards of beauty, I'd believed on some deep level in the myth of white superiority. That was part of my sickness, part of the colonizing of my sexuality. I felt that every white woman who rejected me somehow reaffirmed both my sense of a color line and my sense of debasement" (232). According to David, Fanon believes that his patient needs to both restructure his thinking (stop blaming external causes for his mental condition) and see that "the world must be restructured," the color bar challenged and erased. David's own "cure" for his self-destructive behavior has involved a double adjustment of vision: he now questions the racialized aspects of society rather than internalizing them, but he has also distanced himself from the younger self who perpetually blamed race for his problems.

On a symbolic level, David's promiscuity is a way of combating extinction by claiming many mates. As David suggests, it also seems to be a way of affirming that his virility compares with (or exceeds) that of white men (hence, the need to "score" with so many white women). But, as in the case of Chin's Fred Eng, such promiscuity can be seen as the last-ditch strategy of someone with limited hope of authoring or fathering on his own terms, a sign of true desperation. In David's life, these destructive demonstrations of masculinity ultimately give way, more fruitfully, to David and Susie's formation of a family and to his various literary projects. Among these, the exploration of his previous sexuality in print (at length and in some detail) functions partly as a thinly veiled sexual display ("I was such a cad. I just couldn't stop this powerful engine . . ."). More complex and multidimensional gestures of authorship as self-fathering are the many family narratives that appear in his memoirs and poems, where he imaginatively recreates the experiences of relatives, celebrates the present joyful security of his marriage, and explores the presence and meaning of his three children in his life.

Of course, the writer's strongest defense against extinction is literary authorship, self-fathering. In Mura's work, the creation of a literary identity, the claiming of authorship, is intimately knit to the creation of an ethnic self, an awareness of himself as both American and ethnic, which is again a reaction to his parents' success in assimilating. We must recall that they were born American, and for them this meant reaffirming their Americanness after the setbacks of the war era (when Japanese Americans were constituted as racial others defining the limits of American subjectivity), thereby bequeathing to David a firmly American sense of self. From the viewpoint of Mr. and Mrs. Mura, what I have called assimilation might be expressed as foregrounding their affinity for America and understanding their Japaneseness, not as forms of denial, amnesia, or deracination but as a process perceived as natural, even typically American, in their generation. David, however, sees it differently.

In one of *Memory*'s most lyrical passages, he imagines assimilation as another kind of extinction, the slow death of the ethnic self. Writing of his father's life after the war, he imagines Tom Mura's exposure to two cultures fostering two distinct beings within: "If you're separated from one of the cultures, that being dies, at least for a time. It has no light to bathe in, no air, no soil. It can, like certain miraculous plants and seeds, come back to life, but the longer it dwells in that state of nonbeing, the harder it is to revive" (121). As Tom Mura attends a midwestern American college, living in the household of a white professor, David imagines the thriving of the self attuned to Anglo-American culture and the dwindling of his Japanese-American self: "All those years in Kalamazoo, my father's Japanese self seemed to be gasping for breath, its being gradually forgotten. This self believed in the quickness of spirits, the unspoken messages born of the silence that rests in the Japanese language, in the messages of gestures and hovering implications, in the visions that reside in dreams. This self, like his mother, was becoming a ghost" (123).[12] The Japanese American self dies, in David's narrative, while the other lives on and seems to be the father of David.

Here assimilation is imagined as the extinction of the ethnic American self. In David's own life, entry into the corporate world of his father represents the extinction of the ethnic artist in him, his real self, "something vital." The image of himself hiding his poetry under the desk is an image of self-denial and disguise, of being buried alive, "gasping for breath." In fact,

David's career flowered with the publication of *Japanese,* in which the narrative of himself as a struggling ethnic artist-hero bloomed from the fertile ground of his observations about Japan.

Before David's trip to Japan, his literary heroes were John Berryman, Robert Lowell, Pasolini, and Mishima, writers and a filmmaker notorious for linking literature with madness and dissolution in life and death. In Japan, David finds another model in Bird, the young writer in Kenzaburo Oe's autobiographical novel, *A Personal Matter.* Like his creator Oe, Bird "is finally shaken from his rage, stupor, and dissolution by the birth of a child. . . . In accepting the child into his life, Bird finds a sense of purpose to anchor his world; in the process, he lets go of the aimless rage that has characterized his existence. It is hard not to see this change in traditional terms: Bird grows up" (*Japanese,* 275). Although David is characteristically resistant to this story (especially the ending, in which Bird receives the blessing of his teacher and then goes home to his wife and child "armed with the traditional Japanese concept of gaman — endurance, forbearance" [275]), he makes it his own. Like Bird, he goes home to America from his "instruction" in Japan, where he has revived his latent Japanese self and placed it into dialogue with his American self, thereby redefining what it means to be Japanese American; he and his wife have three children; and he writes three books, *Turning Japanese, The Colors of Desire,* and *Where the Body Meets Memory* (with more sure to follow). Like Oe or an old-fashioned Victorian novelist, he ends all three of his books by tenderly invoking, as the most classical form of narrative closure linking authorship and fathering, the magical presence of his children, as he does in the first: "Each night, in our apartment in St. Paul, before we go to bed, I lay my head on Susie's stomach and feel the kicks of our daughter. Only one pound, she kicks with a sound that has come from nothing, from everything in our past, from my Japanese genes to the genes of my wife, English and Hungarian Jew. . . . This split I have felt between America and Japan, this fusion of two histories, will reside in her, in a different, more visible way. . . . In the darkness, a tiny thump" (*Japanese,* 372–73).

In closing his recent memoirs and anthology with references to his children and implicitly celebrating the endurance of his marriage, Mura constructs himself as the "well-married hero" of bildungsroman that I described as largely absent from Asian American literature, a resolution I find both moving and deeply ironic. For Mura's texts overtly argue that his parents' labors to assimilate — to interpellate themselves as citizens into the narrative of the nation — were compromised, perhaps even vitiated, by their willingness to accept the condition that they forget and deny their specific history of exclusion during the World War II internment and its aftermath in order to join the country club of American citizenship. Mura, for his part, takes it upon himself to claim and articulate what he perceives as the traumas of exclusion and subsequent invisibility, traumas that are increased by their very erasure (or repression) from public and private narratives that might ameliorate their effects by articulating and acknowledging them. The emotional import Mura attaches to such an erasure is conveyed in the detail of Mrs. Mura's white, minimalist decor. While Mura's account of his parents' lives may seem tendentious and judgmental when read in isolation, particularly because David links it with his provocative personal history, the themes of erasure, denial, amnesia, and invisibility that animate Mura's work gain resonance and validity when placed in the context of similar works addressing the experiences of pain and trauma in excess of accepted public narratives and hence silenced by them. Again, the figure of abjection is a good one for the public denial of Japanese American experience depicted and challenged in many of these texts.[13] It is therefore paradoxical that, having devoted three books to foregrounding his family's unassimilability, Mura closes each book with classic bildungsroman tropes for the subject's successful interpellation into the nation: marriage, children, and fatherhood. Like those Victorian novels in which private, romantic resolutions symbolically resolved fundamental social anxieties of the period, and later stories of Americanization by marriage, Mura makes his own marriage to Susan Sencer, a pediatrician of European ancestry, an explicit metaphor for his successful assimilation.

3

Women's Plots:
Edith Maude Eaton and Bharati Mukherjee

[T]he Chinese people may have no souls, no expression on their faces, be altogether beyond the pale of civilization, but whatever they are, I want you to understand that I am—I am a Chinese.—Sui Sin Far [Edith Maude Eaton], "Leaves from the Mental Portfolio of an Eurasian"

I fell in love with his world, its ease, its careless confidence and graceful self-absorption. I wanted to become the person they thought they saw: humorous, intelligent, refined, affectionate. Not illegal, not murderer, not widowed, destitute, fearful. —Bharati Mukherjee, *Jasmine*

Romance and the Immigrant Woman

Previously, I introduced the immigrant romance as a plot paradigm in which the immigrant Asian American man's desire to attain Americanness is mediated through his relationships (real and imaginary) with white and Asian women. In this male paradigm, Americanness is conflated with authorship and white women function less as objects of sexual desire per se than as symbols of America and as cultural mediators (teachers, editors, readers) between the immigrant and his aspirations to claim membership in America through literary authorship. The flip side of this romance is the construction by immigrant and American-born writers of the Asian woman as a maternal figure embodying values associated with the Asian homeland. Disqualified in various ways from participating in the discourse of Americanization, the maternal Asian woman in these texts represents the departure point for the Asian American son's journey toward Americanization, which in turn is crucial to his establishment of adult masculinity and authorship. Thus, the Asian woman is "abjected," constructed as a less

American "other" defining the limits of the male Asian American's subjectivity. In my account of the immigrant romance, then, a racialized triangle emerges: the Asian American son becomes American by renouncing or devaluing the Asian mother (and the aspects of Asia she represents), taking in exchange the white woman, who represents desired aspects of America and American identity, as his new object of desire and the telos of his narrative of formation as an Asian American author and subject.[1]

A second, related kind of plot centers on the Asian American male author's association of American subjectivity, authorship, and fatherhood, a group of associations that implicitly excludes women from functioning as authors or as exemplary Asian American subjects. These plots, exemplified by the critical work of the *Aiiieeeee* editors, the plays of Frank Chin, and the memoirs of David Mura, focus on the Asian American sons' perceptions of their fathers as inadequate or diminishing, as failing to provide them with either paternal recognition (Chin) or sufficiently high expectations for inclusion and leadership in mainstream society (Mura). In these oedipal dramas, Asian mothers and white women alike are secondary to the Asian American male's primary goal, the search for legitimation of his prerogatives as an American male. Among these, one of the most important is the prerogative to author (and implicitly, to *father*) an Asian American literary tradition.

Like the Asian American males, Asian American women writers are concerned with separation from mothers whose task has been to imbue them not only with images of their roles as women but images of their roles as daughters of Asian parents. Unlike their brothers, however, the Asian American daughters are more successful in portraying Asian mothers—that is, women—as subjects in their own right who may also define Asian Americanness. For women writers, the mother figure either cannot be abjected or must be recovered from abjection because the daughter needs to see the mother clearly as a subject in her own right in order to understand her own identity. Asian American women authors emphasize the daughters' need to base their adult, autonomous selves on strong but not overwhelming connections with their mothers; generally speaking, there is a greater emphasis on continuity than on the oedipal tasks of separation or rebellion noted in men's writing.[2]

Earlier, we saw that Asian American male authors had little to say about the helpfulness of Asian American women of their own generation in the task of discursively claiming American subjectivity and authorship. For immigrant writers like Younghill Kang and Carlos Bulosan, this omission may be traced to the combination of more restrictions being placed on the women of their generation in their home culture, reducing their participation in the project of Americanization, and American laws excluding Asian women from entry into the United States. In Bulosan's *America*, for instance, we saw that Carlos's sisters were kept at home, not taught to read, and not taught to support themselves, so they could hardly develop either the financial or the mental independence that was crucial to Carlos's constitution of his Asian American identity. At the same time, the males themselves seem responsible for devaluing those Asian American women who really could be potential allies in their acculturation. In Younghill Kang's *East Goes West*, for instance, the protagonist's friend, the immigrant George Jum, is strangely apologetic about having "settled" for a Korean American wife, even though she is beautiful, a hard worker from a good family, able and willing to support him, and more established in America than he. Yet he writes after announcing this engagement, "I have not failed, . . . I have only not succeeded" (399). Neither the narrator (to whom he writes) nor any critic has asked why George's incredibly good catch (considering his own childish, impractical nature) isn't celebrated by him and his friends as a more obvious success; it seems that the author himself cannot recognize a Korean American wife as an ally in the task of Asian American subject formation. Even some American-born writers who ought to know better seem reluctant to acknowledge women of their own generation as allies (rather than competitors) in the struggle to construct an Asian American identity. John Okada, Milton Murayama, Frank Chin, and David Mura all emphasize the sons' need to shake off mothers' influences and make Asian American women's cultural negotiations peripheral to the main plot of the sons' struggles (Murayama, Okada), seek to invalidate Asian American women's strategies for establishing American subjectivity and authorship (Chin, Mura), or view more recently arrived Asian American women as more Asian and alien than themselves (Chin, Mura), thereby replicating the process I've described as abjecting the Asian mother.[3]

When we turn to the writings of women, we find a greater emphasis on male-female bonds as the basis for immigrants' material survival and success in the immigrant generation. Not only are immigrant women portrayed as central to the survival, success, and continuity of immigrant communities, but their male relatives, especially husbands, figure centrally in these women's immigration narratives. This is in part due to historical realities: Asian women often came to the United States in the wake of more established males who were their husbands or fiancés, and their labor did indeed make the difference between subsistence and the establishment of a more stable and secure life for their families and communities. For such women, acculturation in America would be mediated through relationships with their husbands. In women's immigrant narratives, therefore, the separate subgenre of husband-wife narratives is more developed and diverse than it is in the men's writing.

In the Chinese American texts to be discussed here, male immigrants' conflicting attitudes about assimilation color their views of Chinese women. For the anonymous Cantonese poets presented in translation by Marlon Hom, whose work was anthologized in 1911 and 1915, contradictions in their position as permanent sojourners were voiced in their attitudes toward, and poetic constructions of, Chinese women at home and on Gold Mountain. As a result, Chinese women could be deemed either unfaithful to tradition or too faithful—too backward and old-fashioned for life in the new world. In a collection of short stories published in the same era—1912—the Eurasian writer Edith Maude Eaton (who published under the pen name Sui Sin Far) composed her stories of Chinese immigrant couples so as to question the traditional division of cultural labor in which the husband is charged with Americanization and the wife with preservation of the Asian culture and traditions.

White characters often enter Asian American women's narratives as outside forces in the woman's negotiations with the problem of embracing change while also being responsible for cultural preservation. In Eaton's stories, white women appear as rivals who threaten to divert the Chinese husband's attention from home, as threatening interlopers insensitive to Chinese family customs, and as potential allies in the wife's struggle for the respect of her husband (though even as allies, their influence is problematic). As for white men, Asian American women's versions of the interracial immigrant romance are also distinct from those of Asian American men. Whereas Asian American men portray white women as either trophies or cultural mentors and muses, Asian American women must necessarily contend with narrative paradigms that conflate cultural tutelage with eroticized class patronage (*Pygmalion*) or colonial paternalism (*Madama Butterfly*). That is, they understand that when Asian women seek or accept cross-cultural mentoring by white men they must also respond to the white men's fantasies of Asian women as docile, easily accessible mistresses rather than equals whose cultures, histories, and needs might be as complex, vital, or intractable as their own—the starting point for Bharati Mukherjee's novel, *Jasmine*.

Authorial Perils and Pearls

For women, authorship itself is a pearl of great price, made hard to attain by ideologies of gender and the realities they describe and legitimate. In the Anglo-American tradition, many critics have discussed how women may be deprived of educational capital, the leisure and privacy to write, the liberty to attain the breadth of experience and cultural knowledge that would enrich or legitimate literary endeavors, support for ambitions to publish, and the serious and informed critical study and circulation that contributes to the longevity of a published work.[4] To this we may add Mary Dearborn's observations about ethnic female difficulties in *Pocahantas's Daughters:* "The ethnic female text is often eased into the world by midwives—editors, publishers, friends, authenticators. . . . The tradition of ethnic female authorship is a tradition of mediation, by which novels are introduced and sometimes produced by agents other than the ethnic woman" (33). Mediating may be positive, as in the case of literary mentoring, and it may resemble the mentoring relations that nurture other writers, but it may be also be intrusive or overwhelming in the case of extensive editing or coauthoring. For published texts, devices such as introductions, notes, and glossaries, which ostensibly prove ethnic writers' "authenticity," may also signal the texts' lack of self-evident authority. At the same time, the ethnic woman writer's task of intercultural mediation may drive the writer to submerge her "real" self too completely in dominant discourses or to weave redoubled stories, disguising subversive ideas in conventional codes. A special burden is that of being damned for success itself: "The ethnic woman who mediates too successfully, who writes for the perspective of the dominant culture (which has insisted on her Americanization and conversion to its values) rather than that of [a reviewer's idea of] 'her own' culture, is roundly scolded" (41).

While these hazards are not unique to women, Asian American literature does convey strong differences in male and female expectations when it comes to community support and recognition. For instance, Younghill Kang and Carlos Bulosan take for granted the greater importance of educating males in their cultures, though Kang is a Korean aristocrat and Bulosan a labor activist and the son of a Filipino farmer. In Kang's *East Goes West,* the immigrant protagonist tries to woo his "beloved," a virtual stranger who is herself a poet, by compelling her to take notes on his life for a couple of hours and asking her to get to work drafting his biography—and this is how he hopes to get a second date. Of course, Kang must be poking fun at his hero's quixotic methods, but the inability to distinguish between courtship and demanding service from women appears in other male-authored texts. Playwright David Henry Hwang had his first romantic "hero" rush into a Chinese restaurant and attempt to pick up the owner's daughter with a line that can be summarized as "Bring me some scallion pancakes on the double; I'm a Chinese god."[5] Granted, these are ethnic references and this is a comedy, but at the end of the evening the guy gets the girl. On a more serious note, the hero's literary struggles in Carlos Bulosan's *America Is in the Heart* are supported at various points by his little sister's savings (the precious five pesos), his brother's earnings, and the money volunteered by a dying white girl, Marian, in her last few days of life. Later, the aspiring writer realizes she's earned the money through prostitution. Bulosan's delicacy in presenting this fictional incident suggests that he does not mean it to be taken lightly, but clearly it is introduced as a moving instance of a (white) woman's sacrifice to a worthy cause—the male ethnic artist's survival.[6] In rebellion against such expectations for either gender, Maxine Hong Kingston wrote in her own memoir: "No one supports me at the expense of his own adventure."

By contrast, one finds in the biographies and creative output of women writers not only important material disadvantages (as in the case of Edith Eaton, who helped her parents raise and support her dozen younger siblings and did not publish a book until her late fifties) but also, in many cases, the sense that creative writing is a personal luxury to be pursued only after fulfilling duties to parents, siblings, partners, children, and employers—or, worse, the suspicion that what the writers have to say will not be valued by readers. Like other ethnic women's texts, Asian American texts are often mediated by authenticators, as Dearborn has noted, because they cannot assume that their experience and insights count. On the biographical level, for instance, Elaine H. Kim has recounted how Jade Snow Wong wrote her memoir *Fifth Chinese Daughter* in response to an editor's solicitation; Wong credited her editor with excising two-thirds of the manuscript and her teacher with reunifying the remainder. Similarly, Jeanne Wakatsuki Houston, coauthor with her husband of the internment memoir *Farewell to Manzanar,* countered her "feelings of unworthiness" by relying on her spouse's interview and drafting skills. "I kept saying, 'Who'd be interested in that?' . . . feeling unworthy and feeling that my experience was unworthy," she told Elaine Kim in an interview (71, 84).[7] Writing for money to support oneself and one's family, responding to a solicitation for one's writing, and accepting the mediation of more established literary mentors are all strategies for countering cultural narratives that insist that women's writing does not count. This view is shared by women of many backgrounds, but these writers particularly needed such strategies because they wrote in eras when there were very few published texts about Chinese and Japanese American experiences. Houston in particular had to break through a generation of official silence, willed forgetting shared by mainstream Americans and Japanese alike, about the camps.

The sense of "unworthiness" voiced by Houston is not limited to any one ethnic group but emerges strikingly in other writings by Japanese women of Houston's generation, the nisei generation that experienced internment. Houston's question "Who'd be interested in that?" echoes the self-effacement described so angrily by David Mura in his nisei parents and figured more strongly as the denial of any interior life in David's mother. In the same generation, Hisaye Yamamoto describes the silencing of women artists in her poignant stories "The Legend of Miss Sasagawara" and "Seven-

teen Syllables," and her friend Wakako Yamauchi associates female longings for art or other forms of fulfillment, expression, and joy with domestic betrayal in three stories and a play in her recent collection, *Songs My
Mother Taught Me*.[8] In the most powerful of these, "The Coward," a married woman who has worked all her life for her family is offered artistic
mentoring, and an affair, by an older white man, also married, who insists
that she needs to engage more passionately with life in order to become a
mature artist. Although on a gut level she agrees, she declines the relationship on the grounds that she cannot base her art on hurting others. He calls
her a coward. She replies, with a prim yet sharp diction reminiscent of the
poems of Emily Dickenson, "You did not hurt me, Sir," but her story belies
her words.[9] In these works, Yamauchi depicts self-sacrificing women with
great sympathy and women who leave their families to pursue other things
as leaving grief and chaos behind them; placed together in a single collection, they convey a perception that, for the ethnic woman, art and family
responsibility cannot coexist.[10] Yamauchi's portrayal of the conflict between
family duties and the requirements of art, further complicated by Asian
Americans' marginalization, can be seen as explaining why Asian American
women need particularly strong strategies for justifying the very enterprise
of writing—a need that crosses ethnic and generational boundaries in this
literature.

Within the literature itself, certain tropes also justify female authorship,
which works as a signifier for female authority, independence, and agency.
In the discussion that follows, Edith Eaton's challenges and revisions of male
narratives, her stance of championing the Chinese, and her loyal constructions of her mother (and other Chinese) as a domestic woman (or domestic people) like herself and her readers also serve to legitimate her literary
work as both unselfish, because she is doing it for others, and authentic, because she establishes both her credentials to write about the Chinese and
her literary credentials.[11] Other strategies for legitimation include the scene
of parental authorization; the scene of rebellion and self-authorization ("No
higher listener; no listener but myself," writes Maxine Hong Kingston in
The Woman Warrior); the introduction of multiple narrators, a version of
the "collective protagonist" described by feminist critics; the invention of
communal authorship; and the decentering of authorship.

Bharati Mukherjee's *Jasmine* is not about authorship per se, but it is about
the revision of the bildungsroman as a narrative form for legitimating a
privilege ethnic women's narratives cannot take for granted, the privilege
to become American by giving up or challenging traditional obligations. In
my introduction, I argued that the domestic and sentimental varieties of
English and American bildungsroman legitimated female moral authority
by suggesting that this authority, used properly in the domestic sphere,

was crucial to the welfare of the nation. Many Asian American women, including Eaton and Mukherjee, have written literary texts processing Asian American political and identity issues through representations of Asian American women as upholders of domestic values, seekers of eligible marriage partners, and artful narrators. Since the domestic woman of the bildungsroman is particularly defined by her words, especially her written words, she is also particularly important to a literary tradition in which the authors are searching for devices to justify female literary authority. Such devices may be particularly important because male writers sometimes disparage Asian American women's capacity to deploy American discourses of democratization to construct viable Asian American subject positions. Thus, in the many texts in which Asian American heroines appear as mothers or daughters struggling to keep the family together, as women seeking to establish, maintain, manage, or survive romantic or marital partnerings that situate them as Asian Americans, as aspiring writers and artists, and as moral instructors, the authors are drawing upon bildungsroman constructions of women as heroines and hence, implicitly, as exemplary national subjects.[12]

However, since the domestic bildungsroman also privileges marriage plots as the arbiters of female success, Asian American women join others in challenging and transforming those plot conventions. Asian American writers may demonstrate how traditional family arrangements are transformed by immigrant-related pressures, depict the oppressiveness or failure of patriarchal forms of family and community, recenter genealogies matrilineally, or deconstruct the realist novel and the official histories it underwrites entirely. Although the writers I discuss at length—Edith Maude Eaton, Bharati Mukherjee, Amy Tan, and Maxine Hong Kingston—all use some of these strategies, I include Bharati Mukherjee's *Jasmine* as a particularly explicit and problematic appropriation of the genre. Other writers invoke domestic values in their stories, but Mukherjee more explicitly alludes to the English bildungsroman as a site for constructing the class and gender privileges that, in an American context, her heroine comes to want. By having her heroine triumph through tactics out of keeping with traditional domesticity, such as surviving rape and prospering, fleeing her ethnic community, and accepting white men's eroticized patronage, Mukherjee offends by appearing to celebrate a disturbing form of opportunism. But, I argue, the novel's failures as a "realist" or "domestic" novel ultimately work to expose the ideological limits of the bildungsroman and its unsuitability for Asian American subjects.

Edith Maude Eaton: "Leaves" and the Immigrant Mother

I've described a male version of Asian American subject formation in which Asian motherhood and womanhood are abjected, positioned as Asian others defining Asian American males as more American by contrast. Then, in the second half of the immigrant romance, the Asian American man, seeking to establish an American identity through authorship, constructs white women as objects of desire, calling upon them both to embody "America" and to aid the men in their struggle for authorship, which in turn is symbolic of other aspects of acculturation. For Asian American women writers, this narrative prototype would of course be problematic, perhaps unthinkable. How can an Asian American woman construct her gender and identity on the basis of abjecting her female, maternal, and Asian aspects? If she succeeds, what kind of subjectivity has she claimed? Finally, since this ethnic literary tradition has not always been well known or consciously drawn upon by emerging Asian American authors, and the romance I describe has not previously been recognized as a significant narrative paradigm, what would be the basis for arguing that female Asian American writers must struggle with it?

For an answer, let us turn to the Chinese Canadian author Edith Maude Eaton, who used the pseudonym Sui Sin Far. Eaton's work has been described as "the first expression of the Chinese experience in the United States and Canada and the first fiction in English by any Asian North American" (Ling and White-Parks, Introduction, 2).[13] The daughters of an Englishman and a Westernized Chinese woman, Edith and her sister Winifred (another author) are distinct from other Asian American writers due to their Eurasian background, but Edith's writing is particularly valuable, not only for the uniqueness of her Eurasian, immigrant perspective but because, both as a journalist and a fiction writer, she researched and wrote about the Chinese communities of several North American cities, including Seattle, San Francisco, Los Angeles, New York, and Montreal, where she grew up. In the absence of more direct literary expressions by immigrant Asian women in Eaton's era, and given the skill with which she cast her pro-Chinese advocacy into literary forms acceptable to the public of her day, Eaton's intra- and interracial versions of the immigrant romance are suggestive of the wide variations later women writers would bring to the story, which, as we have seen, was developed more homogeneously by males.[14]

Both Edith and Winifred wrote repeatedly on the themes of interracial romance and cross-cultural contact, and I will argue that in constructing her public persona as a Chinese Eurasian author Edith had to reject numerous cultural forces constructing her mother as Chinese (the Asian mother) and herself as white (the North American daughter); that her work provides traces of the ideological work Edith did, both to construct and to affirm an identity as a Chinese Eurasian author and subject; and that she therefore consciously rejected a strong impulse to "abject" Chineseness, biographically identified with her mother, from her private and public self-constructions. As part of this ideological work, Edith wrote multiple versions of immigrant romances, stories in which sexual and cultural desire crossed the white-Chinese boundary. In doing so, she built a corpus of work in which the immigrant romance is scrutinized critically (before it becomes a recurring motif in the work of later writers) in an effort to locate the obscured subjectivity of the Chinese woman and to question the white woman's symbolic significance and personal interventions. First, however, let us consider how Eaton dealt with the problem of constructing her public persona as an author.

Edith Maude Eaton was born in England in 1865, the second child of a British father (part English, part Irish) and a Westernized Chinese mother. In her early childhood, the family moved to Montreal (by way of Hudson City, New York), where Winifred was born in 1875 (the Eatons had fourteen children in all). Edith is technically a first-generation immigrant to Canada, but in terms of her relationship to China she is more like a second- or even third-generation Chinese American, as she grew up in a highly Westernized household and never visited China. Indeed, Eaton is arguably less Chinese in her cultural upbringing than such contemporary second-generation writers as Maxine Hong Kingston and Amy Tan. Eaton's choice to identify with and write about the Chinese in North America testifies to her emotional commitment to her mother's heritage, but in her writings about her family, she does not describe their Westernized, Eurasian family household as transmitting very much information about Chinese culture or identity to the children. She does mention her love of her mother's "stories of China," for instance, but she identifies only two, both stories about her mother's experiences. Nor does she mention the presence of any Chinese family friends or acquaintances. She admits that she knows no Chinese and that she learned about China mainly from library books and Chinatown business contacts. Moreover, in her published work she describes Chinese cooking with the formality of someone unfamiliar with it.[15] Eaton's Chinese-born mother, Grace Trefusis Eaton, was educated in England and was apparently training to become a missionary when she met Edward Eaton in Shanghai. Marrying him, she moved to his native England as a young wife and mother, apparently never to return to Asia. In Annette White-Parks's *Sui Sin Far/Edith Maude Eaton*, Mrs. Eaton is shown in Western dress (11, 12).[16] The family as a whole appears not to have socialized with other Chinese in England or Canada. On the contrary, Eaton's published memories of her childhood in "Leaves from the Mental Portfolio of an Eurasian" (Far, 218–38) emphasize the difficulties she and her siblings had fitting into various English and Anglo-Canadian social settings as Chinese Eurasians and their shock, when Edith was around six, at seeing their first Chinese laundrymen, the first Chinese they had encountered besides their mother.

I mention all this not to suggest that Eaton is unqualified to be considered a Chinese North American writer; rather, I want to acknowledge the ways in which she is ethnically *unlike* the other immigrant and second-generation writers in this study because her decision to claim Chinese American identity and authorship is more obviously her own deliberate and individual choice. We might say, too, that for her even more than for the other authors in this study Eaton's Chinese American identity was her own invention; Amy Ling credits her with inventing the very term *Chinese American*. In terms of her own identity construction, the more complicated mediation of the term *Chinese* in Eaton's life and work, combined with her gender, translates into a complex literary practice and multiple subject positioning in her stories; that is, her writing usually requires us to examine the text from multiple perspectives (as Ling and White-Parks insist [6]). Yet it is striking how well Eaton, an isolated foremother of the yet to be written Asian American literature, anticipates later writers' concerns with identity, racial and gender oppression, the search for ancestry and filiation, and the problems of Americanization embodied in Asian American versions of the immigrant romance.

It seems common in Asian American literature, as well as in the literature of other immigrant American groups, for the American-born generation to claim their Americanness by contrasting themselves with their immigrant parents. As we saw earlier, male writers seem especially prone to identifying Asian mothers (overseas or in the United States) with the Asian homeland as well as with traits coded as Asian and abjected from the consciousness of their sons in the process of constructing an American identity. In the Eaton sisters' case, there were also strong pressures to distance themselves from their mother's ethnicity. Not only were the children raised and educated under predominantly Western influences, but there were the additional pressures of anti-Chinese racism in England and North America; the advantages of "passing" as all white, which they were well positioned to do; the difficulty of "proving" their Chineseness to the Chinese themselves; and, for Edith and Winifred, the problem of situating themselves publicly as writers.

These pressures are the unifying theme of Edith's published autobiographical essay, "Leaves from the Mental Portfolio of an Eurasian" (Far 218–30), from which three examples may be drawn. In one, an acquaintance admonishes the author against walking with "a Chinaman" in public: "It isn't right," says he. "Not right to walk with one of my mother's people? Oh, indeed!" she replies. The second incident is perhaps the single passage that best epitomizes Eaton's construction of herself as a Chinese Eurasian. In it, she is forced to come out with the secret of her ancestry at a dinner party in a small midwestern town. Having passed as white up to that point, she's impelled to speak by her companions' demeaning remarks about the Chinese:

> My employer shakes his rugged head. "Somehow or other," says he, "I cannot reconcile myself to the thought that the Chinese are humans like ourselves. They may have immortal souls, but their faces seem to be so utterly devoid of expression that I cannot help but doubt."
> "Souls," echoes the town clerk. "Their bodies are enough for me. A Chinaman is, in my eyes, more repulsive than a nigger."
> "They always give me such a creepy feeling . . ."
> "I wouldn't have one in my house," declares my landlady.
> . . . .
> A miserable, cowardly feeling keeps me silent. . . . I have no longer an ambition to die at the stake for the sake of demonstrating the greatness and nobleness of the Chinese people.
> . . . .
> With a great effort I raise my eyes from my plate. "Mr. K.," I say, addressing my employer, "the Chinese people may have no souls, no expression on their faces, be altogether beyond the pale of civilization, but whatever they are, I want you to understand that I am—I am a Chinese." (224–25)

Although her employer immediately apologizes, she leaves town shortly thereafter, for his apology can hardly erase these insults, much less insulate the author from the prejudices of the entire town. Although she says she no longer wishes to die at the stake for the sake of her mother's people, she clearly feels that the only moral choice for herself is to do just that, albeit not literally; to remain there, passing as white, would be to suffer indefinitely from the cowardly, shameful feeling that for her always accompanies silence. In a third incident, a Chinese Eurasian woman—no doubt Eaton herself—breaks off her engagement when her fiancé asks: "Wouldn't it be just a little pleasanter for us if, after we are married, we allowed it to be presumed that you were—er—Japanese?" (229).

Eaton's resolve on these occasions, and her later decision to publicize her ancestry in print, contrast with the choices of her siblings. White-Parks speculates, for instance, that the "acquaintance" asking Eaton not to walk publicly with Chinese men in "Leaves" may well have been her brother. More significantly, the author's sister Winifred built a prolific, successful literary career upon the presentation of herself as half *Japanese*. To protect her own career, Winifred went so far as to claim that their mother was "a Japanese noblewoman" in Edith's obituary and to publish her own memoir, pseudonymously, with strategically guarded references to her true ethnicity (Ling, *Between Worlds,* 25, 34–38).

Taken together, the evidence from "Leaves" and elsewhere demonstrates that Eaton and her siblings faced lifelong pressure to disown their mother's race, a course that would align the junior Eatons with the Americanizing sons discussed earlier. Eaton, however, clearly felt that for herself such a compromise would be more intolerable than claiming and defending her maternal ethnicity. As reconstructed by Annette White-Parks, the story of Edith Eaton's progress as a writer is the story of someone coming more and more into the open about her family background (Introduction to part two of *Mrs. Spring Fragrance and Other Writings*). Having begun her career writing unsigned but sympathetic articles about the Chinese in Montreal (1894–97), she later combined open advocacy with the implicit presentation of herself as a sympathetic white journalist, as in "A Plea for the Chinaman," published in 1896 "during an era of severe Chinese witch-hunts in both Canada and the United States," and signed "E. E.," at a time when she published under the name Edith Eaton and was perceived as an English woman ([Far, 192–98]). Toward the end of her career, Eaton published "Leaves" (1909) under the pseudonym Sui Sin Far, as part of a public presentation of herself and her experiences as a Chinese Eurasian writer, a presentation that would culminate in the publication of her short story collection, *Mrs. Spring Fragrance,* in 1912. Whereas several sons constructed their Asian American subjectivities by abjecting their Asian mothers, Edith's public construction of herself as a Chinese Eurasian seems motivated by her desire to draw closer to her mother, who bequeathed to her both the lifelong status of an outsider and an example for living with that status. Although in many ways still obscure, from the available evidence Grace Trefusis Eaton appears to have been a resilient, adaptive person, both well suited to the rigors of Americanization and unlike the mothers discussed so far.

Earlier, I argued that in male-authored texts young men prove their Americanness by demonstrating their capacity for critical thinking, which the texts code as an American activity. By contrast, the texts construct the Asian mothers as either embodying the unquestioning courage and character needed to survive extreme hardship and nurture others, though largely *silent* (Bulosan), or as *unable to adapt Asian values* appropriately for their families within their American contexts (Murayama, Okada). Asian and American values are thus polarized in familiar orientalist terms, with the Asian gendered as feminine and devalued and the American gendered as male and privileged. In Eaton's "Leaves," by contrast, this gender polarization does not take place. Instead, the values of rebellion and independence, which at once define Eaton's career and implicitly mark her as a North American (influenced by Western individualism), seem implicitly to come from both her father and her mother, whose marriage and multiple emigrations were an affront to both Chinese and English taboos against miscegenation and assimilation.

Edward Eaton must have been a black sheep in his family. Instead of going right into the family textile business, he studied art in Paris. Sent to Shanghai to begin a career in the silk business, he brought home a Chinese wife and a baby (Edith's brother Charles). He went on to father thirteen more children, become a painter, and move to the wilds of Canada. More central to my argument, however, is the character of Grace Trefusis Eaton. Though she was "stolen from her home" as a child ("Leaves," 222), educated in England, and apparently was in the process of being trained as a missionary—a career already connected with the problematic process of Westernizing China and the Chinese—her choices to marry Edward and return to England (where she'd been educated) still must be seen as daring, violating both Confucian taboos (against marrying for love and marrying foreigners) and English norms (against miscegenation). Among other things, "Leaves" traces the socioeconomic consequences of this couple's uncompromising, romantic, personal choices: we see Edith enrolled in school and being attended by a nurse in early childhood but being withdrawn from school to hawk her father's paintings and her own lace at age ten.

Eaton's portrayals of Chinese women as desiring subjects who seek control of their own lives, atypical for her time, may well have been rooted in her close relationship with her mother. The earliest memories in "Leaves" show Edith and her brother encountering whites who behave as though they think being Chinese is a peculiar condition, too disgraceful to discuss openly, and that being half Chinese makes the children curious specimens, as suitable for inspection as animals. In each case, the child Edith is indignant and resistant to this treatment, as if refusing the pejorative labels. When Edith is about six, she and her brother are shocked by their encounter with some Chinese laundrymen, the first Chinese they have seen besides their mother, who dresses and behaves like an educated Englishwoman.

"Oh, Charlie," I cry. "Are we like that?"
"Well, we're Chinese, and they're Chinese, too, so we must be!" returns my seven-year-old brother. (219)

When taunted by a crowd of older, larger children with racist epithets linking them to these rough-looking, queue-adorned, working-class men, the children acquit themselves splendidly, crying, "Better than you" and "I'd rather be Chinese than anything else in the world." Although physically assaulted, the children confidently report to their mother that they have won the battle: "They ran from us. They were frightened," Charles asserts.

Reflecting orientalist stereotypes, Eaton writes, "The white blood in our veins fights valiantly for the Chinese half of us," but actually it seems that within their home her mother promoted valor and her father quiet tolerance. On this occasion, it's Mrs. Eaton who "smiles with satisfaction" at Charles's report of victory and asks Mr. Eaton to listen and respond, while he says only "um" and pretends to be disinterested. In later conflicts, Edith's mother "takes a great interest in our battles, and usually cheers us on," while her father, the family pacifist, "deems it wisest to be blind and deaf to many things." Clearly, the mother's approval legitimates her children's battles against racism and helps to sustain their self-esteem in the face of these insults. With her backing, and her father's tacit consent, Edith learns early that battling racism is energizing and silently tolerating it is shameful.

Despite whites' denigration of Chinese, Edith sees clearly that her mother is "every bit as dear and good" as her father; she also describes her mother as "very bright and interested in every detail of practical life." From her mother's stories, Edith learns to think of China romantically, perhaps as the site of female adventure; we know she liked her mother's stories about being stolen from home (a surprising theme for a childhood story) and meeting and marrying her father, this family's definitive immigrant romance. Though Edith is readily able to deduce from her parents' examples that Chinese and English are equally "dear and good," she seems less sure about Eurasians, a category for which her parents cannot offer examples.

These glimpses of Mrs. Eaton suggest that one reason Edith does not need to abject her mother in order to assert her Englishness (White-Parks suggests that the family was considered English in Canada) is that, unlike the relatively static, discursively inflexible mothers portrayed in many texts, Grace Trefusis Eaton was herself adept at cultural adaptation. She had overcome the dislocations of her childhood and youth and transformed them into exciting family stories. She had adopted the English language and Western dress and manners, and she provided her children with the resources to function within mainstream Canadian society while affirming their Chinese heritage at home. At the same time, we might see the roots of Edith's uncompromising moral character in her closeness to her parents, whose major life choices were also idealistic. Perhaps the children's report of racial persecution in Hudson City, followed by Mrs. Eaton's pointed question to her husband ("Do you hear?"), had something to do with the family's subsequent move to Montreal; perhaps this move was part of the parents' lifelong quest to find a place for the multicultural family they had dared to found.

For Edith, then, there were many pressures to pass as white and deny or distance herself from her mother's culture, but the family history provided a fundamentally different version of the immigrant romance than the male ones I've described. In the Eaton version, the mother embodied both Chineseness and resourceful Westernization. A willing immigrant, she embraced Westernization yet retained affection for China; she crossed national borders and transgressed miscegenation taboos; and, unlike the Asianwhite partners in popular fictions of interracial love, in which the Asians often suffered and died in symbolic retaliation for their romantic audacity, she and Edward Eaton forged an enduring marriage and produced fourteen Eurasian children.

Though Grace Trefusis Eaton's life story is unique in Asian American literature, the example and maternal effects of her cultural adaptiveness are not. The Asian or Asian immigrant mother who adapts well to change appears in many women's texts; this trait both enhances the Asian American offspring's capacity to construct an ethnicized American identity and reduces the offspring's incentive to engage in the distancing psychic or symbolic operations of maternal abjection. In Grace's case, such positive traits may explain her eldest daughter's lifelong eagerness to identify with "her mother's people" and to construct narratives countering the anti-Chinese presumptions that made her feel ashamed when she did not challenge them directly.

Eaton's position contrasts with those of Younghill Kang and Carlos Bulosan, not only because she was female but because she was born to an English father and eventually was perceived as an Englishwoman by other Canadians. For Edith and Winifred as writers, and for all the children as private individuals, the question was how and when to identify as Chinese and how to know what being Chinese meant when by education and in public perceptions they were already coded as English. In "Leaves," Edith not only claims her Chinese heritage but specifically explores the experience of being a Chinese Eurasian, which she depicts as so difficult that she prefers not to have a nationality because the two races are in conflict. Whereas others might have gauged Chinese Americans according to a conversion-based model of assimilation (either all Chinese or all American), Eaton's "Leaves" broaches the then novel idea that Chinese in North America might appropriately be viewed as bicultural subjects capable of transforming North American culture: in short, Eaton's writing begins the process of constructing a new type of subject, a Chinese American.

Eaton's Fictions of Americanization

Eaton's fiction can be seen, then, as an effort to construct in fiction the Chinese subjectivities to which, as the Anglicized daughter of a Chinese mother, she had had limited exposure in her personal life. Her work seems fundamentally designed to refute the public suspicion, so readily voiced by some whites, that the Chinese might not be human, that they lack feeling and perhaps even souls. Despite her withdrawal from formal schooling at age ten, Eaton's fiction and journalism suggest her familiarity with the norms for subject construction in the female-centered versions of the bildungsroman that have been described as domestic novels in England and sentimental novels in America.

As we saw earlier, critics from Ian Watt to Nancy Armstrong have described how the English domestic novel emphasized the private mental life of heroines, through which the texts represented both the heroines' essential humanness and their worth and virtue. In his discussion of Samuel Richardson's novel *Pamela,* Watt describes how the epistolary form enabled readers vicariously to experience the heroine's most intimate thoughts and emotions (*Rise,* 174–207, esp. 188–97), rendering the writing, feeling woman an exemplary subject of fiction. In *Desire and Domestic Fiction,* Nancy Armstrong draws upon Watts's work to argue that the possession of middle-class, domestic virtues such as modesty, diligence, frugality, and chastity came to be privileged as definitive, not only of virtue and inner worth but of subjectivity itself, in English domestic fiction. Armstrong suggests that English fiction and conduct books naturalized the domestic woman as the exemplary English subject, implicitly displacing aristocratic virtues and values and naturalizing the historic ascendency of the "middling" (commercial and professional) classes in England. By placing domestic *women* at their center, this cultural tradition rationalized the rise of these classes in terms of moral and mental virtues (associated with the feminized private sphere) rather than economic and political competition between the upper and middle classes (the harsh realities of the masculinized public sphere). Thus, the domestic woman's virtues could be presented to the English reading public as transcending class divisions and soliciting the identification of various classes of readers with a feminized national subject.

In North America, similar virtues were explored in "sentimental fiction," as studied by critics such as Jane Tompkins and Nina Baym, where somewhat different social divisions would be bridged by readers' identifications with domestic heroines, but the ideological effects of readers' identification with certain characters and predicaments would be analogous. Both traditions were part of that English and American print culture that Lisa Lowe suggests served "in the interpellation of readers as subjects for the nation" by inviting readers to identify with the " 'imagined community' of the nation" and to relinquish "particularity and difference through identification with an idealized 'national' form of subjectivity" (*Acts,* 98).

One need not prove that Eaton pored over specific texts to see that she had internalized these cultural norms for the sympathetic representation of subjectivity in fiction, journalism, and memoir form. But, whereas Lowe suggests that English and American fiction interpellated all readers as implicitly *white* subjects, Eaton undertook to find a place for the Chinese of North America, not as outsiders but as national subjects in the "imagined community" of North American readers created by her writings. One need only glance at "Leaves" to see that Eaton's central ideological points consist of establishing interiority for herself, her family members, and by implication other Chinese, as in the quotation "I come from a race which is said to be the most stolid and insensible to feeling of all races, yet I look back over the years and see myself so keenly alive to every shade of sorrow and suffering that it is almost a pain to live" (221) and through her construction of a psychological history for herself.

As others have demonstrated, the Chinese in North America were publicly constructed primarily as male laborers in competition with "native" white labor or as opium-smoking deviants (the men) and prostitutes (the women). In Canada as well as the United States, public representations of the Chinese as lacking "normal" sexual and domestic feelings may well have contributed to public acceptance of exclusion policies, which resulted in the formation of Chinese "bachelor" communities. The resulting negative perceptions of these communities were then used to rationalize the continuation of these policies. In journalistic pieces such as "A Plea for the Chinaman" (Far, 192–98), Eaton tries to directly confront and refute pejorative stereotypes of Chinese males as undesirable competitors or vicious private citizens. In her fiction, Eaton tends to move the Chinese out of the public realm of economic competition and into the private realm of domestic life, symbolically bridging the gap seen in "Leaves" between the Chinese laundrymen in the street and the Chinese mother at home.

The primary ideological work of the first two stories in the collection *Mrs. Spring Fragrance* (the title story and "The Inferior Woman") is to establish the novel figure of a Chinese American yenta, who is also a writer, in the conventional position of helping young lovers—one pair Chinese, one pair white American—who are separated by parental opposition.[17] As critics have noted, Mrs. Spring Fragrance's quotation of Tennyson, her ambition to write a book about Americans, and her sly critique of American ideological contradictions mark her as "Americanized" both in her mastery of English and in her ability to deploy American discourses for her own purposes: matchmaking, the assumption of cultural superiority inherent in the pose of observing and commenting on cultural others, and the exposure of contradictory attitudes toward Chinese.

The characterization of Mrs. Spring Fragrance poses the collection's first challenge of interpellation, as much for Eaton as for her readers. In the first story, where the only white character is a minor one (Will Carman, the neighbor), the reader is positioned to admire the wit and wisdom of Mrs. Spring Fragrance as she solves a young Chinese couple's romantic problems but is ironically distanced from her and aligned with the omniscient narrator—who knows, for instance, that Mr. Spring Fragrance is jealous of his wife, while she remains oblivious to the cause of his peculiar outbursts and withdrawals. In the second story, Mrs. Spring Fragrance helps Will Carman, a young lawyer, win his beloved, a self-made white woman (Alice Winthrop), by overcoming his mother's class prejudice against her. Since Mrs. Spring Fragrance is more clearly the moving force in this plot, readers might ordinarily identify with her more strongly, but since she, a Chinese immigrant, is correcting the social attitudes of Mrs. Carman, a white American, Eaton carefully has the Chinese lady position herself as humbly quoting, and learning from, another white woman who thinks highly of Alice, Ethel Evebrook. On a visit to Ethel, who lectures publicly on women's issues, Mrs. Spring Fragrance overhears her explaining to her own mother why Alice, the "inferior woman," is actually superior to herself. Instead of announcing her presence, the Chinese American visitor first takes down the conversation, then announces herself, verifies the quotation, gets Ethel's permission to quote it in her book, and agrees to present the whole conversation personally to Mrs. Carman. As Ethel is the "superior woman" Mrs. Carman wants her son to marry, Ethel's approval of Alice (and indifference to Will) carries extra weight and persuades Mrs. Carman to accept Alice as her daughter-in-law. This maneuver is double edged: on one hand, it positions Mrs. Spring Fragrance as only a student of American society and reaffirms the social authority of Ethel Evebrook, who bears the author's own initials. On the other hand, Mrs. Spring Fragrance's skillful use of journalistic etiquette and rhetorical techniques (getting an authority to make her own point while appearing neutral) codes her as American in both her democratic social attitude and her reportorial pose of objectivity. In short, this story disperses the author's perspectives among several points of view: those of Mrs. Spring Fragrance, Mrs. Evebrook, and the omniscient narrator. Her readers, then, are free to interpellate themselves in a similarly fragmented fashion. They are obliged to accept Mrs. Spring Fragrance as a subject comparable to themselves, but she is still represented as a courteous guest, an outsider observing American life.

A journalist herself as well as an author of a book about Americans (namely, *Mrs. Spring Fragrance*), Eaton did not take her responsibility to witness for the Chinese Americans lightly. In the story "Its Wavering Image," the Eurasian heroine Pan, a resident of Chinatown, is romanced by a cynical white reporter, Mark Carson, in order to get the inside scoop about Chinatown life. With Pan as his native informant, Carson finds many otherwise closed doors opened. When he departs and publishes the community's secrets in a paper for white readers, Pan and her father behave as if the reporter has sexually betrayed her. Pan's father "bays" a curse on Mark's ancestors,[18] while Pan reflects:

Ah, well did he know that the sword which pierced her through others, would carry with it to her own heart, the pain of all those others. None knew better than he that she, whom he had called "a white girl, a white woman," would rather that her own naked body and soul had been exposed, than that things, sacred and secret to those who loved her, should be cruelly unveiled and ruthlessly spread before the ridiculing and uncomprehending foreigner. And knowing all this so well, so well, he had carelessly sung her heart away, and with her kiss upon his lips, had smilingly turned and stabbed her. She, who was of the race that remembers. (64–65)

Mark's reporting, likened to both sexual and lethal penetration, both invokes and invites the stabbing gaze of the "uncomprehending foreigner" on the "body and soul" of Chinatown, with which Pan equates herself. (In a typical reversal of perspective, Eaton momentarily interpellates her readers as fellow Chinese Americans by inviting us to share Pan's view of Mark Carson's readers as "uncomprehending foreigners.") Rejecting Mark's philandering attempts to claim her as his because she is "white" and "cannot be both," Pan insists she is Chinese because, as she tells Mark at their last meeting: "I would not be a white woman for all the world. You are a white man, and *what* is a promise to a white man!" (66). As usual with Eaton, the story cuts several ways. For Amy Ling, it continues Eaton's exploration of her "between worlds" positions as a Chinese Eurasian and a Chinese American (Ling, *Between Worlds*, 44).[19] The casual sexism and racism of Mark, who treats Pan and her community as playthings, also makes this a miniature revision of both the Madame Butterfly story and the Asian American immigrant romance.[20] In Eaton's version of the Butterfly story, the Asian woman survives her stabbing (which is only figurative), rejects her white suitor for the scum that he is, and ends up receiving consolation from a fellow Chinese American woman and her child in a symbolic affirmation of her place in her own community. This is one of many stories in which Eaton seems preemptively to criticize the immigrant fantasy in which the eroticized white partner helps the Asian American to assimilate: in the female version of the immigrant romance, the cultural history of white male exploitation of Asian women makes the white male partner a problematic risk.

In the context of our exploration of Asian American self-construction through *authorship*, this story is most interesting as a tale about the potential evil of *reporting*, a task Maxine Hong Kingston has equated with "vengeance" and one that Eaton herself—as well as Kingston—chose as her form of service to her community.[21] If Mark Carson's journalism is forgetful, white, and exploitative, Eaton's will not be; the story itself is silent about the secrets Mark publishes, proving that the author herself will be "all Chinese" in her discretion, a Pan rather than a Mark, despite her acts of reportage and publication.

The story's title, "Its Wavering Image," seems at first to stand for Mark's inconstancy, foreshadowed by the love song he sings to Pan in their (pre-publication) courtship phase:

> The moon and its broken reflection,
> And its shadows shall appear,
> As the symbol of love in heaven,
> And its wavering image here. (64)

"Wavering" evokes Pan's internal conflict about her identity, and the wavering reflection might also be taken as a figure for the remoteness of a "report" from its original subject, particularly if the reader and writers do not see or understand the original. Alternatively, the wavering reflection evokes Eaton's sly mode of representation, in which some details appear, some don't, and others appear in disguise. But most of all, the wavering image of the moon suggests the difficulty for Eaton of transcending race and culture in her own vision of Chinese American subjects. In Eaton's conceit, comparing the moon and its reflection to "the symbol of love in heaven" and "its wavering image here," the moon stands for the ultimate (implicitly feminine!) Subject whose love transcends race but can only be known through the "broken reflection" of fallible earthly subjects and perhaps the wavering images of their cultural productions.

In "The Wisdom of the New" and its counterpart, "The Americanizing of Pau Tzu," Eaton confronts the problem of sympathetically representing the subjectivity of a Chinese woman immigrant to whom Western culture is both unfamiliar and difficult to swallow. In telling the stories, Eaton tries to move beyond the perspective that seems most accessible to her, that of the sympathetic white bystander, to understand both the immigrant husband, whose idealism and readiness to assimilate seem reasonable to her, and the wife, who seems enigmatic but crucial to the author's ideological objectives. As she struggles to find common ground with the fictional Chinese wife, Eaton shifts from a tragic ending ("Wisdom") to a happy one ("Pau Tzu"), makes several problematic stabs at describing the "Chinese" and "American" character and finally comes to construct Chinese female subjectivity using the Anglo-American literary tropes for domestic womanhood.

At the same time, the stories anticipate the romantic triangle we've seen in Asian American men's writing, in which the assimilating Asian male makes a choice between the Asian woman who represents the homeland and the white woman who represents America. While sympathetic to this male conflict, the stories also suggest that the community's survival is threatened by these polarized gender roles, which can be seen as an adaptation to North American immigration policies. When the men's success depends on their ability to assimilate in America, while the women are required materially to perpetuate traditional Chinese customs and symbolically to embody those customs, their separated spheres are bound to be diminished and estranged.

In both versions of Eaton's domestic drama, a smart young Chinese man has established himself on the West Coast and sent for his wife, only to discover that, having spent her young womanhood in his home village, she is unprepared to learn English, adopt American ways, or accept as platonic his close friendships with American women. In both stories, the provincial wife serves as the racial shadow of the semiassimilated husband, the embodiment of values and beliefs that he cannot abandon, though they appear cumbersome and costly, however carefully the author defends the wife's loyalty.[22] In both stories, the seemingly provincial, jealous wife is further defined by contrast with the charming, cultured young white woman, Adah, whose family employs the husband, whose society the husband enjoys, and whom the husband worships as a kind of higher being, a cross-cultural angel in the house. In this semicolonial ménage à trois, the dazzling but sexually unavailable white woman represents both Americanization and entry into the American middle classes from the perspective of the young man. The wife, who is linked to the husband primarily by tradition, rightly recognizes that her husband's desire for his American friend, though carefully contained as platonic, potentially alienates him from her more surely than a mere mistress would, for Adah embodies the real, albeit unacknowledged, object of the husband's passion, ironically called "the wisdom of the new" in the title of the first story and "Americanization" in the other.[23]

In "Wisdom," Eaton carefully describes the factors limiting the husband and wife's intimacy, beginning with her absence from the opening scene when Wou Sankwei, in Confucian fashion, agrees to take a wife as a substitute companion and caregiver to his mother in China so that she will be less lonely when he leaves for America; the theoretical wife's loneliness, of course, is not considered by mother or son. Seven years later, the successful, Americanized Wou is seen confessing to Adah Charlton that he has never written to Pau Lin, his wife, during their seven-year separation; it seems she is illiterate, though he's too delicate to say so. Nor does he admit that he can't remember her face. When Pau Lin comes to America, Adah and her aunt, Mrs. Dean, accompany Wou Sankwei to meet her boat; Pau Lin instantly perceives that he is attached to them in ways with which she can't compete.

Later, Pau Lin is notably less integrated into her husband's working or social life than her undeclared American rival, Adah:

> Pau Lin was more of an accessory than a part of his life. She interfered not at all with his studies, his business, or his friends, and when not engaged in housework or sewing, spent most of her time in the society of one or the other of the merchants' wives who lived in the flats and apartments around her own. She kept up the Chinese custom of taking her meals after her husband or at a separate table, and observed faithfully the rule laid down for her by her late mother-in-law: to keep a quiet tongue in the presence of her man. Sankwei, on his part, was always kind and indulgent. (46)

There follows a list of material amenities Sankwei provides for his wife (treats, clothes, genteel transportation, and a household "chapel" for her religious practices, not theirs), thereby establishing him as a kind and generous provider, an acceptable husband in Confucian terms despite his remoteness. Thus, Eaton supports her case that by American standards Pau Lin is more like an accessory than a wife to Wou Sankwei.

Sankwei accepts Pau Lin's disinclination to become Americanized, explaining diplomatically to Mrs. Dean that "the time for learning with her is over" (47), but, as he is only twenty-six and she is probably younger, Wou's words suggest either that she isn't very intelligent as an individual (something he wishes to avoid saying) or that uneducated Chinese women cease to learn and adapt by the time they're thirty—that is, that they essentially lack the adaptive qualities needed for successful Americanization. While both readings are possible, the latter is reinforced by other details within the story (such as the portrayal of the other Chinese women) and the already established stereotypes of the Chinese. The portrayal of Pau Lin as a relatively wooden, inflexible person, more a type than a rounded character, links her with both white stereotypes of Chinese women and the images we've seen in male Asian American writing, where Asian women tend to function as icons of an unchangeable Asianness rather than as subjects. As a result, Pau Lin is rendered less credible, both as a fictional heroine and as a potential American subject.

The story's fundamental conflict—between the Americanizing husband and his unassimilable wife—is played out in the problem of their son's education. Clearly perceiving her narrow function in her husband's life, Pau Lin understandably believes that Americanization would estrange her son from her as well. The first conflict sets the pattern, as Sankwei implicitly overrules his wife's attempts to prevent "little Yen" from speaking English, which Pau Lin calls "the language of the white women," her rivals. Later, when Pau Lin discusses the incident with her female friends, we learn that one of them has a son who married a white woman, with the result that "his children passed their granddame on the street without recognition" (48), hinting that letting Yen learn English will make him as remote a son as Sankwei is a husband. Next Sankwei takes Yen to have his queue (a sign of loyalty to the Chinese emperor) cut off. Surveying the damage, Pau Lin scolds the boy: "I am ashamed of you; I am ashamed!" "Never mind, son," says Sankwei. "It is all right" (50).

The following scenes provide further justification for Pau Lin's jealousy, as Sankwei rejects his wife's critical observations but accepts the same comments when they are offered by Adah; at the same time, they set up claims for the couple's complex interior life, which are meant to establish them as thinking and feeling like Americans. When the narrator explains why Pau Lin is more insulted by Adah's influence over her husband than she would be if he took other wives, Eaton is suggesting that Pau Lin is "American" in her psychological sophistication: "But oh! the humiliation and shame of bearing children to a man who looked up to another woman—and a woman of another race—as a being above the common uses of women. There is a jealousy of the mind more poignant than any mere animal jealousy" (51).

When Pau Lin complains to Sankwei that Adah, who has neither loved him nor borne him sons ("gives nothing"), has nonetheless "taken all your heart," he inadvertently confirms her charges by rebuking her for speaking of Adah as if she were also a woman rather than, as he puts it, "a pure water-flower—a lily!" When he leaves the room carrying Adah's portrait of their boy, the triangle is complete. Sankwei's preference for Adah's art over Pau Lin's presence suggests how powerfully the idea of Americanness ("the wisdom of the new"), represented by Adah, has displaced Chineseness in his heart. By consistently rejecting everything Pau Lin *says*, Sankwei signals his disregard for her mind and his construction of her primarily in terms of the physical care they render each other. By contrast, Sankwei idealizes Adah, the symbol of American culture, attempting to deny her sexuality and seeming to hang upon her words. When Adah takes Sankwei aside and voices the same objection Pau Lin has made—that, in effect, he is too Americanized, thinks too much of "other women" (a euphemism for herself and her aunt), and takes his wife too much for granted—Sankwei listens attentively, asks questions, and resolves to change his behavior. In this sense, Sankwei has too deeply imbibed Western assumptions privileging the subjectivity and moral sway of white women and casting into doubt those of Chinese women; by criticizing these attitudes, the story seeks to reaffirm the subjectivity of Pau Lin, who in that sense stands for Chinese women in general.

So far, the story has aptly anticipated the romantic triangles discussed earlier, in which white women, as cultural meditators in the process of Americanization, become objects of the immigrant man's desire, while Asian women are rejected as embodiments of the Asian and inept interpreters of American democratic ideology. Though Sankwei must be very practical to succeed in business, his idealization of Adah is distinctly reminiscent of Han's feeling for Trip and the narrator's feeling for Miss O'Reilly. Indeed, we're told along the way that "even the most commonplace Chinese has yearnings for something above everyday life," and Adah, who is compared in the course of the story with a pure water-flower, a lily, the moon, and "the angel with the flaming sword" (51, 55, 59), clearly fulfills this function in the young immigrant's life because she is associated with Americanness. His feelings for Adah, and for America, are indirectly expressed in the rather Romantic apotheosis to the moon that Adah hears chanted and translated at a Chinatown harvest festival, which ends, "but I, who have ever been a pilgrim and a stranger in the realm of the wise, offer to thee the homage of a heart which appreciates that thou graciously shinest — even on the fool" (55).[24] Combining Asian ceremonial humility with the self-abegnation of the Western courtly lover, this passage invites us to think of Sankwei as a pilgrim, stranger, and fool — an outsider — in America, the "realm of the wise." This moment seems meant to correct perceptions of Chinese as material men, soulless workers, by attributing to Sankwei the kind of interior life and sublime longing found in novels and poetry.

The story comes to a head when Sankwei privately decides that he'll withdraw Yen from American school if Pau Lin objects once more but fails to tell her so. Locked out of discussion of her son's future, Pau Lin poisons the little boy the night before he is to enter school: her irrefutable act will make up for her disregarded words. As Sankwei correctly reads the boy's still body and the emptied cup as signs of his wife's dissent, Eaton's lyric narration balances between the pathos of his loss and an ironic construction of the wife's "giving" and "taking" of life as poetically just: "The thing he loved best in all the world — the darling son who had crept into his heart with his joyousness and beauty — had been taken from him — by her who had given." Pau Lin explains that she has saved her son "from the Wisdom of the New," and insists: "The child is happy. The butterfly mourns not o'er the shed cocoon." While it's true that any child of this couple was headed for a rocky life, the prevailing impression is that Pau Lin has gone melodramatically mad. In response, Sankwei "put[s] up his shutters" — closing his marriage off from further white scrutiny — and writes a cryptic farewell to

Adah, announcing his intent to return to China with his wife, "whose health requires a change" (61). In protecting his wife and renouncing his dream of Americanization, the husband implicitly accepts responsibility for contributing to the tragedy. While sympathetic to Sankwei's passion for "the wisdom of the new," the story suggests that the Chinese American community cannot survive a highly polarized approach to assimilation, in which one gender is trained to assimilate while the other is left behind.

For some critics, this is one of many stories in which Eaton credibly and sympathetically gives voice and agency to Chinese women, whose voices were not often heard and understood by whites in Eaton's time. In such a reading, the story clearly backs the wife and criticizes the husband for being "too Americanized" and, moreover, arrogant and insensitive to his wife, as Adah charges. More importantly, Eaton conceives of Chinese women here and elsewhere as desiring subjects who work to achieve what they want. The limits of Eaton's imagination can be noted, however, without denying her innovative work in this area.

Throughout the story, Eaton seems caught between the desire to convey respect for the Chinese custom of arranged marriage and awareness of its stark emotional implications: Pau Lin is bound by tradition to spend her life in a few rooms, living with, loving, and raising the children of a man who has fallen in love with a world she cannot enter. As a self-appointed cultural ambassador, however, Eaton has to avoid condemning this kind of marriage outright, which would merely support Western readers' view of Chinese customs as barbaric or inferior. One strategy for voicing this ambivalence is to dramatize it in a debate between Adah and her aunt, Mrs. Dean. The latter explains that, although Americans might find a separation of seven years with no correspondence "dreadful," it isn't so to the Chinese. "Everything with them is a matter of duty. Sankwei married his wife as a matter of duty. He sends for her as a matter of duty." When Adah wonders if this account squares with the wife's experience ("I wonder if it is all duty on her side"), her aunt chastises her for being "too romantic" (45). This brief conversation raises several problems. On one hand, the aunt's well-meant explanation requires us to accept that the Chinese lack ordinary conjugal feelings. Not only do we know from Cantonese sources (such as poems lamenting the separation of sojourners from their wives) that this isn't so, even in the case of this established immigration system, but we know from Western sources such as the memorable dinner in "Leaves," where this "they don't mind" conversation leads politically: Americans can dine calmly while Chinese are shipped out of town in railroad cars, secure in the knowledge that it's different for "them." On the other hand, Adah's question might lead to conclusions that would reinforce readers' preconceptions about the backwardness and inferiority of Chinese culture: the Chinese do suffer as a result of their arranged marriage customs, and therefore Chinese customs are oppressive, especially to women. But because Adah's query is presented early on as a *question* rather than a conclusion, readers can interpret the rest of the story as an answer to the questions "What does the wife feel?" and "How would she describe what she is feeling?"

In "Wisdom," the implicit ideological aim of representing the Chinese wife as a talking, feeling subject is ultimately undermined by the author's inability to enter Wou Pau Lin's perspective fully. The character's "normal" feelings for her husband and son are emphasized, but when they are presented in an exaggerated form linked with conventional expressions of madness, she becomes reminiscent of Charlotte Brontë's madwoman in the attic, the colonial other against which Jane Eyre's more privileged subjectivity is constructed. Although Eaton makes Pau Lin articulate and pathetic, she also gives her such alienating, illiberal traits (from the perspective of sentimental fiction readers) as illiteracy, suspicion of Adah's portrait ("She would cast a spell!") and by extension art, opposition not only to American education but implicitly to education itself, possessiveness, jealous laughter, dementia, and, of course, maternal murderousness.

In this sense, Pau Lin becomes a foil for Adah, who takes the traditional heroine's role of giving moral instruction to the hero but also takes the white domestic angel's role of giving solace and instruction to her social inferiors, which in Anglo-American culture would include supposed racial inferiors. In "Wisdom," Sankwei is clueless about his wife's unhappiness until Adah explains his own heart to him, partly because he's deaf to his wife's perfectly lucid complaints. Although Adah is introduced as "a young girl," neither a wife nor an immigrant, she is nonetheless positioned as the arbiter of truth by the story, in a feminized version of the colonial formula voiced archly in another context by Gayatri Chakravorty Spivak as "White men are saving [trying to save] brown women from brown men."[25]

In "The Americanizing of Pau Tzu," Eaton seems to revisit the same romantic triangle with different attitudes toward assimilation, the Chinese, and the proper role of white friends in Chinese American domestic life. As a result, the story's critical view of the husband's devaluation of his home culture seems more persuasive and internally consistent, while Adah, the white female character, is given less moral authority. The story begins with the assimilating immigrant, Wan Lin Fo, announcing to his white friend, Adah Raymond, a young relative of his firm's American partner, that she has inspired in him a love — for his Chinese fiancée. Charmed with Adah's performance as a domestic "angel in the house" ("dispensing tea and happiness to all around" [84]), he hopes to remake his young fiancée, Pau Tzu, in her image. Here Eaton's artful dodging of the dreaded specter of miscegenation may be compared to the sublimated desires of Carlos Bulosan's narrators and with her direct treatments of the issue in "The Story of One White Woman Who Married a Chinese" and "Her Chinese Husband."

In this happier version, Eaton takes care to stack the deck in favor of the Chinese wife and the happy resolution of the couple's conflicts over assimilation. For one thing, both partners are younger: Lin Fo at twenty-two and Pau Tzu at nineteen are more impressionable than the slightly older Wous of "Wisdom." Adopted to be Lin Fo's future wife, Pau Tzu (Pearl) has lived with his family for years, so the couple are well acquainted and have only been separated for a few years. She is pretty, happy, childless, beloved by Lin Fo (who calls her not only "my wife" but "heart of my heart"), and capable of transforming their American flat into an "Oriental bower," which is depicted as a Chinese version of Adah's bliss-inducing domestic realm. When Pau Tzu entertains Wan Lin Fo's friends, "the Misses Raymond," they readily adopt her as their protégé despite the language barrier. Wan Lin Fo, whose mother in China is sustained by a brother and his wife instead of dying off as Mrs. Wou did in "Wisdom," comes from a more affluent family than Wou Sankwei; as a result, Pau Tzu is imagined as having leisure in China for embroidery, lute playing, and "sipping tea and chatting with gentle girl companions" (again rivaling Adah as a domestic angel in Chinese terms) in contrast to hapless Wou Pau Lin, who is pictured as attending her baby and mother-in-law in poverty and isolation.

In short, Eaton constructs a sympathetic subjectivity for Pau Tzu, and by implication other Chinese women, by invoking codes for that privileged subject of sentimental fiction, the domestic woman. She makes a similar move in the two stories in which she depicts the immigrant, Mrs. Spring Fragrance, as humorous, cultured, Westernized, liberal, and a fluent, even crafty, reader and writer of English. In "Wisdom," Eaton attempts, and I think fails, to create a heroine whose subjectivity is coherent and sympathetic but not Westernized; the heroine of "Americanization," who is aligned more explicitly with Victorian ideals of femininity, represents a second attempt at this kind of "Americanization." If, as I think, this attempt largely succeeds, it's because Eaton has subtly upgraded the heroine's social class, and the key to that upgrade is that Pau Tzu is a skilled speaker and writer of her own language, as evidenced by her singing and her farewell letter to Wan Lin Fo, both of which are "translated" by the narrator into faultless (though stylized) English. In one scene, Pau Tzu solicits her husband's concern by singing about a silk fan, which, like a fair-skinned wife, is lovely and white and used for a season, then readily discarded. The lyric, though attributed to some ancient imperial wife, is plainly Eaton's composition, for it adheres gracefully to the nicest conventions of Victorian lyric poetry, ending with:

This silken fan then deign accept,
Sad emblem of my lot,
Caressed and cherished for an hour,
Then speedily forgot. (90)

Though strikingly Victorian in prosody, diction, and sentiment, the lyric incorporates a bit of Chinese symbolism (the association of white with death), as it uses the fan's whiteness to link the wife with both purity *and* death (a conjunction widely favored by Victorian poets). The song also moves the plot along by communicating Pau Tzu's fears that Lin Fo will discard her if she fails to assimilate because he really desires to marry Adah.

When Lin Fo fails to see the root cause of Pau Tzu's unhappiness and mysterious wasting illness, she runs away, sending him "a dainty, flowered missive" that announces her willingness to be divorced, "as is the custom in America," so that her husband "may be happy with the Beautiful One," whom she recognizes as the model for her own Americanization. Lingering illness, of course, is a classic trope linked with Western romantic heroines (not to speak of Victorian women writers, including Eaton herself). It is also famously associated with female sensibility in the eighteenth-century Chinese classic *The Dream of the Red Chamber,* in which the passionate, tubercular heroine dies of a broken heart. Letters of renunciation, usually followed by death, are another such trope.[26] Thus, Pau Tzu's pathetic epistle, with its undertone of suicidal intent, marks her as a proper sentimental heroine, as American (i.e., Western) as any white heroine in the delicacy of her feelings and language. By dissociating American subjectivity in this story from cultural assimilation per se (i.e., Christianization, the use of English, the adoption of Western dress and manners, and so on) and identifying it instead with fictional codes for (implicitly middle-class) feminine domestic virtue, this story renders Pau Tzu intelligible as a sympathetic subject whose emotional experience crosses cultural barriers. The centrality of Pau Tzu's literacy to this characterization can be underscored by comparison with the denouement of "Wisdom." In terms of plot structure, Pau Tzu's letter takes the place of the murder that compels readers to reject (or abject) Pau Lin as a deviant subject, an attic madwoman in whom racial and mental alterity are conflated.

Eaton also revises the husband's "Americanization" to include continuing love of his homeland, thereby maintaining the symbolic links between Asian women and Asian homelands that we've seen in "Wisdom" and many male-authored texts. In "Wisdom," Wou Sankwei is emasculated by his inability to work in China and is deeply enamored of America. When Adah tells him to pay less attention to her and her aunt, she is figured as an angel evicting him from paradise, which stands for both her presence and

America itself. At the story's end, Wou's plan to return to China reads like an exile and a defeat. Wan Lin Fo, by contrast, views Americanization somewhat more pragmatically. In his heart, he remains a "*true son* of the Middle Kingdom," secretly pitying those "who were born away from its influences," though he admires "much about the Americans" and is willing to adopt their ways in the spirit of touristic good manners, adopting the motto "When in Rome . . ." (86, emphasis mine). In his search for Pau Tzu, he vows not to care "if she never speaks an American word" and to take her "for a trip to China, so that our *son* may be born in the country that Heaven loves" (92, emphasis mine). These quotations, including the healthy hint of pro-Chinese chauvinism and the confident reference to his nonexistent firstborn as "our son," establish Wan Lin Fo's intention to perpetuate his lineage as a true son of China but also hint that he thinks he can do this on American soil. Why else would he plan to take Pau Tzu "for a trip to China" instead of simply "home"?

Thus, Pau Tzu still embodies China, but now, with her claims to Western, bourgeois subjectivity (domestic virtue, sentimental heroinism) knit into the fabric of the story, she need not Americanize outwardly in order to compete with Adah. Americanization is redefined for Wan Lin Fo, too. Instead of a country bumpkin seeking membership in America, for whom Adah is like a sublime moon goddess (as she is to Wou in "Wisdom"), and his wife an unwelcome reminder of his obligations to home, he is the cosmopolitan son of "the country that Heaven loves," borrowing American ways to make his way in this country but also emotionally attached to his wife and homeland and seeking to construct a family that "marries" Chinese and American cultural virtues. In both stories, then, the husband's feelings for the wife are metaphoric of his feelings for his homeland.

In this spirit, Adah is deposed from her problematic double role as American icon and paternalistic marriage counselor. In "Wisdom," chauvinistic Wou Sankwei rejects his wife's very clear explanations for her unhappiness until Adah, pulling racial rank to gain his attention, enlightens him. "What am I to do then, Miss Adah?" asks Wou Sankwei, whose docility is lauded as Chinese openmindedness (57–59). (Why doesn't this "young girl" address the Chinese men as "Mr. Wou" (her senior) or "Mr. Lin Fo" in these stories?) In "Americanization," by contrast, Wan Lin Fo seems quite capable of understanding his wife's missive unassisted and seems to resist Adah's presence as intrusive. Adah's castigation, while somewhat clarifying, is also satirized, as Wan Lin Fo wonders "how he could ever have wished his gentle Pau Tzu to be like this angry woman" (91). The goal of Americanizing Pau Tzu is challenged more directly when Adah, stepping down from her pedestal, admits that *she* could hardly Sinicize herself within a few months, and the narrator implies that most of the couple's Chinese friends sympathize with Pau Tzu's flight from Wan Lin Fo. And, instead of having Adah explain to the husband that he is unconsciously in love with her (awkward even for heroines not named after their authors), Pau Tzu's jealousy of Adah is communicated indirectly by Wan Lin Fo himself when Pau Tzu's whereabouts are discovered, as he gently asks Adah not to preside over his reunion with his wife.[27] Unfortunately Eaton couldn't end the story there or with Adah's silent understanding; she gives Adah the last words of explication, and they are "Poor, brave little soul!"

Together, the two versions offer a glimpse of Eaton's progress in constructing and claiming subjectivity, in terms accepted by European Americans, for Chinese men and women. At the same time, she seems to progress in understanding her own position in relation to these Chinese characters. From the perspective of the Chinese husband, Eaton takes the story of the man who wants to shed Chineseness (embodied by his wife) and acquire Americanness (symbolized by his white lady friend) and revises it so that the husband's desire ultimately returns to his homeland and his wife, affirming his positive self-image as a true son of China. We might read this as a political deficit, arguing that the stories confirm that the Chinese really cannot become Americanized and that the wives embody an inconvertible Chinese essence that every immigrant carries within. But in a broader sense Eaton seems to be questioning the husband's model of Americanization, as she suggests that Wou Sankwei's passion for the "wisdom of the new" is lethally insensitive and that the "Americanizing of Pau Tzu" should not and need not require the discarding of Chinese cultural identity. The latter story's ending suggests that being a true son or daughter of China need not, with time, be inimical to life in America.

In both stories, Adah is positioned not only as the catalyst for the couple's problems but also as their Western observer: her responses stand in for those of the "English" author and her readers. Despite Adah's insight and sympathy, she proves unable to solve the couple's problems in the first story and her efforts are satirized in the second. The latter demonstrates greater sensitivity to the potential for Adah's harmful intrusiveness and expresses greater confidence in the Chinese couple's ability to manage their own affairs.

The representation of the Chinese wife is perhaps most problematic because Eaton has to justify a character who resists Westernization to a Western audience. In the first story, she tries to accomplish this by redefining *American* in terms of romantic love and companionate marriage. Although Adah argues that women's needs and perceptions transcend race ("I do not believe there is any real difference between the feelings of a Chinese wife and an American wife. . . . A woman is a woman with intuitions and perceptions, whether Chinese or American, whether educated or uneducated"), this moment of universalism is undercut by the assertion that follows, that "for all her ignorance, I can see that the poor little thing become more of an American in that one half hour on the steamer [when she realized that her husband was more attached to Mrs. Dean and Adah than to her] than Wou Sankwei . . . has become in seven years" ("Wisdom," 53). In Adah's conclusion, Pau Lin is more American than Sankwei because she understands her husband's platonic friendships better than he, and because she is dissatisfied with marriage to a man who is unconsciously in love with another woman and whose primary interests exclude her.[28] Adah's argument, which appears to be the author's, is offered to refute her aunt's stereotypical assumptions about Chinese: that they are accustomed to doing everything according to duty, that they do not expect mental intimacy or romantic love in their marriages, and that Chinese women are content with less (45, 53). Yet Wou Sankwei appears to share these presumptions, at least until they are corrected by Adah. Are we to read Wou Sankwei's presumptions about his wife's limited needs as Chinese, male, or purely individual? To argue that Pau Lin is American because her feelings are finer than the norm for Chinese women, or that Chinese women have the same feelings as Americans but Wou Sankwei is being Chinese when he ignores those feelings, is to single out Pau Lin, who expects more from her marriage after observing American ways, as different from other Chinese women, an exception that leaves the rule intact. Moreover, the central premise of the story is altered by the sensational ending. When the neglected wife described by Adah becomes the mother who so fears change and education that she prefers to kill her son rather than risk his estrangement, Pau Lin becomes pitiable and morally deviant in either culture. The project of recuperating Chinese female subjectivity as "like" ordinary American subjectivity is at best suspended, in this particular story, when we come to the murder of the little boy Yen. (At worst, the story might be read as confirmation of Chinese moral perversity and unassimilability if the couple are somehow construed as typically Chinese.)

"Americanization," by contrast, constructs the Chinese wife as resistant to the externals of "Americanizing" but ultimately more assimilable because she is fundamentally an oriental (childlike, ultrafeminine) version of the "domestic woman" already constructed by Anglo-American culture as an exemplary national subject. Pretty, happy, obedient, culturally refined, and willing to change, though unable to make herself into Adah, Pau Tzu more readily solicits the sympathy of Eaton's imagined community of white American readers through her innate similarities to Adah, the domestic angel. Although the story flatters American readers with the characters' shared assumptions about Adah's superiority, it undercuts these assumptions at the story's end when Wan Lin Fo's turn from Adah toward his wife is reinforced with his positive reclamation of Chinese identity. Thus, Pau Tzu and Wan Lin Fo combine American and Chinese virtues in different, strongly gendered ways that move Eaton toward a new concept of a genuinely Chinese American subjectivity.

Here, then, at the beginning of Asian American fiction, are a struggle and a question that continue to this day: the struggle to construct the Asian American *as* American, or, more properly, to transform the connotations of "American" to include those of Asian descent; and the struggle to create imaginatively the elusive subjectivities of the immigrant generation, those who came before the writers and did not leave verbal records of their thoughts or who never crossed the chasms that separate private utterance from published English texts.

Eaton now seems both prescient in her concern to establish the Chinese as subjects whose interiority resembles that of her American readers and constrained in her ability to either transcend the perceptions of her day or get her distinctive perceptions into forms deemed acceptable for publication. In particular, the problem of representing Asian woman immigrants who have not left written or oral records of their own remains a concern of scholars and creative artists. The relative obscurity of Eaton's mother Grace amid all the writing of this literary family gives rise to Eaton's hurtling her imagination against a fictional wall—what do Chinese women think? It is difficult to write about people like one's parents but harder still to write about people unlike them in class, life experience, or education.

One of the stories told about Chinese women is the other face of the Asian male immigrant's romance with America: the story of the woman left at home. Because the Chinese women of the exclusion era (1882–1943) do not "speak" for themselves in many published English texts, their stories appear in muted and mediated forms in Asian American literature. Edith Maude Eaton is ahead of the game in telling this story in abbreviated form at the outset of "Wisdom," when the Chinese son's arrival in America is prefaced by his departure from somewhere and someone: he leaves behind a mother, sister, wife, and child. Adah picks up this story, which the husband seems to have forgotten, when he evokes the scene of Pau Lin caring for Wou Sankwei's aged mother and newborn son, unaided, for the seven years of his absence.

Ultimately, the apparent reticence of Grace Trefusis Eaton in her daughter's work resonates with the silence of the mother, the sisters, the sisters-in-law, the unmarried Filipinas, and the prostitute in Bulosan's memoir. Although the particular histories of China and the Philippines diverge in many ways, the women in the new world and the women left behind offer the same challenge to English-speaking readers and writers about Asian America.

These stories evoke a division of cultural labor in the families of Cantonese immigrants that seems intertwined with the American policy of admitting laborers but barring their wives: the custom arises of casting the women as the bearers of tradition and the men as the family's sanctioned explorers. I've suggested that in these two stories Eaton takes the figure of the wife who comes to embody China in her husband's mind and demonstrates that the contradiction of the husband's situation—asked to assimilate *and* remain Chinese—is symbolically displaced onto the figure of the wife in his eyes. Whatever the politics of having Adah voice this perception, Eaton's articulation of the injustice of this is uncannily prescient.

But how could Eaton have known that Asian women would fill this iconic function in the representations of writers not yet born when she published her book? She had only to turn to the functions of women in the Anglo-American literature of her own time. If the domestic woman in Anglo-American fiction stood for the national subject, she also stood as the guardian of national morality and cultural values. In the male imagination, this iconic function underlies the American cultural tropes described by Nina Baym, in which (white) women stand for the socializing and constraining forces that male protagonists, in search of freedom and self-realization, need to evade. In the female imagination, both the payoffs and the costs to individual women of accepting such a role are explored. Not knowing Chinese, Eaton could not have known that a similar iconization of Chinese womanhood had taken place in the collective Cantonese imagination, but she may have learned of the narrow social scope sanctioned for Chinese women on both sides of the ocean through her personal contacts with Chinese men and women in North America. In the following section, I want to suggest that the turn of the century poetry published by Cantonese American men provides a continuity between Eaton as the first woman writer to address Chinese immigrant concerns and later Asian American male writers such as those discussed earlier. These songs of Gold Mountain, as Marlon Hom names them, suggest that the positioning of immigrant men as the subjects of Asian American assimilation narratives, and white and Asian women as literary foils for their stories, which I have found runs through the works of a range of later male writers, is a theme that was already present in the Chinese American cultural community by the time Eaton published *Mrs. Spring Fragrance.*

Songs of Gold Mountain: Male Views in Eaton's Day

As a cultural expression that also served ideological functions, Marlon K. Hom's 1987 *Songs of Gold Mountain* is intriguingly double voiced.[29] On the one hand, we have the turn of the century Cantonese literary community of the West Coast, centered in San Francisco, writing Cantonese-language poems addressed to each other, holding contests, and publishing anthologies. On the other, we have the contemporary cultural historian Marlon K. Hom, who has collected, selected, translated, and published the poems with introductory material situating them within Chinese America social history and also in relation to Chinese literature and Cantonese folklore. Hom's project is clearly to refute a number of pejorative stereotypes about these communities. His work conclusively refutes the presumption that the immigrants had no culture of their own as well as the presumptions, addressed by Eaton, that the Chinese either lacked domestic and sexual feelings or that their feelings were abnormal (whether perverse, vicious, or undeveloped) and that these lacks and abnormalities were intrinsic to the Chinese. Hom's selections, then, provide a moving counterpoint to Eaton's work. Not only do they offer access to the writings of Chinese men of the same era as Eaton's (Hom's selection is made from two anthologies dated 1911 and 1915, while Eaton's collection was published in 1912), but we have a range of male voices writing about Chinese women.

By placing the Gold Mountain poets in dialogue with Eaton's work, we can clarify two things: the literary conventions through which these male poets viewed and portrayed Chinese women at home and abroad and their attitudes toward Chinese female gender roles. Hom's selections tell us, first and foremost, that these Chinese poets had understandable feelings and attitudes toward women, including feelings of great tenderness, respect for Chinese women, longing for their wives, sexual fantasies that were romantic as well as passionate, and in a few cases tolerance for Western ideas about female equality and emancipation. (Hom says little or nothing about themes of homosexual bonding, desire, or identity.)

The sequence of poems Hom has offered as "Lamentations of Estranged Wives" is a telling counterpoint to Eaton's portraits of cross-Pacific marriages. In them, the male poets assume the voices of the women married to Gold Mountain sojourners and left behind in China. These poems, startling in the directness of their expressions of sexual longing, convey at once the sojourners' own sexual feelings, their sympathy for their wives at home, and their consensus about the wives' proper role: to remain at home, maintain the family, and keep their desires focused on their absent husbands. In many poems, the wives are imagined to argue that gold is not sufficient to compensate for the misery of de facto widowhood, thereby contradicting another stereotype of the Chinese as greedy or practical to the exclusion of other feelings and values. While the poems express some criticism of the system, they are also strikingly resigned to it. Most importantly, they demonstrate the sojourners' wish that their wives will remain totally focused on them during their absence. These male writers prefer not to consider the possible calamity of female infidelity, a threat to their system, and they seem unable or unwilling to write about a female culture or one in which the marriage bond is peripheral to the wife's daily life (Hom, *Songs*, 47).

By contrast, the "Ballads of the Libertines" suggest that this community not only tolerated but expected the men in America to seek and enjoy sexual experiences. Hom acknowledges the Chinese men's patronage of prostitutes in the United States, but he presents these habits, along with the consumption of pornography and the expression of sexual fantasies, as understandable expressions of normal sexual feeling in the face of years of enforced womanlessness. As Hom explains, this relaxed attitude, an appropriate adaptation to their circumstances, was typical of the Cantonese men's standards for themselves. Typical of these "ballads" are no. 163, which urges a "young man" to loosen up and think about "places of merriment"; no. 164, which expresses readiness to "have a taste of the white scent while there's time"; and no. 166, which invites the speaker's beloved, "sweet sixteen," to seize the day and enjoy love while they are young:

> Sweet sixteen, that's the right moment.
> Happy times should not be lightly abandoned.
> Youthful days, once they have slipped away, cannot be detained.
> Dear lady, do you realize this opportunity is golden?
> A union of clouds and rain—
> Most wonderful at the young and tender age.
> If you don't catch the fun while it's here,
> It won't taste as sweet in later years. (Hom, *Songs*, 259)

Other poems rue the speakers' romantic entanglements as costly distractions from their proper manly tasks, but the basis for regret is financial rather than moral. "Flower debts are endless," laments one speaker, employing a common euphemism for the expenses of womanizing, while another sighs, "My savings are exhausted; what choice is there for me?" (nos. 173, 174). A series of poems figure the speakers as heroes ensnared by love; no. 172 is a particularly playful version of this theme, in which the sex act itself is figured as a martial encounter:

> The gorgeous woman is just too much:
> Her tender passion is a tiger-cage prison.
> With an army I challenge her, showing her the weapons.
> To my surprise, I am flattened by her soft, whirling whips.
> Soar no more;
> A defeated general stranded on a narrow path.
> Water flows from the ravine, flooding the grass.
> O, how can a powerless man make his escape? (265)

The speaker's mock dismay at the defeat of his "general stranded on a narrow path" suggests the community's underlying acceptance of nonmarital sexual activity, for this poem's double entendres imply a readership well versed in deciphering such codes and accustomed to sexual candor.

This tolerance colors the poems celebrating liaisons with prostitutes (nos. 214, 215), who are portrayed sympathetically as women with normal sexual feelings and urged to reform (through marriage) before it is too late; by contrast, respectable women who act too independently are criticized for a wide range of unsubmissive acts in the "Songs of Western Influence" and accused of behaving like prostitutes. In poem no. 130, a wife's lack of obedience, her self-adornment, and her "acting cute and charming" are condemned as signs of promiscuity and incipient prostitution; no. 126 condemns a "lawless shrew" for bullying her (admittedly) "inept husband," divorcing him, getting their property, and remarrying; while no. 127 condemns "emancipated women" for speaking English and going out freely with men (127). Finally, no. 128 suggests that "the charming girl" is spoiled and Westernized because she wants to be equal and select her own mate; she's therefore said to dally with him before marriage, which the speaker describes as "shameless," an adjective noticeably absent from accounts of male sexual activity in the "Ballads of the Libertines." This speaker complains that they'll all be deprived of the "roasted pig" (a dish that for some reason symbolizes the bride's purity) at the charming one's wedding; it's clear, however, that there will be plenty of sour grapes.

To be fair, the collection includes poems that celebrate the emancipation of women from conventional codes of property and arranged marriages. In one, a female speaker flouts convention by urging her friends to wear "different and colorful clothes" and circulate freely, insisting defiantly that "We are all as pure as white jade, without a blemish whatsoever" (no. 133), while engaged lovers in another poem happily anticipate the changing of the community's mores to match their own emancipated decision to marry for love:

> Remember this firmly:
> We have secretly vowed our matrimony.
> Someday, as we sing in harmony in our bedroom,
> We'll laugh that we were way ahead of our time. (224)

Though by no means unanimous on all issues, the Gold Mountain poets as a group portray their prolonged sexual segregation as one of the more painful aspects of their lives in America. Within their own community, they adjust their sexual standards pragmatically: according to Hom, they are far more tolerant of male promiscuity and the use of prostitutes than they would be at home. However, they do not make corresponding adjustments in their expectations about their wives' conduct at home. Instead, the readers and writers of this community seem to gain a kind of imaginative pleasure and reassurance from the figure of the sexually tortured but chaste wife at home. There are mixed feelings, too, with respect to adaptive behavior seen in Chinese women in America. On one hand, tolerant attitudes toward prostitution are expressed, while on the other "emancipated" female behavior is condemned in another class of Chinese- and American-born women. I've suggested that some of this ambivalence may simply reflect sexual frustration with the shortage of available women. But there is also a feeling that these men, so hard pressed in this alien culture and so far from home, respond with a nostalgic evocation of "home" and their womenfolk as stable, unchanging, loyal, and supportive, that this image within helps them to stabilize their sense of self in the new country and thus to survive. In this context, the modern demands of the women portrayed with distaste as too emancipated and Westernized seem to threaten these men, as if the modernizing women are somehow competing with them, and beating them, in the race for cultural adaptation in America. This unspoken sense of competitiveness with Asian American women is palpable in the works of later writers such as Frank Chin. For the Gold Mountain poets, the prospect of American-born daughters setting their own terms for dress, socializing, and marriage, implicitly rejecting the values of the older generation, would be deeply disturbing because it implies the sojourners' loss of connection both to certain sexual possibilities and to future generations—the same fear that drives Pau Lin to kill her son in Eaton's melodramatic story.

As an editor, Hom has shaped the collection to emphasize the diversity of men's views about women, but an underlying conservatism is clear: the poets as a group see themselves as agents of change, for whom adjustments to America are fitting, but they want and need to see Chinese women as stable, unchanging embodiments of the way of life they've left behind, keepers of the cultural flame. In this way, the Gold Mountain poets anticipate the nostalgia attached to the Filipino mother by an immigrant writer like Bulosan as well as the use of the idealized Asian woman as an unchanging "other" who helps to define the male immigrant's self as embroiled in change and adaptation in America—one version of the psychic process I've called abjection.

In this context, Eaton's work stands at the beginning of an alternate tradition in which Asian American women writers both challenge this division of labor (in which men adapt and wives are asked to both maintain the old ways and absorb the men's ambivalence about these ways) and replicate it in their own representations of Asian and immigrant women as wives and mothers. Taken as a whole, Eaton's collection *Mrs. Spring Fragrance* also challenges the stereotype of the Asian woman as intrinsically less adaptable than her male counterpart by depicting women who are culturally more adept at assimilation than their husbands yet true to their home culture.

Reinventing Bildung: Bharati Mukherjee and the Jasmine Controversy

I now turn to a contemporary author who undertakes ideological work similar to that chosen by Eaton and Hom, with very different results: Bharati Mukherjee. Like Eaton, Mukherjee is an immigrant to the United States, formally educated in English and American culture, who has chosen the role of fictively giving voice to other, far less privileged immigrants. In particular, Mukherjee's controversial novel Jasmine, about the transformation of a Punjabi village girl into a sophisticated middle-class American, undertakes the work of fictively constructing a subaltern subjectivity; of imagining how such a subject could become truly "American," not only in her attainment of material security or success but in her internalization and mastery of American ways of thinking; and of commenting on the cultural presumptions that govern romantic encounters between whites and Asians.

As we shall see, Bharati Mukherjee's positioning of herself as an Asian American writer who seeks to speak for immigrants from many countries and class backgrounds is viewed as deeply problematic, particularly by readers focusing on the politics of postcolonial representation. The recurring and interrelated questions of her work's authenticity and quality, and the basis for her right to speak for these subaltern others, is epitomized by critical commentary on Jasmine. The Jasmine controversy touches on the recurring problem of educated Westernized or American-born writers seeking to give voice to the subjectivities of less privileged others with whom they feel a bond and the question of what standard legitimates such efforts. To the usual concerns about social and psychological plausibility, I will add the view that Jasmine is a negotiation between preexisting narrative conventions of plot and character construction—an attempt to marry American myths of upward mobility to the constructions of such myths in the English domestic novel. Where Jasmine fails or offends as a realistic portrayal of class dynamics, immigrant experience, or female agency, I suggest, the failure points productively to gaps or contradictions in the mobility myths Mukherjee deploys. In this sense, the novel may function as a stimulant to the reader's critical rethinking of these myths, and therein lies its real contribution to the debate.

In her creative writing, as well as in public appearances and published essays, Bharati Mukherjee portrays herself as acutely aware of the cultural baggage of colonialism and the responsibility to speak for those less privileged than herself. Having announced this political agenda, and having written about the experiences of immigrants to North America from many cultures, Mukherjee inevitably invites readers to judge her work on the basis of whether it credibly and responsibly represents the immigrant experience. In her recent book, *Jasmine*, Mukherjee tells the story of a young widow from a Punjabi village who emigrates to the United States and successfully enters the American middle class, but this entry is contingent upon plot conventions drawn from an English literary tradition, the domesticized nineteenth-century version of the bildungsroman. As a result, this novel has been harshly criticized for purporting to speak for immigrants yet trivializing the real obstacles they face by making Jasmine's rise so swift, so easy, and so dependent on her sexual appeal as an oriental woman.

The novel has drawn the ire of Indian critics, who fault both its stereotypical representations of India and Indian immigrant communities and its representation of Jasmine's consciousness and opportunities. Debjani Banerjee, for instance, accuses Mukherjee of "catering to a First World audience while still mining the Third World for fictional material" (173). She cites this novel's portrayal of Sikh nationalists (as insatiable, irrationally malicious purveyors of random violence) as one instance of the author's general tendency to gloss over the complex political history of India's postcolonial period, thereby protecting Western readers from having to confront the "uncomfortable moments of complicity" that would arise from a more demanding analysis and "trivializing . . . the complexities of the postcolonial condition" (170). For Banerjee, Jasmine's flight from India and her willingness to assimilate by presenting her past selectively to complacent American mentors and admirers is symptomatic of Mukherjee's escapism as a writer. Both Jasmine and her author profit, she charges, from a collaboration with sentimental liberal readings of Third World politics that figure Indian history "in terms of a lack, an absence or an incompleteness that translates into an inadequacy" (Dipesh Chakrabarty, qtd. in Banerjee, 171). Jyoti/Jasmine's improbable insistence on coming all the way to Florida Tech solely to commit *sati* and her unsympathetic view of family life in the Flushing ghetto have been considered similarly obtuse, implausible, and simplistic (Grewal, "Born," 188–90).

Criticism of the novel's first-world biases extends to the heroine herself. In addition to Banerjee's complaint that Jasmine "acquiesces to her own exoticization as an Indian princess," Gurleen Grewal charges that, to the extent that *Jasmine* portrays Indian women as ignorant, oppressed victims awaiting rescue, the book leaves intact the simplistic binary thinking that posits "western women as secular, liberated, and having control over their own lives" and third world women as their opposites (Chandra Mohanty, qtd. in Grewal, "Born," 187–88). Finally, Grewal contests the coherence and plausibility of Jasmine as a character on class grounds:

Mukherjee blurs the distinction between someone like herself, a member of an Indian elite, well groomed in British colonial education, and a peasant woman like Jyoti-Jasmine. . . . Mukherjee attributes to an underprivileged immigrant woman (Jyoti-Jasmine) the dispositions and options available to an Indian woman privileged by class and education (Jazzy-Jane). For women of the class and education of Mukherjee, assimilation into the American mainstream is possible. However, to assume that unskilled, illegal women immigrants like Jasmine — who are not fluent in the English language — have the same opportunities as upper-class, educated immigrant women is to make a mockery of their lives. It is to brush aside the realities of class, whose lines of hierarchy in both America and India can be as unyielding as the Indian astrologer's lines of fate. It is, in short, to write a romance novel. (192)

These complaints can best be understood by viewing the novel as Mukherjee's attempt to imagine a female immigrant version of the American Horatio Alger myth.[30] To imagine how an uneducated, unskilled Asian woman can replicate this myth, Mukherjee falls back on the romance plots of English novels of education, perhaps because they form a well-known, compelling tradition that assumes that women with no economic or political power can still attain social status, security, dignity, and freedom. These plots work hard, with very persuasive results, to depict their heroines as earning and deserving privileged social status through their private personal characters rather than their contributions in the public work force. So it is understandable that Mukherjee has appropriated them for her own purposes.

However, *Jasmine* illustrates some significant ideological problems with both the English novel of education and the American Horatio Alger myth. Nowadays, the English genre is seen as both elitist and colonialist, biases that Mukherjee does not adequately address or overcome in her American adaptation. Moreover, Mukherjee's jump to the romance plot allows her to evade the central problem that characterizes American success myths: they deny the obstacles faced by real-life workers, both illegal immigrants and many Americans, in achieving even basic levels of personal security and comfort. By retreating to the romance plot, Mukherjee tacitly demonstrates that she knows she is evading this problem, and she seems unwilling to acknowledge it directly in her novel. Instead, the protagonist's story affirms the United States as a country in which middle-class life is both desirable and available to newcomers. To its credit, *Jasmine* provides plenty of information that contradicts the myth of America as an open society. Ultimately, however, Mukherjee is reluctant to distance herself from the British and American success myths, and her novel suffers from that refusal. Unlike some critics, however, I don't consider this lapse a sign of Mukherjee's failure or bad faith. Rather, the glaring contradictions that result from her conflicted purposes productively illustrate the working of ideology within the American success myth. The novel registers, often aggressively, the author's perceptions of lives that contradict the myth. It subordinates those stories to a success story that supports it, illustrating the author's overt ideological intent. Yet in the end it undercuts this very intent. By providing a recognizable, yet clearly untenable version of an American romance plot, *Jasmine* teaches readers to recognize and view with suspicion the ideological work that such myths do.

Let me begin by clarifying my usage of the term *romance plot,* which refers not to American or English Romanticism but to the marriage-centered plot conventions of the English domestic novel or novel of education. Briefly and somewhat simplistically, I'm thinking of a tradition of eighteenth- and nineteenth-century novels such as Jane Austen's *Pride and Prejudice,* Charlotte Brontë's *Jane Eyre,* and Charles Dickens's *David Copperfield.* In these works, the protagonist's moral and social development is represented in terms of his or her negotiations with various romantic possibilities. David Copperfield, for instance, learns to appreciate Agnes Wickfield's balanced personality only by recognizing the limits of his charming child bride, Dora. During the same period, he becomes a wiser judge of character, matures as a writer, and becomes more socially secure, but the primary vehicle for representing all this development is the narrative of his disillusionment with Dora and his growing love for Agnes. In *Jane Eyre,* the reality of Jane and Rochester's mutual regard is tested and proven when each declines to marry an eligible alternative: Blanche Ingram in Rochester's case and St. John Rivers in Jane's. For heroines, in particular, romantic success, figured as marriage to a worthy and loving mate of equal or higher social class, represents the resolution of all other issues: thus, Jane's union with her erstwhile master, Mr. Rochester, also resolves the issue of her vocation because she will devote herself to caring for him.

The specifically English versions of this Cinderella story are invoked in *Jasmine,* in which the heroine compares herself to Jane Eyre and also mentions *Great Expectations* and *Pygmalion,* texts that comment caustically on English romance plots and the protagonists' dreams of becoming a gentleman or a lady. The English tradition has clearly been part of Mukherjee's own elite postcolonial education, and it is of course intimately bound to the Anglo-Indian colonial history that conditions Jasmine's life and aspirations. The genre is also a significant, albeit distant, ancestor of the slick commercial genre that has been perfected by Harlequin and studied by Janice Radway as the genre of the "romance novel," which Grewal uses as a term of disparagement.[31]

In their emphasis on marriage as a vehicle for upward mobility, such plots provide a feminine contrast to American success myths, which teach that outsiders to American society can achieve success through sheer hard work and character. Such myths were strikingly invoked, for instance, in President Clinton's first presidential campaign (in which the multiterm governor of Arkansas, a graduate of Yale Law School and a Rhodes scholar, was figured as a marginalized underdog and outsider) with great success. One problem with uniting English and American success myths, however, is that they don't agree about whether courtship and marriage count as hard work. In the implicitly male, populist American myth of upward mobility, as well as most works of American naturalism, *work* means physical or economically gainful labor; this implicitly excludes courtship and marriage. In English novels, by contrast, romance really was work, either because it was the genteel heroines' primary vocation or because her marriage subsumed and represented all the other work she hoped to accomplish. In Elizabeth Gaskell's *North and South,* for instance, the heroine's romantic relationship with a mill owner is intertwined with her efforts to improve the lives of his workers; both are resolved when she marries him and turns him into a model employer. Thus, *Jasmine* invokes—and harshly rewrites—a tradition that codes courtship and marriage as legitimate "work" for a fictional heroine, potentially offending readers who consider marriage plots obsolete and readers who are offended by Jasmine's pragmatic use of her sexuality, her calculated rewriting of romantic plots.

Second, *Jasmine* suffers from its acceptance of the English genre's elitism. To illustrate this, I'll describe an archetypical English heroine's career, then suggest briefly how this translates into the American context. In constructing this composite, simplified account, I am thinking of Richardson's Pamela Andrews, Austen's Elizabeth Bennett, and Brontë's Jane Eyre, three early and influential heroines, and I am passing over the many domestic novels that complicate, criticize, or satirize this archetype. In my mininovel, the heroine is a gentleman's daughter who is economically impoverished but whose innate virtue, refinement, intelligence, articulateness, and independent spirit mark her as both a lady and a worthy heroine, a character we can like and take seriously. After a series of mishaps, her intrinsic but undervalued merits are recognized by a worthy and well-positioned suitor. Eventually, he offers her a socially advantageous match, which proves what we have always known, that despite outward reverses she is inwardly a lady, a person whose moral and mental refinement is intrinsic and unchangeable. My novel ends when she accepts the offer. My heroine is upwardly mobile, and her unstated objective is to affirm her gentility. Romance and marriage provide the plot vehicles for her moral testing and maturation. Finally, she is rewarded with privileged class status for having a sensibility that in these novels she could only have if she already belonged to a privileged class. Elizabeth Bennett, for instance, has a superior grasp of fine moral and social distinctions, but her experience of the world is limited; much of her knowledge has been derived from reading novels, a sign of literacy and leisure.

In short, these elaborate Cinderella stories imply that through marriage upward mobility is available to any woman of intrinsic merit—any "true lady." But that merit is defined in psychological and genealogical terms that require that she already be a lady. Indeed, gentle birth—roughly speaking, middle-class birth—is usually a prerequisite for becoming an English novel heroine. When the novels are successful, however, this exclusivity is obscured by the fact that the heroine's social status is supposedly both secondary to her essence and inseparable from it. For Pamela Andrews, Elizabeth Bennett, and Jane Eyre, the outward achievement of gentility emanates from their essence.

American versions of this myth do not require gentle birth and education so explicitly, but I believe they function similarly to obscure the mechanisms by which privilege is made accessible primarily to those who already have it while promoting a rhetoric of egalitarianism. Mukherjee, in conceiving of her heroine as a Punjabi-American Jane Eyre, illustrates perfectly the veiled elitism inherent in the original novels of education as well as the American ideology of an open society.

The third relevant element of these novels I will simply call colonialism. Here I am thinking of the many ways that the historical force of British colonialism both pervades the Victorian imagination and is marginalized by it. The British colonies are ever-present at the peripheries of these texts: they supply places to send convicts and other English outcasts, such as Dickens' Mr. Micawber and L'il Em'ly; they supply wealth without visible labor, as in the case of Jane Eyre's beloved Mr. Rochester, who has gained his wealth through a profitable marriage in the West Indies; and they supply an exotic and inhuman other, like Mr. Rochester's insane West Indian wife, Bertha Rochester. The first Mrs. Rochester is portrayed as having a body, passions, and economic value but lacking a mind or soul; hence, neither her death nor the loss of her wealth are mourned by Jane and Rochester. She is one of innumerable dark-skinned fictional characters who more or less embody the colonies in British and American literature. Inevitably, the cultural meanings of liaisons between white men and dark women cannot be isolated either from the history of European and American imperialism, nor from the accumulated force of cultural representations of such women as exotic curiosities. *Jasmine* confronts this cultural legacy with mixed results.

Mukherjee's novel is a self-conscious revision of Charlotte Brontë's *Jane Eyre*, which in its time was both successful and controversial. For the sake of brevity, I will not describe all the plot parallels but merely suggest that some of the elements that have most irritated Mukherjee's critics are clearly to be blamed on her apparent inability to draw upon the genre, even in the fragmented, ironized mode she adopts, without also accepting some of its controlling assumptions. For instance, Debjani Banerjee has criticized *Jasmine*'s cursory, unsympathetic treatment of Sikh nationalism and terrorism in the Punjabi heroine's homeland. In this decision, Mukherjee follows the bildungsroman's tendency to portray political issues as peripheral to individual ones and to view third-world politics from a first-world point of view, with problematic results.

Most importantly, the book's heroine, Jasmine, is a grammar school dropout from a Punjabi village who enters the United States illegally with no job experience or skills. Privileges and opportunities are repeatedly granted to her because, like a Victorian heroine, she's perceived as innately special. A Florida woman who hides and helps illegal immigrants, for instance, says to Jasmine a few weeks after her arrival: "Jazzy, you don't strike me as a picker or a domestic. . . . You're different from those others. . . . You're a very special case, my dear" (120). The implied dismissal of "those others," which is echoed elsewhere in the text, is both disturbing and characteristic of novels of formation. In short, difficulties arise because Jasmine has been constructed as a tough, modern, third-world version of an English novel heroine. But because the genre by definition marginalizes the working classes to which Jasmine supposedly belongs in the United States, the protagonist becomes a marriage of opposites.

As the novel's narrator, Jasmine herself points out this contradiction when she introduces Taylor Hayes, the liberal Columbia professor with whom she falls in love and ultimately elopes: "The love I felt for Taylor that first day had nothing to do with sex. I fell in love with his world, its ease, its careless confidence and graceful self-absorption. I wanted to become the person they thought they saw: humorous, intelligent, refined, affectionate. Not illegal, not murderer, not widowed, destitute, fearful" (151–52). The novel strongly implies that Jasmine is all of the latter things (illegal, murderer, widowed, destitute, fearful) but that she is able to become all of the former (humorous, intelligent, refined, affectionate—in short, a middle-class intellectual) because of her own will to survive and improve. As Gurleen Grewal has noted, this transition can only be represented fictionally by authorial sleight-of-hand. Instead of sticking to the consciousness that a person of Jasmine's history really would have, Mukherjee provides Jasmine with a worldly, forceful, ironic temperament more typical of an educated, privileged person like the author herself.

I concur that Mukherjee's portrayal of Jasmine is inconsistent, sometimes offensively so. However, I see these contradictions as symptomatic not so much of Mukherjee's limits as of the entrenched contradictions of the success myths she is invoking. By giving us a nominally conventional story of a Punjabi immigrant making good in America, but riddling it with implausibilities and contradictions in character, the text forces the skeptical reader to recognize that this Cinderella story could never really happen. It's a cultural myth, and Mukherjee knows it. True, my reading may be contrary to Mukherjee's stated intention, which is to celebrate that myth. But she deliberately figures Jasmine's rise in this novel as exceptional, not typical. The immigrants who don't make it into middle-class comfort and culture are minor characters, but they are also far more numerous in the novel. Moreover, the America this novel depicts is hardly Edenic; in Florida, Flushing, and Iowa, it is hostile to and suspicious of immigrants and refugees and cruelly disappointing for many of its natives. The susceptibility of American men to Jasmine's supposed charms not only connotes their predisposition to stereotype her; it is a measure of their deep disappointment in their lives and their longing for a richer existence. Mukherjee's critics think that the obvious impossibility of Jasmine's story is a mistake; I suggest that it is the novel's saving grace.

This implausibility, and the discomfort we may feel as readers, are compounded by Jasmine's tendency to climb the social ladder by sexually attracting most of the men she meets. Granted, advancement via romance is inseparable from the English novel of education; still, the early readers of those novels would have been thoroughly affronted by this novel's plot, in which *four* men fall in love with the heroine on first sight. In addition, Jasmine's advancement depends on her willingness to accept the advances of two men who are specifically attracted to her as an oriental woman, the Columbia professor and Bud Ripplemeyer, a successful Iowa banker. Both men wish to possess her—as pupil, protégé, mistress, and finally wife—in a well-intentioned but clearly paternalistic way that is strongly reminiscent of an orientalist mentality. I do not, of course, wish to imply that all cross-racial couples should be viewed reductively as metaphors for European or American colonialism. But Mukherjee explicitly demonstrates that for these two characters Jasmine signifies experience of the third world in a form that enhances rather than challenges their superior status as white men. She deliberately presents herself as an impressionable, dependent, and deferential young woman, and she tacitly agrees to conceal the things that would expose their innocence and naïveté as middle-class Americans—such as the fact that she has been raped and has murdered her rapist. The irony is that this orientalized femininity also wins her the love of Taylor, the person whom she thinks sees her as humorous, intelligent, and refined.

Indeed, Jasmine tells us that it is precisely the men's innocence that attracts her, that she wishes to support, protect, marry, and assume as an American. Thus, when a ruined debtor shoots and maims Bud, the banker loses the possibility of making Jasmine love him, not merely because his health is ruined but because he has lost this innocence. He has entered the world of random violence, sacrifice, and hopelessness that Jasmine knew at home and seeks to escape and forget in America.

Brontë's Jane Eyre loves Rochester for his inner spirit, an essence that survives his social and physical ruin; her compelling portrayal of this spiritual kinship and her Romantic view of the self as constant and ineffable make it convincing and inevitable that Jane will love Rochester even after he has lost everything. By the end of that novel, social roles and class distinctions are mere shells to be cast off; that's one reason why it was deemed so scandalous. By contrast, Jasmine's attachments to Bud and Taylor are based on mutual perceptions of exoticism and alienness and on her view of identity itself as a social construction, not an essence. Thus, when Bud ceases to be the "pillar of Baden" in the eyes of other Iowans, he is no longer the same man to Jasmine. Similarly, the love Jasmine feels for Taylor has little to do with his essence, for in a sense he has none. Rather, she defines him entirely through the social milieu he represents and loves him for offering her a means of entering that world: "I fell in love with his world, its ease, its careless confidence and graceful self-absorption," that is, its insularity. It's understandable that Jasmine prefers to enter this haven, to cast off the responsibility of her past and her knowledge of the world as savage and fallen, both in Asia and in the United States. It's understandable, too, that many readers are offended by her flight to innocence as well as Mukherjee's willingness to define the male characters in terms of their social status and to celebrate Jasmine's defining trait, her willingness and alleged ability to remake herself in response to each new situation. But are Jasmine and her novel really so naive? Doesn't the novel really say that the United States is just as dangerous, its educated and supposedly freer citizens just as irrational, fearful, and adrift as the people in the Punjab? Doesn't Mukherjee invite us to see Jasmine herself as a scarred and damaged survivor, incapable of the naive and hopeful first love she offered her husband Prakash (or the deeply knit spiritual kinship Brontë claimed for her hero and heroine) and deeply saddened by the compromises she makes (as indicated by the pointedly joyless depiction of her sex life with Bud)? If this novel problematically misrepresents certain realities—and I grant that it does—it also raises some usefully obstinate questions about the immigrant success myth it seems at first to celebrate.

Both Eaton and Mukherjee grapple with a double problem: the problem of inscribing the subjectivities of Asian immigrant women into national literatures (English and American) that conventionally position Asians as racial outsiders; and the problem of combating masculine conventions for representing Asian women. In particular, we see them rewriting existing scripts privileging the formation of the Asian American subjectivity in masculinized terms. For Eaton, the Chinese American woman must emerge from behind the barriers posed by white nineteenth-century prejudices against the Chinese, her own position outside the community, and the wavering image of what she could and could not learn about Chinese Americans—not to speak of what she could and could not write about them. Ultimately, Eaton takes a male-centered paradigm of assimilation —the desiring male immigrant, the idealized white woman, and the unassimilable Asian woman—and rewrites it so that the Chinese American woman's voice is stronger, her vision clearer. She claims subjectivity for Chinese American women both by inscribing them as desiring subjects in her stories and by rendering herself—an apparently white subject—as one who is also Chinese American.

For Mukherjee, the problem of reading a subaltern female subject as an Asian American subject also involves a bridging of impassible class boundaries through the medium of domestic fiction. Though her Asian Americanized, double-voiced rescription of English stories of social mobility in *Jasmine* permits the novel to be read as both celebrating and fundamentally questioning the myth of American upward mobility, in the end she shares with Eaton the difficulty of imaginatively extending subjectivity to those beyond the norms usually privileged in the bildungsroman genre. It is this problem of breaking the boundaries while retaining the upward trajectory of the English model that leads to the gaps of which Mukherjee's critics complain.[32]

I have focused on Eaton and Mukherjee partly because both writers seem to combine an awareness of the class and race presumptions of the specifically English literary tradition with attunement to issues of race and class in North America and its literature. Though other Asian American women writers may be less British in their education, most know the English tradition as part of the Anglo-American one. To the extent that Eaton, as a Victorian woman writer, and Mukherjee, as a writer with a postcolonial education, are influenced by the Anglo-American bildungsroman's construction of the domestic woman as a model for establishing Asian American subjectivity, it is difficult for them to escape or subvert the genre's privileging of white, middle-class, female subjectivities entirely: we see them changing variables without transforming the equation as a whole. If we take Eaton and Mukherjee to stand for a body of Asian American texts that counter white and Asian literary objectification of women by claiming a form of subjectivity found in the feminized values of the domestic bildungsroman, we might well ask whether this strategy, with the dividends and liabilities I have described, is the only one Asian American women writers have found. For an answer, I now examine the efforts of three prominent Chinese American writers (Amy Tan, Maxine Hong Kingston, and Frank Chin) to construct the Chinese American subject by placing Chinese American "experiences" in dialogue with narratives of Chinese experience and literary narratives of Chinese heroism.

TWO

Constructing Chinese American Ethnicity

4

"That Was China, That Was Their Fate": Ethnicity and Agency in The Joy Luck Club

"In Your Bones": The Mother-Daughter Romance

My discussions of Eaton and Mukherjee have emphasized the cultural work they do in attempting to find a way to portray Asian women that addresses various ideological agendas. The prime agenda is to interpellate the Asian woman immigrant as a subject whose interior life is not only accessible and sympathetic to American readers but whose story in some way redefines Americanness. By using the codes of sentimental and domestic fiction, both authors seek to complicate their readers' ideas of American subjectivity by presenting Asian women immigrants as already possessing, or readily understanding, deeply American ideals of love, self-determination, and individual happiness; such narratives seek, ultimately, to establish the newcomers not only as less alien but as quintessential American subjects. Amy Tan's best-selling first novel *The Joy Luck Club* (1989) contributes to this project by introducing life-defining episodes from the lives of four Chinese immigrant mothers and their American-born daughters. Although Tan's novel is one of numerous matrilineal Asian American texts published in the last ten years, its extraordinary popular success suggests that Tan has been particularly successful in positioning herself and her work in relation to readers who are not Asian American.[1] Indeed, students of various ethnicities in my contemporary American literature courses have described the book's portrayals of mother-daughter relations as universal stories with which they themselves identify.

Whereas Eaton used the short story form and Mukherjee a highly compressed, episodic format to convey insights into the multiple experiences of various immigrant characters, Tan's innovation is the use of the four-player mahjong club to structure the development of four mother-daughter pairs. One critic has suggested that the introduction of multiple narratives about two generations of Chinese American women is inherently challenging to stereotypical readings that treat Chinese women as fungible because they share a defining Chinese "essence," and Melanie McAlister argues, along the same lines, that the novel's complex representation of Chinese American subjectivities requires careful attention to the full range of temperaments, class variations, and differences in personal history, particularly among the four mothers.[2]

In *The Joy Luck Club,* Tan's contribution to the problem of narrating Asian American subject formation lies in her elaboration of an established form, the mother-daughter plot, in which the immigrant mother's desire for America becomes focused on her American-born daughter. In this plot, the American offspring fulfills multiple functions that I have previously linked with white romantic partners in narratives about immigrants for whom marriage and child rearing are seen as remote and unlikely. For instance, Tan's daughters both personify America and mediate their mothers' assimilation into American society. Though the mothers' desire for their daughters' love and understanding is not sexualized, it tends to displace the mothers' heterosexual relationships in importance and to be charged with the burden of compensating for multiple losses, including romantic disappointments and a range of losses attributable to emigration, war, and natural disaster.[3] Because of the intensity attributed to mother-daughter relations in such stories and the structural similarities these dyads bear to romantic partnerships in earlier assimilation narratives, I consider such mother-daughter plots another form of the narrative I've described as the immigrant romance. From the daughters' perspectives, the functions of the immigrant mother are similarly complex. Tan's novel is typical, but usefully explicit, in spelling out these functions in *Joy Luck.* The mothers both personify China and Chineseness in their daughters' minds and mediate as the daughters seek to construct narratives of Chinese female subjectivity that will be enabling to them in their task of Chinese American self-formation.

At the same time, *Joy Luck* challenges this sense of intergenerational differences by suggesting that the mothers and daughters are united by blood and gender. The "in your bones" trope of kinship as an organic, ineffable link is reinforced by the allusions to the common issues the book attributes to the characters' gender socialization. The majority of the stories deal with the protagonists' feelings of helplessness in the face of oppressive domestic relationships; this internalized helplessness is then addressed primarily as a psychological hurdle that must be overcome through individual efforts of will.

By looking at the ways Tan first constructs her generational dialogues as intercultural ones and then seeks to envision rapprochement between the two poles for each mother-daughter dyad, we see that ultimately the imagined similarity turns on the problem of women's agency and that the portrayal of women's agency as essentially the *same* in both the United States and China rests in this novel on a kind of historical amnesia about twentieth-century Chinese political and social history. Such amnesia, I suggest, is neither unique to Tan nor a sign of individual deficiency on her part, but it is suggestive of the ways in which American culture selectively takes in and constructs Chinese culture. Because I read the novel's ending as gesturing beyond intercultural understanding within America toward a horizon of international cooperation between China and the United States, the terms on which the novel suggests such an understanding might be built are suggestive of larger cultural assumptions governing perceptions of Asians and Asian Americans.

Let's begin, then, by speaking briefly about the relationship between the "mother-daughter romance," as I shall call it, and the utopian myth of the immigrant's Americanization that underlies it, noting that Tan's version shares with the generic myth certain values central to American thinking: the belief in America as a land of opportunity, the bonds between parents and children, and the power of the individual to control his or her own future through acts of will (agency).[4] In the immigration myth, immigrants abandon an old world, which, like the home of a mythic hero, has become incomplete, disordered, or intolerable, to brave the journey to America, which is figured as a promised land of greater economic and social opportunity as well as greater freedom and justice.[5] Although the immigrant may encounter substantial difficulties in America, he or she typically overcomes these difficulties by remaining true to the initial dream of American society's fairness and openness, working hard, and looking forward to the greater success and assimilation of his or her American-born children. This narrative typically emphasizes the power of the immigrant's agency and the ultimate attainability of the American dream and denies that obstacles such as racism or economic exploitation are systemic or insurmountable. This utopian view of American immigration is the foundation of Tan's text.[6]

Built directly upon this foundation is the mother-daughter narrative, which affirms the desire of each generation for the respect and understanding of the other, and the importance of maternal legacies of wisdom and character transmitted from mother to daughter. This plot, in which each mother guides her daughter to claim greater agency in her own life, tallies nicely with the immigration plot. Together, the two plots comply with a fictional condition deeply embedded in American popular culture, the premise that heroic individuals can triumph over all obstacles.

The novel opens with a short episode — a prelude to the first four stories — that epitomizes the whole book's skillful blending of the mother-daughter romance and the immigration myth. In the mother-daughter romance, mothers seek their daughters' understanding and offer in turn a legacy of gendered, ethnically marked identity and empowerment. On one level, the text insists that this legacy is transmitted instinctively and genetically — "through the bones," as one character will say — but the text as a whole makes *narrative* the prime medium for transmission of the maternal legacy. The primary function of the prelude, then, is to signal that the stories to follow will fulfill the crucial functions of cultural transmission and translation. This opening story also embodies three components of the maternal narratives that are shortly offered at greater length: first, a narrative in which girls and women are educated to accept social powerlessness as their due, first in long-ago China and then in contemporary America; second, a counternarrative of female empowerment through individual efforts of will; and third, a narrative of successful immigration and assimilation, processes that provide avenues of escape from the closed system of Chinese society. As we shall see, these elements all return us to the problem of conceptualizing Chinese women's agency.

In the story, an old woman remembers a swan she once bought in Shanghai, which, according to the vendor, had transcended its original identity as a duck by stretching its neck in the hope of becoming a goose. Instead, it became something better: a swan "too beautiful to eat." As the woman carries the swan to America — both travelers stretching their necks in aspiration — she fantasizes:

> "In America I will have a daughter just like me. . . . Over there nobody will look down on her, because I will make her speak only perfect American English. And over there she will always be too full to swallow any sorrow! She will know my meaning, because I will give her this swan — a creature that became more than what was hoped for."
>
> But when she arrived in the new country, the immigration officials pulled the swan away from her, leaving the woman fluttering her arms and with only one swan feather for a memory. And then she had to fill out so many forms she forgot why she had come and what she had left behind.
>
> Now the woman was old. And she had a daughter who grew up speaking only English and swallowing more Coca-Cola than sorrow. For a long time now the woman had wanted to give her daughter the

single swan feather and tell her, "This feather may look worthless, but it comes from afar and carries with it all my good intentions." And she waited year after year, for the day she could tell her daughter this in perfect American English. (unpaginated)

This Chinese American "ugly duckling" tale captures a number of ideas central both to this text and to other narratives of immigration: the old world as a place of limited possibility; the immigrant as the one duck who will not accept her appointed place in that society; America as the site of the immigrant's dream of transformation, the land of unbounded possibility; the blurring of the immigrant's vision and sense of self when confronted with the realities of an alien and inhospitable land; the transference of hope (the swan feather) to the immigrant's offspring; the dream of vicarious assimilation through those offspring, who will be both like and unlike their parents (fully comprehending the parent yet fully assimilated); and, finally, the fear of alienation from and rejection by the offspring. The daughter's affinity for Coca-Cola and unfamiliarity with sorrow serve as shorthand for issues to be elaborated in the novel: the danger that the material comfort, even luxury, symbolized by the drinking of bubbly, unnourishing Coca-Cola will also lead to malnourished character development, a callousness and lack of imagination bred by the very prosperity, and shelter from suffering, that the mother has risked so much to offer. The story ends with the immigrant mother poised between hope that her daughter may still be brought to understand the world of meaning symbolized by the swan's feather and fear that the moment for transmitting that legacy may never arise.

The opening chapter, which follows this passage, emphasizes this interweaving of the mother-daughter and assimilation plots. June Jing-mei Woo, whose mother, Suyuan, has just died, is invited by her mother's friends ("aunties") and her father to take her parent's place at the weekly meeting of the mahjong club her mother founded, the Joy Luck Club. Like bridge, mahjong is a four-handed "card" game (played with engraved tiles rather than cards). June knows she is to play her mother's hand at this meeting, but this turns out to be true on more levels than one. After the game, her father and "aunties" reveal that June's half-sisters, lost in China in their infancy, have at long last been located. Alas, it has happened too late for them to meet their mother, Suyuan. Thus, June is to go to China to greet them in her mother's place, break the news of her death, and bear witness to her life. When June doubts that she knows her mother well enough to perform this task, her aunties erupt in dismay:

"Not know your own mother?" cries Auntie An-mei with disbelief. "How can you say? Your mother is in your bones!"

"Tell them stories she told you, lessons she taught, what you know about her mind that has become your mind," says Auntie Ying. "your mother very smart lady. . . ."

"Her kindness."

"Her smartness."

"Her dutiful nature to family."

"Her hopes, things that matter to her."

"The excellent dishes she cooked."

And it occurs to me. They are frightened. In me, they see their own daughters, just as ignorant, just as unmindful of all the truths and hopes they have brought to America. They see daughters who grow impatient when their mothers talk in Chinese, who think they are stupid when they explain things in fractured English. . . . They see daughters who will bear grandchildren born without any connecting hope passed from generation to generation. (40–41)

Thus, June, a drifting copywriter who has not yet found her true subject, is officially assigned the task of remembering and representing her mother (both speaking for and portraying her). By implication, she is chosen to be the chronicler for her mother's generation. Clearly, June is Amy Tan's fictional surrogate, for she inherits not only the immigrant offspring's classic call to remembrance but the writer's call to authorship. Male writers, like James Joyce's Stephen Dedalus, are often portrayed as eagerly seizing the hammer and anvil of authorship ("to forge in the smithy of my soul the uncreated conscience of my race" [*Portrait of the Artist,* 276]); by contrast, women writers, especially ethnic women writers, often need the legitimation of outside authorization for their writing.[7] Here Amy Tan offers her alter ego, June, official family cover for taking up the perhaps unwomanly or unfilial task of writing for publication: it is a duty to her mother, family, and community. The link between June and the author is further suggested by this novel's dedication, which addresses the book to Tan's mother and grandmother and offers it as a kind of memory in response to remembered conversations. In short, the charge of *The Joy Luck Club* initiates a roundelay of interlaced first-person stories in which June, as the author's surrogate, imagines the voices and stories of the mothers and daughters. Only Suyuan, being dead, does not voice her own first-person narrative; instead, June takes her two turns in the narrative as well as the mahjong game.

The Two-Worlds Problem

Both the immigration and mother-daughter plots turn upon the tension between sameness and difference: the immigrant passes from an old world defined as a dystopia of exhausted possibilities and tragic narrative outcomes to the utopian new world, where opportunity and happy endings beckon. This scheme is evident in the immigrant attitudes summed up respectively by An-mei Hsu, an immigrant, and June Woo, speaking for her mother Suyuan:

> [An-mei:] My mother, she suffered. She lost her face and tried to hide it. She found only greater misery and finally could not hide that. There is nothing more to understand. That was China. That was what people did back then. They had no choice. They could not speak up. They could not run away. That was their fate. (241)

> [June:] My mother believed you could be anything you wanted to be in America. You could open a restaurant. You could work for the government and get good retirement. You could buy a house with almost no money down. You could become rich. You could become instantly famous. . . .
> America was where all my mother's hopes lay. She had come here in 1949 after losing everything in China: her mother and father, her family home, her first husband, and two daughters, twin baby girls. But she never looked back with regret. (132)

The thread that links these two disparate worlds is of course the story of the immigrant herself, whose consciousness mediates between the two cultures, and potentially unites them, as he or she moves from one place to the next. The coexistence of loss, transience, and change, on the one hand, and the will to establish continuity and progress, on the other, is the essence of the immigration plot; the image of the old woman's swan feather gains its resonance from this tension.

In the mother-daughter plot, the tension between sameness and difference resides in the mother-daughter dyad itself, as each party struggles to overcome perceptions of the other's differentness and to locate the qualities they have in common. Such a plot is ideally suited to examining how ethnicity is constructed as a source of intergenerational difference as well as commonality ("Your mother is in your bones!" [40]). The text constructs its implied reader as occupying the American pole of Chinese-American binarism, so that we readers share the American daughters' search for the essences of their respective Chinese mothers. That search brilliantly folds together the two plots defining both ethnicity and femininity while providing a basis for assessing Tan's success in negotiating with existing preconceptions about Chinese womanhood. In this regard, the text expresses two opposed impulses: the impulse to expose and distance itself from American stereotypes of Chinese as un-American, nonrational, or backward and the tendency to reinforce these stereotypes by accentuating the alienness of Chinese thinking and character.

When the novel invokes the old world/new world opposition we saw in the quotations just discussed, its positioning of China as an inferior term that helps to define American modernity and progressiveness is reminiscent of the East/West split that raised such sharp critical questions in Bharati Mukherjee's *Jasmine*. As we have seen, critics attuned to the complexity of South Asian social and political history were affronted by that novel's tendency to portray India primarily as the negative term in a first world/ third world comparison that ultimately celebrates the United States as the more modern, civilized society where women are more assertive and better treated, and even terrorists' motives can be cogently explained (as justified economic frustration, in the American gunman's case, and as opposed to knee-jerk religious fanaticism in the Sikh nationalists' case). In scrutinizing Tan's negotiation of the problem of first-world bias in her representations of pre-Communist China, let us draw upon Johannes Fabian's concept of "allochronism," or temporal distancing, in anthropological writing.[8] According to Rey Chow's succinct summary of this concept, anthropologists tend to position themselves and their subjects as "coeval," inhabiting the same temporal world, while in the field, with the implication that the writers and their subjects are equally modern and equal in other ways as well. When the scholars depart and write up their notes, however, this sense of "shared time is replaced by a more linear, progressive use of time that enables the distinctions between 'primitive' and 'developed' cultures" in which the subjects of study, placed in a static, "primitive" time, are thereby distanced from the progressive, linear temporality of the writers. In Chinese area studies, Chow argues, this "casting of the other in another time" has contributed to a reverence for classical China and an attitude of "realpolitik contempt" toward modern China, with a corresponding lack of interest in the full psychological complexity of modern Chinese as postcolonial, diasporic subjects.[9] I want to suggest that what Chow describes as Western disinterest in the complex subjectivities of modern Chinese people—that is, resistance to modernity in the Chinese—resembles the historical American resistance to the ideas of Americanness and assimilability in Asian Americans because both are rooted in a conceptualization of Asia as "other." This othering, and the tendency to fall back on familiar, static stereotypes (such as those of classical China or the inscrutable Chinese), may take place partly because it is easier to conceptualize a subject one is writing about as static, rather than dynamic, and of course it is easier to draw upon existing concepts than to create new ones.

The Joy Luck Club is in many ways an effort to disturb and challenge orientalist conventions for representing Chinese women, yet Tan's decision to emphasize retrospective maternal narratives of pre-Communist China, addressed to daughters who stand in for a late 1980s American readership, necessarily raises the specter of allochronism, and the risk of representing the Chinese mothers as belonging to a fundamentally different, and other, narrative universe from their daughters.

It's in the daughter's stories, set in contemporary America, that Tan is most overtly concerned with debunking orientalist stereotypes about Chinese women, and as a result her portrayal of the mothers' nature is divided. In these scenes, we find the American-born daughters struggling with the tendency to view their mothers in ways that combine immaturity (in the form of uncertainty about their own independence) with orientalism. That is, they see their mothers as powerful, controlling beings whose psychology is unfathomable both because as daughters they still retain an exaggerated image of their mothers' powers from childhood and adolescence and because, rightly or wrongly, the daughters chalk up seemingly unfathomable differences to the fact that their mothers are Chinese. The novel is winning and persuasive when it suggests that images of the mothers as superhuman others are largely projections of the daughters' own fears and fantasies, as in the story where Waverly Jong learns to see her mother, not as a malignant adversary scheming to break up Waverly's new romance but simply as an old woman waiting for her daughter's acceptance (184). In addition to these moments, which humanize the mothers by highlighting their vulnerability, Tan undercuts Western stereotypes in the mothers' narratives. For instance, Lindo and An-mei identify fortune cookie epigrams as "American" nonsense (262), and Ying-ying St. Clair (the daughter of a wealthy family) explains that she was unimpressed by the trinkets offered by her American suitor as gifts but pretended to make a fuss over them so as not to disrupt his illusions of cultural superiority (250).

However, the text also provides scenes that serve to validate orientalist stereotypes of Chinese alterity by portraying the mothers as guardians of ancient Chinese wisdom or powers—powers their life stories cannot adequately explain. This sort of problem occurs, for instance, when Ying-ying St. Clair, on a visit to her unhappily married daughter, Lena, proposes to help by drawing upon her own "tiger spirit"—a manifestation of her and Lena's Chinese birth sign—to release Lena's (252). Given that the four stories devoted to Ying-ying and Lena have portrayed Ying-ying as a psychically fragile person (permanently traumatized by an abusive first husband, an abortion, a well-intentioned but uncomprehending American husband, and a miscarriage), that she has always been rather remote from Lena, and that she has been passive in her two marriages, the text's insistence on her underlying "tiger spirit" feels like an attempt to substitute a romantic, generic ideal of Chinese folk wisdom for a conclusion more consistent with her previous, individualized psychological profile. By awkwardly forcing this romanticized element into an ostensibly realistic chapter about Lena's failing romantic relationship, the text ends up implying that the mother is culturally and psychically alien — of a different universe — after all. At such moments, the text ceases to critique the orientalism of particular characters and becomes orientalist itself.[10]

Lindo's Agency

This text, then, continues the Asian American exploration of the problem of defining Asian American difference within a broader claim of commonality with other Americans. On what terms, the text seems to ask, can we recognize these mothers as American in their core values yet still retaining values that are Chinese? Most importantly, which values, common to subjects in both cultures, transcend the "East is not West" fallacy?

Tan's answer to this problem draws upon feminist thinking to invoke the struggle for personal agency — control of the decisions that define one's life — as common to girls and young women in both China and America. In the end, I think Tan's difficulty is that she bases her understanding of female agency on her experiences as a middle-class American in a post-feminist era without being fully aware of how privileged this position is. In the stories of two yuppie daughters (Lena and Rose), the key to regaining self-respect, claiming better treatment from males, and beginning a new life is simple self-assertiveness. Thus, Rose Hsu Jordan, whose passive dependence on her husband has extinguished his interest in her, learns that she can force him to make a generous divorce settlement, and even scare him, merely by deciding to become self-assertive again. "The power of my words was that strong," she concludes (196). Rose's passivity, explained as both an individual psychic deficiency and a symptom of feminine conditioning, vanishes so quickly that one wonders why she didn't clear it up sooner. Although somewhat simplistic, such solutions are appropriate for these characters because, for women of their class and era, other elements necessary for their "liberation" from debilitating marriages are available to them: education, the possibility of supporting themselves, family support, legal rights, and a well-established public ideology of women's equality. The novel doesn't really need to acknowledge this environment as the product of the American women's movement because this social context is familiar to American readers. On the other hand, because the novel lacks historical self-consciousness about the enabling conditions for female self-assertion in America, it naively universalizes its lessons about self-empowerment, disregarding the more serious obstacles to autonomy faced by Chinese women, as we shall see by exmaining the circumstances for self-empowerment described in Lindo Jong's story, "The Red Candle." Whereas a sense of self-worth may be a necessary condition for women's survival or liberation in China, it isn't a sufficient guarantee of either unless other conditions also prevail. Thus, the novel's understanding of female agency, and its efforts to compare Chinese and American female oppression, are dependent on simplistic analogies between two groups of women whose differing social conditions aren't fully clarified by the book's optimistic treatment.

Before assessing what is marginalized by Tan's narrative method, it's only fair to acknowledge what is achieved: clear plots in which heroic young women, undergoing trials by ordeal, arrive at epiphanies of character that carry them through their ordeals and, implicitly or explicitly, to America. Lindo Jong's story, "The Red Candle," is the most compact and winsome version of this type of story. It goes like this: she is betrothed at age two to marry into a rich family, the Huangs. When she is twelve, her peasant family is ruined by river floods. They have to move far away but leave her to be brought up by the Huangs. Before leaving, her mother insists that Lindo uphold the family honor by devoting her life to fulfilling the family's marriage contract. Lindo's natal family then disappears completely from her life. Although the Huangs treat her more like a servant than a family member, Lindo remains and does her best to please them, both because of her mother's wishes and because there is no alternative. After her marriage at sixteen, she's relieved to find that her husband, who's slightly younger, avoids touching her. This means she can sleep in peace but can't produce the required male heir despite the threats and confinement imposed by Huang Taitai, her mother-in-law. Having recognized that a servant girl whom she likes is concealing an illegitimate pregnancy, Lindo uses bogus supernatural tokens to persuade Huang Taitai that the family will be cursed by her continued presence and blessed if they trade her in for the servant, whose pregnancy the Huangs have not yet noticed. The Huangs accordingly bribe Lindo to accept a quiet divorce and leave town; they marry their son to the pregnant servant and thereby (it's implied) get their heir (so to speak). Lindo escapes with honor and a nest egg, to Beijing and thence to America, rescues the servant from ruin, and saves the Huangs from patrilineal extinction in the process.

    The features of Lindo's story that recur, with variations, in those of her friends are these: a young girl or young woman is forced to face extreme adversity or injustice, either alone or with the support of a powerless mother. Aside from her mother, the heroine has no friends or allies either within or beyond the family circle. The heroine's initial condition of hopeless victimization is represented as emblematic of the condition of all women in

China, which is basically seen as a static feudal society. Each heroine, however, discovers within herself a reservoir of self-esteem, resourcefulness, and
dissatisfaction with her prescribed low status, and each finds a way to escape
her entrapment and come to America.

These positive qualities, which appear in each mother's story at some
point, are most clearly defined in the case of Lindo. The text portrays her
in-laws, both son and mother, as a self-absorbed pair who see her as a combination of servant, breeding stock, and chattel (indeed, many traditional
Chinese proverbs compare the taking of a wife to the purchase of livestock).
But Lindo survives and ultimately escapes the marriage because of outstanding personal qualities, which are depicted as intrinsic to her and are, in
terms of the social milieu depicted, inexplicable. These qualities, the greatest of which is courage, define Lindo; they are also, I would argue, definitive
within this text of the immigrant sensibility—that which marks the Chinese mothers as unfit for their old world milieu and destined to become
Americans. In the Chinese scenes, almost everyone else accepts the status
quo and criticizes those who don't. Only the young protagonists have a version of "Hamlet's dis-ease": they recognize that the world is out of joint.
But whereas Hamlet, as a prince, feels "born to set it right," these young
women are placed in a fictional Chinese world where both individual justice
and systemic social change seem impossible. They cannot set things right;
they can only seek survival, then freedom, for themselves. Therefore, they
must come to America.

The sign of this Americanizing discontent is usually a scene in which
the young woman rallies her spirits and determines to take charge of her
future. In Lindo's story, the possibility of controlling her own fate comes to
her as an epiphany of psychological autonomy, which takes place, appropriately enough, before a mirror. In Lindo's life, the Fen River represents
the inevitability of fate; it's a Fen River flood that ruins her peasant family,
forcing them to leave town and abandon her to the Huangs' tender mercies.
Four years later, as she considers casting herself into the river to avoid her
wedding—a gesture combining defiance with defeat—she's distracted and
heartened by the power of the wind, which exerts terrific force on both the
river and the humans in her view. Her formative scene of self-recognition
follows: "I wiped my eyes and looked in the mirror. I was surprised at what
I saw. I had on a beautiful red dress, but what I saw was even more valuable.
I was strong. I was pure. I had genuine thoughts inside that no one could
see, that no one could ever take away from me. I was like the wind" (58).
Here Lindo grants herself the subjectivity no one else has offered her. In the
story, she has been conditioned all her life to deny her desires, imagination,
and will, a schooling the novel identifies with Chinese female experience.
Now she alone recognizes and values her own interiority, the intelligence

that both parents and in-laws have systematically sought to stifle lest it foster discontent and rebellion. Strikingly, intelligence is linked by Lindo with
a new perception of her sexuality as something strong and good that she
herself commands. Because Lindo's intelligence and the mental freedom it
adds to her life are unrecognized by those around her, it is an invaluable
weapon in her struggle for survival and freedom. This invisible source of
strength, as well as the real freedom she seeks, is henceforth linked with the
wind, which has the power to manipulate the river of fate and the power to
carry her to America.

Similar scenes of courage and decisiveness, definitive immigrant traits,
appear in all the mothers' stories. Suyuan Woo, waiting out the Sino-Japa-
nese War in Guilin, takes charge of her life by forming the original Joy
Luck Club, a mahjong club, to keep her hope alive at a time when the Chinese are being slaughtered by the Japanese. This carefully nourished hope
in turn enables her to flee to safety and to preserve the lives of her two infant daughters. Nine-year-old An-mei Hsu takes her future into her hands
when she accepts her mother's invitation to leave her uncle's house ("full of
dark riddles and suffering that I could not understand," like China in this
book) and follow her mother into an unknown life elsewhere (218). And
even Ying-ying, whose spirit has been broken by her abusive first husband in
China, holds the attention of Clifford St. Clair, her American suitor, for four
years until her first husband's death frees her to marry St. Clair, her ticket to
America. These moments of decision define the young women both as subjects capable of articulating themselves in narrative and as agents who seek
to control their lives and set them apart from the nonimmigrant Chinese
who appear in the book.

An-mei Hsu's stories, "Scar" and "Magpies," describe a similar reversal
of fortune in another traditional Confucian household. An-mei's mother,
the young widow of a scholar, has been tricked into accepting a position as
the fourth wife (actually, the third concubine) of a wealthy merchant named
Wu Tsing. When An-mei's mother was freshly widowed, she had met Wu
Tsing's second wife at a Buddhist shrine. Second Wife, who wanted to find
a docile concubine to keep her husband at home, invited the young widow
to spend the night as their guest, sent her husband to rape her, and spread
rumors that the guest had seduced the host. As a result, the young woman
was cast out by members of her family, who believed the rumors rather than
seeking and crediting the account of their daughter. (The family of An-mei's
father is not mentioned.) With nowhere else to go, An-mei's mother has
grimly accepted her new position in order to survive. By bringing An-mei
with her, she expresses love for her daughter—according to Tan—yet also
seems to guarantee that An-mei's prospects will be bleaker than her own.
(I wonder what mother would really have done this, for by bringing An-

mei from her family's household into Wu Tsing's, she transforms An-mei, for practical purposes, from the orphan of a scholar being raised by her kin into the daughter of a slave.) For, although An-mei's mother is young, well born, and attractive, her status—already at the bottom of society—is low even among Wu's concubines. She is too virtuous and refined to combat the manipulative tactics of Second Wife, who works constantly to ensure her own preeminence at everyone else's expense.

In the story's denouement, An-mei's mother commits suicide and dies two days before the first day of the lunar new year. Although the ghost of the departed traditionally returns to settle accounts on the third day after death, this return is particularly threatening, it seems, when it falls on the first day of the new year because of the Chinese understanding that on this day "all debts must be paid, or disaster and misfortune will follow" (240). In mortal terror of this supernatural threat, the prodigal husband Wu Tsing dons the Chinese equivalent of sackcloth and ashes, vows to honor his fourth wife as his first and only wife and the mother of his only son, and declares that he will treat An-mei as his own legal daughter. As a result, An-mei recalls this as the day she gained both a voice and the agency it symbolizes: "And on that day, I learned to shout" (240).

This story relies upon the same narrative trick used in "Red Candle" with deeply problematic results. Having stacked the odds against her victim, re-inforcing the impression of young women's total isolation in traditional Chinese society, the text fails to provide a plausible source of assistance or escape for her heroines. Therefore, a "happy" ending involving some resti-tution, however incomplete, can only be effected by the extreme means of threatening to invoke the wrath of supernatural forces. In An-mei's case, we are asked to believe that, after years of dominating Wu Tsing and his house-hold, Second Wife will give way permanently to the nine-year-old An-mei out of deference to her mother's ghost, although An-mei has never been taught to fight by her excessively self-effacing mother. An-mei's mother, who isn't even named in the story, has always accepted injustice with resig-nation and never fought directly for anything, even her mother's respect, before committing suicide. It's said that in Chinese society a young woman's suicide was often investigated, and publicly perceived, as a sign of family abuse, and so suicide was the ultimate form of protest available to young women (Wolf, *Women* 112). But An-mei's story doesn't broach this level of social reality. By insisting on the importance of the timing, it implies that the fear of ghosts alone—not the fear of public censure or the awakening of Wu's nonexistent conscience—will permanently set right the household, which for so long has been distorted by Wu's abuse and abrogation of his moral authority and Second Wife's exploitation of his flaws. Moreover, An-mei's idea of justice is (understandably, but severely) limited by her acceptance of the household's gendered power relations: she looks forward to putting Second Wife in her place but never considers Wu Tsing to have been the true author of her mother's tragedy. Nor does it occur to her to question the demeaning ranking and competition set up among the various wives and their children. Of course, she is in no position as a child to question the social order so fundamentally, but the story is, after all, recounted by the adult An-mei many decades later in an effort to incite her daughter Rose to stand up to her adulterous husband.

Later, when the adult An-mei recounts her mother's suicide as a triumphant endgame that protected the child An-mei's interests (240), she places her mother in a tragic world much like that of many European operas in which young women's greatest triumphs are as victims, their agency confined to dramatic acts of self-destruction. For An-mei, her mother's tragic world is remote, mythical, and quintessentially Chinese. An-mei, having lived forty years in America, has escaped this world but is a respectful witness to it. In a passage already quoted, she concludes that, although things are different in modern China, in the China of her youth her mother's story was typical: "My mother, she suffered. . . . That was China. That was what people did back then. They had no choice. They could not speak up. They could not run away. That was their fate" (241).

What Lindo Knows

The "just say yes" fable of self-determination, which can readily be recognized by American readers as simplistic but not entirely removed from reality for the middle-class American daughters, is more problematic in a story like Lindo's because Tan cannot assume an equivalent understanding of the Chinese social context in her American readership, nor does she provide quite enough context in this story or elsewhere in the novel. As a result, Tan's novel tends to give the impression that Lindo Jong, An-mei Hsu, and to a lesser extent Ying-ying St. Clair passed readily from a very traditional Confucian society into the American middle class with little mention of such mediating forces as the questioning of traditional family structures by Chinese reformers, feminist movements within China, the influence of Western education and ideas on Chinese elites, and the struggles of Chinese on many levels—including the level of domestic social structures—to modernize their country.[11] Such forces, which are reduced to the level of rumor in a story like "The Red Candle," would help prepare Chinese women and men of the educated classes for immigration to America and a relatively easy transition into the professional classes here, in contrast to others, who, coming to the United States without English or readily negotiable professional credentials, connections, or capital, would probably enter the ranks of the working poor.[12] In Tan's novel, the characterization of the fourth mother, Suyuan Woo, is most free of the problem of improbable discontinuities in class identity. Since she was trained as a nurse and married to two professional men (a Kuomintang officer and then a journalist, June's father) in China, it's easier to imagine Suyuan picking up English and sending her children to college. What is present in the American stories, but absent from most of the Chinese ones, is the middle term identified by Rey Chow, the Chinese woman as a modern subject, and what that subject represents, the vision of early-twentieth-century China as a country in which modern and traditional elements coexist, a country that, like the United States, is constantly changing.

One way in which Tan occludes this period is by making the Chinese mothers a generation older than they logistically need to be: because the American daughters are the children of *second* marriages, the mothers' childhood memories describe a China one generation earlier, and hence less touched by modernization, than the story's two-generation format requires.[13] Other issues raised by Lindo's story are the exaggerated contrast between her mind and those of the other characters in her story and the issue of social support for her rebellion.

Lindo, for instance, undergoes a highly conventional education yet independently develops values and intellectual resources that might reasonably be expected of a more educated, cosmopolitan person. From age two onward, she is told that she is going to be the property of the Huangs and that the family honor demands that she fulfill this marriage contract by sacrificing her body and will. She is subjected to a number of fortune-telling sessions, taught domestic skills, asked to believe that her worth depends on her usefulness to the Huangs, and lectured inexplicitly on her reproductive duties. What does Lindo teach herself? Despite her youth and isolation, she knows not only about sex but about sexual behavior, she knows her own worth and the worthlessness of the Huangs' words and she knows how to assess and manipulate evidence independently (such as the matchmaker's lying about the candles, her husband's disinclination to touch her, the signs of the servant girl's pregnancy, and the "signs" she invents to convince the Huangs to release her from the marriage). Moreover, she transcends her conventional moral education when she is kind and affectionate toward her bratty husband (despite their inimical positions in an exploitative family structure, she recognizes his humanity), and compassionate toward the hapless servant despite the girl's "promiscuity" and their difference in status. If we relied on this novel, Lindo's reliance on empirical observation rather than conventional class or moral prejudices would seem to set her apart from almost everyone else in China — or at least from everyone else in "The Red Candle." In addition, her practice of judging people by their conduct rather than their class status might be considered in the light of arguments that the very idea of an "inner self" distinguishable from one's outer social status is arguably a Western one. Lindo's empowering emphasis on her mental life — her "interiority" — is certainly not without Chinese literary precedent, but it also aligns her with Western fictional heroines whose mental purity transcends the limits or mortifications of their flesh.[14] Finally, she seems to be the one disbeliever in a community where everyone else takes the authority and supernatural power of dead ancestors literally. If the Chinese people around her are really so homogeneous in their thinking, how does Lindo, an isolated girl confined to these two households, arrive at a mind set so different, so seemingly Western?

When we next see young Lindo, she's in Beijing, copying English words and planning to enter the United States as a college student (of theology, no less). Arriving in America, she amuses herself with jokes about the signs in Chinatown, gets a job in a fortune cookie factory, and uses night school English classes to woo her future husband. Given the Huangs' feudal approach to female education, when did she learn to read Chinese and manage money? How did she learn of America, much less decide to come here? Once here, how does she jump from a cookie assembly line into the middle class? Glossed over are the obstacles to legal entry, and physical and social mobility, faced by most working-class immigrants. Instead, Lindo's lighthearted initiation into America seems more like that of an exchange student with a work-study job.

Such questions, however, beg a more fundamental one: how could Lindo have survived in China after she left the Huangs? Her own mother had preemptively refused to shelter her, and everyone in the village would have known she was the Huangs' daughter-in-law. Even had she found a way to reach the city, who would have sheltered, fed, or hired an unknown young woman from the provinces with no references? The absence of social support for runaway or castaway women is to become a central concern, and a central explanation for wife abuse, in Tan's next novel (*The Kitchen God's Wife*); in *Joy Luck* that absence implicitly explains the high tolerance for domestic abuse of Lindo, An-mei, and Ying-ying. It doesn't, however, explain how Lindo survived the sudden independence for which she had never been prepared.

In Lindo's case, Tan simply attributes an educated, arguably American, consciousness to her character. This serves the optimism of the immigration plot well, because it overstates the possibility of upward mobility in the United States. It serves the task of portraying actual immigrant' experiences less well, however, for it understates the working-class immigrant's struggle to survive (particularly when language barriers and race-based obstacles come into play) as well as the foreign student's loneliness, cultural isolation, and financial anxiety. Admittedly, the class disparity between the narrator's mind and her ostensible background is greatest in Lindo's narratives, and the resulting overstatement of the character's freedom and agency, while historically implausible, is part of the book's charm. Given the difficulty of Tan's cross-cultural project, it seems better that she has chosen to overstate rather than understate Lindo's intelligence and agency. It is merely regrettable that "The Red Candle" depends on portraying other Chinese characters as self-absorbed, maliciously exploitative, and unthinking in their adherence to the letter, but not the spirit, of their traditional religious beliefs.

By contrast, Tan's characterizations of An-mei and Ying-ying make more developmental sense but risk understating their intelligence and agency. Given the traditional upbringing each describes, it's plausible that these two internalize and unwittingly pass on the ethos of self-denial that this text characterizes as a female Chinese legacy. An-mei, for instance, approves of her mother's extreme acts of self-sacrifice (48, 240), and Ying-ying, even while criticizing and manipulating Clifford St. Clair's orientalist view of her as a helpless female in need of rescue, also colludes with that view by concealing her real past from him. In the United States, she permits him to mistranslate her name, birth date, personal history, and thoughts to fit his condescending view of her (104, 106, 109, 250–51), thereby driving her to mental illness and reducing her, in her daughter's eyes and her own words, to a ghost.

At the same time, since An-mei and Ying-ying come from more privileged families, it's disappointing that Tan seems to conceive them as both uneducated and indifferent to public events. Ying-ying, for instance, comes from a wealthy scholar's family, grew up not far from a major port (Wuxi, close to Shanghai), marries an Irish American, and lives in the United States for about forty years before ostensibly offering her life story to her daughter in "Waiting between the Trees." Yet, when she recalls the tumultuous era of her birth and infancy (1914–18), a period when the fall of the last Chinese dynasty was about to herald thirty years of continuous warfare, she describes 1914 as "the year a very bad spirit entered the world," a spirit that, according to her, "stayed in the world for four years" and caused people to starve and die (248). Ying-ying explains her survival, in similar terms, as an astrological accident: born in the Year of the Tiger, she happens to be endowed with the superior tiger spirit she's now passing on to Lena. I've already discussed the representational and psychological problems with this "just say grr" empowerment scene; I want now to question the speech's assumptions about Ying-ying's historical consciousness. What "very bad spirit" is Ying-ying recalling? If she's thinking only of local disasters, why say "the world" to her American daughter? It's true that in the West World

War I may have ended in 1918, but China's struggles to resist Japanese imperialism, which begin in 1914, became worse in 1919, when the Western powers' failure to honor Chinese interests in the Versailles peace treaty provoked student demonstrations and fueled the nationalist May Fourth Movement (Chow Tse-tung, *May Fourth*, 84–116). On the "world" level, China's troubles neither began in 1914 nor ended in 1919. It's true that Ying-ying would have been only an infant at the time. But she's supposed to be the child of a scholar as well as someone who cagily survived a traumatic wartime marriage and found a way to immigrate. Having introduced these details, which seem meant to give Ying-ying both psychological specificity and complexity — she is both a sometime victim and an adaptive survivor — the novel then trivializes them by having the character think and speak as a generic peddler of stereotypical folk wisdom. And, since this is an *internal* monologue presumably conducted in Chinese rather than English, why should it be represented in ersatz pidgin English?

A Chinese Account: Pa Chin's Family

The line between wishing for Chinese characters to be portrayed in a manner that presumes a modern consciousness — avoiding the temporal distancing of Chinese women as passive, accepting victims in a primitive, static culture — and asking that all Chinese be portrayed as having enlightened, arguably Westernized minds free of traditional beliefs construed by Westerners as "superstitions" — is admittedly a fine one. I have argued that several portions of Tan's novel are problematic. First, it portrays a majority of Chinese as unquestioning and rather literal in their acceptance of traditional social hierarchies and traditional beliefs in evil omens, ghosts, astological signs, and the like, which when presented as divorced from the fuller social context seem to function as markers of alterity, producing, as Sau ling Wong has remarked, a pleasing "Oriental effect" of congruence between the text and the reader's orientalist expectations ("Sisterhood," 187). In my reading, such moments, combined with gullibility and meanspiritedness (in "The Red Candle") or faux pidgin English and psychological and historical incoherence (in "Waiting between the Trees"), contribute to an underestimation of the heterogeneity and sophistication of Chinese minds. In addition, the Chinese narrators fail to convey a sense that their stories take place in a country where conventional wisdoms are questioned and discussed, not only by elites but eventually by people in all walks of life. Finally, these lapses contribute to distortions in the novel's conception of the necessary and sufficient conditions for young women to escape unhappy marriages and control their futures in China. To give the book its due, some chapters gracefully avoid these gaffes and work toward conveying a sense of the characters' modernity. I find the stories about Suyuan Woo, for instance, moving and persuasive.

To flesh out this discussion about agency and Chinese consciousness, a useful comparison might be made with a domestic novel by an influential Chinese writer born in 1904, a text that addresses one of Tan's central themes, young people attempting to rebel against the tyranny of their elders. *Family,* an autobiographical novel composed by the radical Chinese writer Pa Chin in 1931, is said to be his masterpiece.[15] According to Olga Lang's introduction, it was an immediate hit with Chinese readers, who responded to its attacks on the old Chinese family system, which "deprived the young of their freedom of action and their right to love and marry according to their own choice" (Introduction, viii). After the Communist revolution of 1949, Pa Chin's work was perceived as having helped "to create among the intellectuals an emotional climate which induced them to accept the Communist revolution," and so it continued to be read, for another seventeen years, until the Cultural Revolution (xxi–xxii). Set in a provincial capital city, Chengtu, in 1931, and incorporating the novelist's experiences during the 1920s, the novel depicts the struggles of three brothers (Chueh-hsin, Chueh-min, and Chueh-hui) to claim autonomy within a wealthy clan ruled by their elderly grandfather (or *Yeh-yeh*), the Venerable Master Kao. The brothers, their cousins, and their friends attend cosmopolitan schools, read Western literature, and are caught up with the new social ideas of the May Fourth Movement. Chueh-hui, the youngest son, often seems to speak for the author, an anarchist, in his youthful intolerance for hypocrisy and oppression. His character is established early in the novel in a typical diary entry:

> That book *Yeh-yeh* gave me—"On Filial Piety and the Shunning of Lewdness"—was still on the table. I picked it up and skimmed through a few pages. The whole thing is nothing but lessons on how to behave like a slave. It's full of phrases like "the minister who is unwilling to die at his sovereign's command is not loyal; the son who is unwilling to die at his father's command is not filial," and "of all crimes, lewdness is the worst; of all virtues, filial piety is the best." The more I read, the angrier I became, until I got so mad I ripped the book to pieces. With one less copy of that book in the world, a few less people will be harmed by it. (85–86)

By pitting the younger generation against the elder and focusing particularly on the effects of arranged marriage and forced concubinage, the novel makes the simple point that Chinese attitudes toward traditional beliefs varied even within generations and classes. In contrast to the empowering suicide in "Magpies," for instance, Pa Chin describes the suicide of an adolescent slave girl, Ming Feng, who loves Chueh-hui but is chosen by the Venerable Master (the one who so disapproves of lewdness) to be sold as a concubine to another rich elderly man. Although her mistress disapproves, she refuses to help, claiming that she can't go against the patriarch's word. Her sweetheart, Chueh-hui, has secretly promised to help and even marry her, but he is not told of the plan and when she tries to tell him is too busy with his exams and his radical paper even to find out what is troubling her. Pa Chin writes: "Her hopes were completely shattered. They even wanted to take away the love she depended upon to live, to present her verdant spring to a crabbed old man. Life as a concubine in a family like the Fengs' could bring only one reward: tears, blows, abuse, the same as before. The only difference would be that now, in addition, she would have to give her body to be despoiled by a peculiar old man whom she had never met. . . . After eight years of hard work and faithful service that was her only reward" (204). When Ming-feng drowns herself in the family's lake, her action has no effect on old Master Kao. He simply sends another maid in her place and purchases a third to do Ming-feng's chores for the Kaos. There is no scandal, no investigation, no fear or thought of her ghost; the death is hushed up within the family compound, and only the few who care remember her. At the same time, Pa Chin describes a greater range of responses to the problem than we hear of in Tan's stories. In the days before the "wedding," Ming-feng often overhears others disparaging the transaction, such as the angry woman in the kitchen who cries, "A young girl like that becoming the 'little wife' of an old man who's half dead! I wouldn't do it for all the money in the world!" (210). (Only in the kitchen does anyone refer to the money old Master Kao will receive for Ming-feng.) Ironically, all this disapproving gossip deeply humiliates Ming-feng but never reaches Master Kao's venerable ears.

The phenomenon of covert, passive dissent among decent people who confuse compliance with virtue is bitterly dissected in this novel. In the novel's climax, which sheds further light on traditional Chinese beliefs, a pregnant woman is sacrificed to protect the supposed interests of the Venerable Master shortly after his death. It seems the women of the elder and middle generations have become obsessed with the belief that, if Jui-chieh, the wife of the oldest brother, Chueh-hsin, should give birth while Master Kao's corpse is still in the house, she would emit a "blood-glow" that "would attack the corpse and cause it to spurt large quantities of blood" (296). This can only be prevented by sending the pregnant woman to give birth beyond the city gates on the far side of a bridge. Pa Chin describes "the curse of the blood-glow," a superstition that overtly places the interests of the dead over those of the living, as something most people in the household discount but are too timid to criticize openly. Lest we think that only the educated, Westernized youth question the myth, the author includes a scene in which Chueh-hsin's middle-aged servant begs the third brother to avert the move: "I don't think she ought to go, Third Young Master. Even if she must, it ought to be to some place decent. Only rich people have all these rules and customs. Why doesn't First Young Master speak up? We servants don't understand much, but we think her life is more important than all these rules" (299). Despite the urgent (but prudently covert) pleas of this servant and of his brothers, Chueh-hsin fails to defend his wife for fear of being called "unfilial." The rest of the household follows his cues, and the expectant mother dies in agony in an isolated house outside the city. Later, Jui-chieh's mother clearly holds the Kaos responsible for her death.

By contrast, Tan has An-mei Hsu describe a cannibalistic gesture of her mother's with apparent approval. After An-mei's family has cast her mother out, forcing the young widow to become a concubine, the mother returns to nurse her mother, Popo, on her deathbed, where she uses flesh and blood from her own arm to brew a medicinal broth for the dying woman. An-mei cites this not only as a metaphor for filial piety but as a gesture that she personally witnessed, recognized as an ancient Chinese custom, and admired; she came to "love her mother" by witnessing this scene:

> My mother took her flesh and put it in the soup. She cooked magic in the ancient tradition to try to cure her mother this one last time. She opened Popo's mouth, already too tight from trying to keep her spirit in. She fed her this soup, but that night Popo flew away with her illness.
>
> Even though I was young, I could see the pain of the flesh and the worth of the pain. (48)

King-kok Cheung wonders whether this is an actual Chinese custom, and so do I.[16] While we might ask the same question about Pa Chin's "curse of the blood-glow," my point is that the two writers position ordinary Chinese very differently in relation to the questionable practices evoked. Moreover, Tan positions herself here as an inside authority instructing her readers about Chinese culture, just as An-mei is supposedly instructing Rose; given such positioning, the text does not signal that the custom described may be an invention or a metaphor. By contrast, Pa Chin implicitly addresses an audience of fellow Chinese who are presumably equipped to assess the literal or poetic truth of his "curse" within Confucian family life.

Unlike Tan, Pa Chin portrays traditional beliefs as held selectively in accordance with existing social hierarchies. The interests of old, rich, powerful men are invoked even after death, while the ultimate protest of a pure-hearted slave girl goes unheeded. Why does the superstition of the blood-glow require the removal of the living rather than the dead? Could it be that this is a way for the middle generation to parade their filial piety at a time when they are struggling over the estate? Or is this action one more battle in the Third and Fourth Households' undeclared domestic warfare with the First Household, now led by Chueh-hsin? Clearly, the death of the patriarch makes this a good time for the other households to test and destroy the influence of Chueh-hsin, the eldest son of his generation, which this move accomplishes. Since the story of Jui-chueh's death is the culminating incident in the novel, the ghoulish curse is also clearly selected by the author to epitomize the older generation's abuse of the young. No doubt Pa Chin was influenced by reformers such as the eminent writer Lu Hsun, who chose cannibalism as a metaphor for the oppressiveness of the Chinese feudal system in his notorious satire, "The Diary of a Madman."[17] In contrast to such moments in Tan's novel, where acts or beliefs that would be considered foolish, bizarre, or unbelievable in a Westerner are justified as Chinese customs, traditional beliefs in *Family* are interwoven with other interests—as Christian beliefs might be in an American story—and are observed according to individual interests and temperaments. The curse of the blood-glow, for instance, is readily discounted not only by the "Westernized" masters and the younger generation but by their servants and Jui-chieh's mother, who are ruled by their feelings for Jui-chieh. Thus, Pa Chin's novel, like Tan's, depicts prerevolutionary China as a site of questionable traditional practices, hypocrisy, and cruelty, but it does not ask readers to misapply cultural relativism by justifying these things as acceptable to Chinese.

Family also conveys the difficulty of resisting custom, even for the wealthy, educated heirs of the clan. In one chapter, the brothers' favorite female cousin, Chin, an admirer of Ibsen, contributes a feminist editorial advocating short hair for women, but she lacks the nerve to cut her own hair. Her timidity isn't without cause; when she broaches the subject to her mother, the latter casually threatens to take her out of school and marry her off early to a rich stranger. In this period, elite female education was still valued primarily for its influence on women as future wives and mothers, an attitude conveyed by Mrs. Kao's resistance to Chin's attempt at critical thinking (Croll, *Feminism,* 153–84). Coached by a freethinking schoolmate, Chin is able to see her mother's threat in collective terms:

Before long there suddenly appeared a lengthy highway stretching to infinity, upon which were lain spreading corpses of young women. It became clear to her that this road was built thousands of years ago; the earth on the road was saturated with the blood and tears of those women. They were all tied and handcuffed and driven to this road, and made to kneel there, to soak the earth with their blood and tears, to satiate the sex desire of wild animals with their bodies . . .

Then, last but not least [came the question]: "Are you willing to give up the one you love, and hand yourself over to be the instrument of sexual satisfaction to some stranger?" . . . Justice was so dim, remote and uncertain. Her hope was completely dashed. (202)

Chin resolves privately to "take a new road," but she is so inexperienced in testing authority that she cannot even tell if her mother's remarks are serious, or communicate her vision to her.

Fortunately, Chin's principles are not put to the ultimate test faced by Ming-feng because her male cousins finally are motivated by earlier family tragedies to resist this sort of coercion. When her sweetheart, the second son, Chueh-min, is threatened with an arranged match, he runs away and stays away until Venerable Master Kao (still alive at this point in the novel) agrees to suspend the engagement, altering the family climate so that Chin is left free to continue her studies and to marry Chueh-min later. However, this resistance is only possible with the support of the brothers' radical schoolmates, who hide him for several weeks; Chin, whose consciousness has been raised by her classmate's discussion of these issues and by witnessing other unhappy lovers; and Chueh-hui, still enraged by the recent death of Ming-feng. Fortunately, the grandfather capitulates and reconciles with Chueh-min before either disowning him or dying.

The novel suggests that, oppressed as young men are by the system, they are still less isolated than their female peers. Throughout the novel, it is the young men who are invested with the possibility of saving themselves and others, and the young women who wail, suffer, and die for their mistakes. It is so much harder for the women to rebel that the brothers are held doubly responsible—for themselves and their loved ones. Chin, the most privileged and feminist of the cousins, hesitates to write a feminist article until she is coaxed by Chueh-hui, the journalist; she dares not even cut her hair or argue with her mother. However, during Chieh-min's exile from the Kao household, she is sustained not only by friends but by access to the modern ideas she has imbibed at school and in her cousins' company. Ming-feng, by contrast, lacks both an ideology of freedom—she longs for it but does not understand herself to be entitled to it, as Chin does—and a network of supporters.

While this highly autobiographical novel is clearly more concerned with male agency, the women's weaker resolve and more limited scope for action seem to reflect not only the author's individual perceptions, and his synthesis of Chinese and Western literary conventions for portraying female agency, but also an underlying recognition of women's greater oppression. Ironically, the only heroine who exercises real agency in *Family* is Ming-feng, whose suicide refuses and indicts the Venerable Master and steels

Chueh-hui's resolve to rebel. When the family system becomes too intolerable for Ming-feng, she can only rebel and escape through suicide, whereas Chin has the support of her classmates and cousins and Chueh-hui finds ways both to rebel at home and eventually to flee to Shanghai, there to pursue his studies, activism, and literary work.[18]

By examining a Chinese novel that treats the same period Tan claims for her Chinese characters' girlhood and youth, we can gain additional perspective on the stories Tan chooses to tell: we see that the oppressive family system Tan describes in her novel was being questioned on a national level by Chinese reformers (the brothers in Chengtu read Beijing-based publications and correspond with like-minded students in Shanghai); that traditional beliefs in ghosts, ancestors, astrology, and the like were held literally by some (arguably, by older and less-educated people), disbelieved by others, and applied selectively by others; and that acts of rebellion and resistance—the claiming of individual agency—required not only individual will (Ming-feng has that) but a network of supporters. Such a network needed to be sustained both by a coherent alternate ideology, strong enough to counter the moralistic condemnation of Confucian thinking, and by material resources. By this novel's standards, the view of Chinese female agency in Lindo's story, "The Red Candle," and An-mei's "Magpies" must be considered incomplete and simplistic. At the same time, Pa Chin's sinocentric perspective sets off more clearly Tan's shaping of her Chinese stories to fit the demands of her (Asian) American genre, the mother-daughter romance. Set in a Chinese society that is distant and picturesque, yet contained by the novelist's simplifying representational choices, the mothers' stories serve to complement and set off the daughters' more familiar, arguably more banal problems as middle-class American women. The women's claiming of agency as a central theme in a majority of the stories serves agreeably to unite the stories of the two generations.

The Mother-Daughter Romance

I have suggested that in Tan's intricate mother-daughter version of the immigrant romance the repeated rapprochements of mothers and daughters who discover they are not so very different is one way of addressing, in a sentimental plot, contradictions inherent in American attitudes toward immigration—specifically the contradiction between the country's ideology of inclusion and its systematic mechanisms for excluding unwelcome newcomers. In this context, the novel's doubled presentation of the mothers as both alien and familiar is central to its ideological force as a set of utopian immigration stories: the mothers must be sufficiently alien to provide "diversity" but sufficiently American to enter mainstream society without radically disturbing or transforming its flow. The text works by giving substance to the American daughters'/readers' combined attraction to, and anxieties about, the mothers' alienness and then relieving those anxieties with assurances of underlying sameness. A good example of this is "Best Quality," in which June worries that her mother, Suyuan, may have done away with her tenants' cat, a fear reminiscent of anti-Chinese literature emphasizing exotic/repulsive practices from footbinding and opium smoking to the consumption of cats and dogs. As June moves toward recognition that her late mother remains close to her because she is, figuratively and literally, in her bones (197–209), the cat reappears, further dispelling June's vague fears about her mother's differentness. In this regard, the text's representation of a group of middle-class women as exemplary immigrants and citizens serves a reconciling function; the class of these mothers and daughters renders them readily assimilable into middle-class American life, while their gender somewhat distances them from the negative images of Asian males that have been generated by nineteenth-century observations of working-class male sojourners, on one hand, and Asian soldiers and leaders in modern wars in Asia and the Pacific Rim on the other.

The final chapter, in which June takes her late mother's place in a reconciliation with her long-lost half-sisters in China, carries the logic of symbolic reconciliation one step further, offering an image of understanding between (ethnic) Americans (June and her father) and Chinese (their relatives) in an era of increased American interest in future ties with China. In this chapter, June's successful first contacts with her Chinese relatives capture larger American attitudes toward China. The basis for June's happy encounters, and metaphorically for cross-cultural understanding, is, in brief, that the Americans come to value ethnic diversity (both outside and within themselves) while the Chinese become familiar, seemingly "the same" at heart, through their acceptance of global capitalism. Thus, the sixty-year estrangement of June's father, Canning Woo, from his aunt is eased by the amenities of their Westernized luxury hotel, Polaroids, hamburgers, and apple pie. Even Coca-Cola, the symbol of American callousness in the novel's opening, is recoded as a sign of China's reassuring Westernization when it appears in the Woos' hotel room bar with other familiar name brands. Belying the remote, impoverished China of the mother's tales, Mr. Woo's elderly aunt tells him that her sons are cleaning up and conspicuously consuming without fear in China's newly liberalized economy: "My sons have been quite successful, selling our vegetables in the free market. We had enough these last few years to build a big house, three stories, all of new brick, big enough for our whole family and then some. . . . You Americans aren't the only ones who know how to get rich!" (296). Even at this moment of seeing China as a modernizing country, the return of the two-worlds problem can be heard in the elderly lady's dialogue: Chinese success is described in comparison with American norms. Described through a tourist's eye, June's perceptions of contemporary China generally share this presumption of a framing American perspective. Conveniently occluded from this perspective are questions about the Chinese government's policy of embracing capitalism but not democracy; ironically, Tan's book was published in 1989, the year the massacre at Tienanmen Square dramatized the limits of official tolerance for democratic movements in the People's Republic of China.

Finally, how does this novel construct Chinese American ethnicity? In the concluding image, the Polaroid portrait of June with her half-sisters, the Chinese sisters prove to be uncanny replicas of the absent mother, both alien and familiar. The alien in manageable form, they appear with June to enact Suyuan's long-cherished wish of assimilating her Chinese past and her American future: "The gray-green surface changes to the bright colors of our three images, sharpening and deepening all at once. And although we don't speak, I know we all see it: Together we look like our mother. Her same eyes, her same mouth, open in surprise to see, at last, her long-cherished wish" (288). From the mother's perspective, the Polaroid represents the happy denouement of the immigration myth set forth at the novel's beginning. Through June and her father, the mother has told her story. The American daughter has understood, will become a successful American version of her mother, and will carry forward her tradition, her wishes, her lineage. And, in terms of the immigrant romance, the American daughter who listens and honors her mother both stands in for the American reader and mediates the mother's self-presentation to that reader.

From June's perspective, the "return" to China represents a return to origins. She begins the novel by taking her late mother's place at the mahjong table, described as "the East, where things begin" (41). In "Best Quality," she comes to a temporary resolution in her mourning by recognizing her mother's presence within herself (209), but this is not quite enough. By ending the book with "A Pair of Tickets," depicting the "reunion" with the lost sisters in China, Tan suggests that the Chinese American's work of remembering the mother/motherland is incomplete without this return and that there is something still unknown about the mother that can only be found in China—something that is represented by the unknown sisters. June's nervousness about the meeting with her half-sisters seems driven by fear that, because they came first and grew up in China, they will judge her as a substitute for her mother and will find her deficient in ethnic consciousness and moral character—traits that the novel as a whole conflates with Chinese life experience. By appearing at this moment in June's story—a few months after her mother's death—the sisters threaten to assume in June's mind the role of the demanding, judgmental mother of June's childhood, the mother described in "Two Kinds" (132–44). The mothers and half-sisters stand for both China and Chineseness, then, and for a psychologically significant other June is seeking to internalize in building a whole adult self. The sense is that part of that self is an inherited core of Chineseness, or of the Chinese feminine (the missing siblings cannot, in Tan's novel, be *brothers*), but that completion of her adult self requires the integration of that aspect within a subjectivity that will be strengthened by acknowledging its presence—this is the work of the Chinese American daughter. The recognition of affinity captured by the Polaroid, then, functions as a sign that June has passed the test of the motherlike sisters' inspection and that the work of mourning/reconstruction represented figuratively by the novels' many maternal narratives has been successful. The American daughter has constructed her Chinese aspects appropriately, lending complexity to her American self without rendering it fundamentally different; the threat of radical difference is embodied by the mothers and their stories—enough to be enjoyed—but is contained in a narrative frame emphasizing the daughter's psychological work and the sentimental story of the finding of the long-lost sisters. Thus, the phrase "your mother is in your bones," which might once have meant that Chinese Americans could not be considered American, now means they share with other Americans an enriching access to a matrilineal heritage of protofeminist individualism and enterprise.

5

TRIPMASTER MONKEY, *Frank Chin,*
and the Chinese Heroic Tradition

The reason he had the radio on was that whenever he stopped typing, he heard someone else nearby tapping, tapping at a typewriter, typing through the night. Yes, it was there, steady but not mechanical. . . . An intelligence was coming up with words. Someone else, not a poet with a pencil or fountain pen but a workhorse big-novel writer, was staying up, probably done composing already and typing out fair copy. It should be a companionable noise, a jazz challenge to which he could blow out the window his answering jazz. But, no, it's an expensive electric machine-gun typewriter aiming at him, gunning for him, to knock him off in competition.—Maxine Hong Kingston, *Tripmaster Monkey: His Fake Book*

Constructing Ethnic Heroism: The Kingston-Chin Debate

It is no accident that when Wittman Ah Sing, the protagonist of *Tripmaster Monkey: His Fake Book,* sits up all night to begin his first play he is haunted by the tapping of a rival's typewriter. His author, Maxine Hong Kingston, has responded to over a decade of hostile criticism by creating Wittman in the image of her harshest critic, Frank Chin. Like Chin, Wittman Ah Sing is a Chinese American playwright, idealistic and enraged over racism, with the persona of an angry young man who can be exasperating—especially in his sexism—but is fundamentally decent. Though this portrait could be considered a personal attack, it is best understood as providing a mediating voice through which Kingston expresses her own anger over American racism. This anger, however, is only one of several concerns that Kingston shares with Chin and explores throughout *Tripmaster Monkey.*

Kingston's novel is considered here in terms of an ongoing debate between Kingston and Frank Chin. This debate, about the proper place of

Chinese texts in the construction of an emerging Chinese American literature, has been central to Asian American literary studies.[1] It is also crucial to Asian American literature, whose survival and growth depend in part on the writers' ability to inscribe an ethnic consciousness that is distinct from Asian and Euro-American cultures yet not isolated from them. Also at stake is the question of whether any particular body of literary texts can reasonably be cited as definitive of an ethnic group's consciousness; the selection and significance of particular Chinese texts, which Chin has claimed as definitive of Chinese American ethnic consciousness; his claim that some texts, versions, and readings are "real" while others are "fake"; and, most importantly, who is authorized to determine these issues. In short, I read *Tripmaster Monkey* as a meditation on the nature of the Chinese "heroic tradition," as it is redefined by the two authors, and its relation to Kingston's authority as a Chinese American woman writer.

Kingston employs various devices to situate *Tripmaster Monkey* as an American novel set in Berkeley, California, in the 1960s, including references to Vietnam, the drug culture, and local sites and writers. Crammed with allusions to Western cultural markers such as James Joyce, Rainer Maria Rilke, Walt Whitman, the Beats, and American pop culture from vaudeville to *West Side Story,* the novel also incorporates numerous stories from the Chinese classics *Three Kingdoms, The Water Margin,* and *Journey to the West.* In doing so, Kingston engages sympathetically but skeptically with Frank Chin's construction of a Chinese heroic tradition that emphasizes martial heroism and a masculine code of honor.

This heroic tradition is best understood as Chin's response to the anti-Asian racism that he and others find rampant in mainstream American culture. In several essays, some cosigned by friends who have coedited Asian American anthologies with him (Jeffrey Paul Chan, Lawson Fusao Inada, and Shawn Wong), Chin has explored the effects of this racism on the Asian American community, focusing especially on cultural denigrations of Asian masculinity.[2] Chin's most influential argument has been that Asian American consciousness and literary production have been hampered by mainstream stereotypes of Asian Americans as docile, effeminate, and exotic. In a typical passage of the 1970s, Chin bitterly rejects the conditions of whites' "racist love" for Asian Americans:

It is clear that our acceptability, the affection and renown we supposedly enjoy, is not based on any actual achievements or contributions we have made, but on what we have not done. We have not been black. We have not caused trouble. We have not been men.

The Asian culture we are supposedly preserving is uniquely without masculinity; we are characterized as lacking daring, originality, aggressiveness, assertiveness, vitality, and living art and culture. What art and culture we do enjoy is passive in the popular mind—we don't practice it, we preserve it and are sustained by it. And our lack of cultural achievement and expression in America is explained by the fact that we are sustaining a foreign culture . . .

Our supposed Asian identity is used to exclude us from American culture, and is imposed upon us as a substitute for participation in American culture . . . ("Backtalk," 556)

While Chin's initial desire to claim American masculinity by rejecting Chinese culture outright is understandable, it contrasts both with Kingston's early, enduring interest in adapting Chinese sources and with Chin's own insistence, starting in 1985, on defining Chinese American cultural identity through heroic Chinese narratives. That year, Chin argued that the rebels and outlaws of certain Chinese classics, handed down through popular forms, were appropriate heroes for modern Asian Americans, especially males. In contrast to Kingston, whose response to cultural exclusion has generally been to recast cultural narratives to be more inclusive, Chin's impulse has been more directly confrontational. Both his critical and his creative work depict American culture as a site of ideological warfare in which Chinese American and other Asian American communities are being culturally erased (see, e.g., his novel *Donald Duk*). In Chin's words, the resulting choice for Asian American writers is one between "personal integrity" and "historical extinction." While not all of his claims have been accepted, the existence and effects of anti-Asian racism have been widely discussed and have become framing assumptions for numerous studies, both cultural and material;[3] Kingston's *Tripmaster Monkey* is both a continuation of her own work and another such study. By incorporating a steady analysis of racial dynamics in American culture and revisiting the Chinese classics, Kingston admits that Chin's desire to inscribe a Chinese American consciousness in American literature, and to expose and counteract demeaning stereotypes of Asian men, also accords with her own goals; but in terms of the Chinese classics, she substantially alters his paradigms and questions his assumptions.

Kingston's novel challenges Chin's readings of heroic texts on two levels. In terms of content, she questions his idealization of this tradition's hypermasculine, martial ethos, the seething "ethic of private revenge." In terms of Chin's model for literary interpretation, she questions his tendency to portray these Chinese texts as completed verbal icons of Chinese culture and character whose meaning is self-evident; instead, she dramatizes an interactive reading strategy that emphasizes the texts' collaboration with various communities of readers. To borrow Roland Barthes's terms, she favors "writerly" texts, which readers help to "write," over readerly texts, which readers passively consume in traditional readerly fashion (Barthes, 4).

Kingston's emphasis on the indeterminate, evolving nature of texts is at the heart of Chin's quarrel with her approach to Chinese myths. Throughout her career, she has challenged the authority of both Chinese and American traditions by inscribing Chinese, American, and European narratives into her work, yet transforming and subverting them in ways that have been, or could be, described in terms of feminist revision or postmodern parody.[4] Kingston's texts have emphasized the labor of interpreting cultural narratives that may be oppressive rather than accepting those narratives as authoritative fables whose meaning is self-evident. Her suspicion of dogmatic and prescriptive textual readings and her postmodernist subversions of such readings are consistent with her suspicion of institutionalized authority and her awareness of the individual subject's capacity to internalize that authority. By contrast, Chin's polemical essays and some of his fiction and drama tend to construct repressive authority and agency as something monolithic and removed from himself; just as he refuses to scrutinize the more oppressive actions of his Chinese heroes, he tends to deny that he might be complicit in the system he attacks or in any other system of oppression. Whenever he rhetorically positions himself as the sole arbiter of truth, he signals that authority itself is not oppressive to him as long as it is in the right few hands. For Kingston, by contrast, the very ideas of authority and cultural authenticity are suspect.

Chin's strongest disagreement with Kingston's work centers around her liberal adaptations of well-known Chinese stories that both writers have referred to as "myths" to elucidate the Chinese American experience.[5] Kingston, best known for her provocative feminist revision of the woman warrior myth, has been criticized by Chin for her view of Chinese myths as folklore that has been forgotten, changed, or improvised to comment on new circumstances. Articulating an assumption central to his earlier work, Chin wrote in 1990, "Myths are, by nature, immutable and unchanging because they are deeply ingrained in the cultural memory, or they are not myths. New experience breeds new history, new art, and new fiction. The new experience of the Anglo-Saxon in America did not result in confusing Homer with Joan of Arc but in new stories . . ." ("Come All," 29). He has accused Kingston, and others who follow her example of postmodern revisionism, of colluding with white racist stereotypes by portraying the Chinese as less literate and more forgetful of their ancestral culture than other immigrant groups. For him, to tamper with Chinese myth, a component of "true" Chinese American culture, is to invent a "fake" Chinese American culture that will sell better to a racist mainstream public.[6]

Kingston, by contrast, is essentially a writer of postmodern parody in the terms defined by Linda Hutcheon (*Politics*, 93–177): in freely improvising variations on themes taken from Chinese or other texts, she both celebrates and criticizes her originals. On the whole, she seeks to vest authority in individual readers or communities of readers. While Chinese and other narratives are valuable to her, she sees the texts themselves as open-ended sketches, like the themes and chord progressions in the "fake book" that a musician uses as the basis for improvised performances or the story outlines offered by the traditional promptbooks of Chinese storytellers. She herself is an improviser whose work enriches and revitalizes her originals by adapting them to address the needs of her audience. Deliberately inverting the negative charge that Chin attributes to "faking" Chinese culture, her novel's subtitle (*His Fake Book*) takes the trope of jazz improvisation as a metaphor for her view of the Chinese heroic tradition (as well as Western cultures) as a rich but open ended source of inspiration for her Chinese American cultural creation.

The Communal Text

Kingston's view of representation as a collaborative matter, and texts as the product of collusions (and collisions) between authors and readers, is illustrated within *Tripmaster Monkey* by her representation of Wittman's own art as a collective rather than individual achievement. This is hinted at by Kingston's naming of her writer-protagonist, Wittman Ah Sing, after the poet Walt Whitman. Wittman, of course, seeks to found a Chinese American tradition that will enter into dialogue with the American tradition of which Whitman is deemed a founder. In addition to "fathering" an American tradition of lyric poetry, Whitman also fathered, or remade, himself as a great American poet; thus, the pun is also an indirect reference to Chin's dramatic and critical work, in which, as we saw earlier, Chin sought to cast himself as a heroic author and father of a new Chinese American tradition. Accordingly, Kingston Sino-Americanizes Whitman's name, replacing the "whit[e] man" with a man of wit. The Chinese American vocative "Ah Sing," evokes Whitman's bardic self declarations in *Leaves of Grass*, "I sing the body electric" and, more importantly,

> I celebrate myself, and sing myself,
> And what I assume you shall assume,
> For every atom belonging to me as good belongs to you. (28)

Whitman's poetry projects a poetic persona that understands and subsumes all Americans by imaginatively identifying with their experiences and giving voice to them, thereby representing his poetic self as an expanded, collective consciousness. The ideal of democratic inclusiveness is challenged throughout *Tripmaster Monkey*, as Wittman voices Kingston's critique of the ways the "universal" texts of American culture subtly exclude or marginalize people of color. On the whole, however, *Tripmaster Monkey* celebrates the ideals of both political and cultural inclusiveness, seeking to envision a new community that is more truly inclusive, and it uses the career of its hero, Wittman, to illustrate how a collective consciousness enlivens a writer's work.

A typical scene of composition begins with Wittman, at the end of an all-night party, telling friends about the week-long play he wants to stage with their help. He proposes to begin by inviting the audience to a barbecue, one designed to remind the audience that the Chinese leaders who helped to tame the American West were themselves American pioneers. Though the barbecue trappings are American, the proposed fare—a freshly killed black ox and white horse—commemorates a famous scene from the novel *Three Kingdoms,* which is also a favorite source for Chinese opera. In this scene, the three heroes celebrate their oath of newly declared fraternity by sacrificing the ox and horse, which they then consume in a bonding ritual with their newly recruited army. As Wittman makes clear, the Chinese opera tradition that the Cantonese brought to the United States is for him (and Kingston) a long-lost *American* tradition. Moreover, the ritual slaughter and feast celebrates the widening of the kinship circle to unrelated people who are united by a common enterprise. In *Three Kingdoms,* the new clan established by the newly bound "brothers" is their army; the enterprise is the reunification of China and the founding of a dynasty. In the nineteenth-century American West, the clan is the Chinese American community, the enterprise the making of America and Americans. In Wittman's play, the clan is an interracial community brought together to perform and watch the play. This play, in turn, is a metaphor for the Chinese American cultural tradition that Kingston seeks to create.

Among the entertainments Wittman wants to include is an enormous fat lady, a tattooed wrestler who will dance exuberantly naked (146–47). For Wittman, the fat lady represents untrammeled female energy and power, and her presence onstage will not only revive a kung fu opera tradition (according to Wittman) but will challenge the equation of female beauty with thinness as well as stereotypes of Han people (ethnic Chinese) as puritanical nondancers and fat people as weak, asexual, and generally unfit for stardom. His female listeners (Wittman's potential actors) object, however, that the exposure of so much female flesh is too much like a woman jumping out of a cake at a stag party. Rejecting Wittman's more radical arguments that fat and nakedness signify freedom, strength, beauty, and sexuality, the women reject the fat lady because of her failure to conform to the bourgeois standards of beauty and propriety she is supposed to disrupt. In deference to their reading, Wittman edits the lady from his text—but not from

Kingston's—and moves on. She remains in Kingston's novel as a sign of the ambiguity of texts.

The fat lady incident is not only an act of collective interpretation, however. Because the group is in the process of composing and casting a play, it also represents artistic creation as a dialogic process in which the putative author, Wittman, must incorporate the views of "readers" who are both critics and artistic collaborators. In this case, and in several others, the collaborative process results in the editing (or censorship) of the most radical ideas by more moderate (or conventional) thinkers. In numerous other scenes, Kingston depicts Wittman expanding his audience by responding flexibly to his critics. For instance, he agrees to eliminate references to human dumplings and "bow" (steamed buns with filling), which would be bad for Chinatown businesses, in exchange for access to a Tong hall as venue for his play (261–62), and he incorporates his actors' ideas into his play (179–82, 286). In addition, he ends his play with a monologue in which he comments on the critical reception of his work (307–10), pointing out the inadvertent racism of critics who reviewed the play in terms of Chinese food, colonialist quotations from Kipling ("East is east and west is west"), and stereotypes about Asian American exoticism, foreignness, or inscrutability: "There is no East here. West is meeting West. . . . Do I have to explain why 'exotic' pisses me off, and 'not exotic' pisses me off? . . . To be exotic or to be not-exotic is not a question about Americans or about humans" (308). This monologue identifies Wittman closely not only with Chin but with the author herself, who published an article ("Cultural Mis-readings by American Reviewers") making the same points about the reviews of her first book. Wittman's discussion provides a model for the exchange between Kingston and her critics: among other things, this novel incorporates and replies to their voices, including Chin's.

Though *Tripmaster* depicts the collective fashioning of a play, it also clearly acknowledges novel writing as an intertextual process. I cannot detail this book's formidable range of Asian and Western references here, but Kingston's arch acknowledgment of Chin's influence may illustrate my point. In the epigraph, we saw how Wittman, who until this point has written only poetry, finds his late-night attempts to compose his first play disturbed by the presence of a competitor. If we continue reading this passage, we find additional commentary about Kingston's relationship with Chin:

It should be a companionable noise, a jazz challenge to which he could blow out the window his answering jazz. But, no, it's an expensive electric machine-gun typewriter aiming at him, gunning for him, to knock him off in competition. But so efficient—it had to be a girl, a clerk typist, he hoped, a secretary, he hoped. A schoolteacher cutting mimeo stencils. A cookbook writer. A guidebook-for-tourists writer. Madam Dim Sum, Madam Chinoiserie, Madam Orientalia knocking out horsey cocky locky astrology, Horatio Algiers Wong—he heard the typing leave him behind. (41)

Here Kingston suggests that, contrary to Chin's film noir–style assertions about the isolation of all Asian American writers ("You write alone, kid" ["This Is," 129]), neither she nor Frank Chin writes alone. Even when composing late at night in their separate garrets, each hears and responds to the other's work, thereby creating a tradition. Using the metaphor of jazz, Kingston distinctly suggests that she and Chin should work as colleagues and collaborators, but instead they remain separated by a wall. Why? In a parody of Chin's attacks on Kingston, Wittman "tunes out" and tries to dismiss his neighbor as a "girl," whose gender marks her as no true literary rival. Incapable of conceiving original work, the unknown typist is fit (in Wittman's wishful thinking) only to engage in mechanical reproduction of others' words or to prostitute herself with cookbooks, tour books, model minority myths, and other debased genres pandering to orientalist tastes.[7] At this point in the novel, Wittman is resistant to intertextual dialogue; nor would the jazz metaphor of improvisation within a tradition appeal to him. No wonder, then, that Kingston, the "workhorse big-novel writer" takes aim at Wittman/Chin and "leaves him behind."

Still, the questions remain: what kind of tradition will be constructed by this peculiar dialogue? And how can Kingston take into account Chin's views, particularly his attempt to define Chinese American culture in terms of a few important but ideologically selected texts, without compromising her feminist vision? In order to support Chin's efforts to rehabilitate Asian American manhood, must she (and we readers) also ignore the chauvinism and the absolute tone of such typically Chin-ese assertions as this? "Good or bad, the stereotypical Asian is nothing as a man. At worst, the Asian American is contemptible because he is womanly, effeminate, devoid of all the traditionally masculine qualities of originality, daring, physical courage, and creativity" (Chin et al., "Introduction," 14–15). When we assess Kingston's incorporation of Chin, and of Chinese heroic texts, into *Tripmaster Monkey,* we must keep in mind that Kingston herself has always mined Chinese sources for models of Chinese American heroism and has always conveyed, through her revisions, her understanding that the old Chinese stories need to be adapted to convey her personal perspectives to an American readership. When Chin came to recognize the richness and importance of such stories, however ("Autobiography," 1985), he disavowed Kingston's eclectic, feminist presentations of Chinese stories, insisting instead on the preeminence of three feudal texts in which women were largely irrelevant to, or disruptive of, a predominantly male code of honor: Sun Tzu's *Art of War* (a war manual), Luo Guanzhong's *Three Kingdoms* (a novel), and Shi Nai'an's and Luo Guanzhong's *Water Margin* (a novel). *Water Margin,* which features the torture and execution of several unfaithful wives, is the most blatantly misogynistic, but *Three Kingdoms* and *Art of War* also place women firmly outside the central heroic concerns of war and leadership. In the two novels, even heroic and outlaw women are defined as good only as long as they obey patriarchal authority.[8]

How, then, can Kingston reinscribe such texts within her novel without sharing complicity with the "heroic" values her novel dissents from, notably their patriarchal assumptions about gender and their celebration of war? In the space remaining, I'll discuss two distinct tropes through which Kingston comments on this issue: the female hero and the empty scrolls.

The Female Hero and the Classic Homosocial Text

I borrow the term *homosocial* from Eve Kosofsky Sedgwick to describe the primacy of social bonds between heterosexual men within patriarchal (and implicitly homophobic) social systems. Following Sedgwick, my argument will discuss *Three Kingdoms'* celebration of such bonds as constitutive of male heroism and Kingston's attempt to appropriate the story's heroic values without accepting its sexism. Although this sixteenth-century Chinese novel, like the other works touted by Chin and Kingston, clearly doesn't belong to the English literary tradition that inspired Sedgwick's analysis, both groups of texts depict societies in which male homosocial bonds are strengthened, and heterosexual bonds rendered subordinate, by patriarchal social structures. Although the homosocial relationships of fraternity, mentorship, fealty, and rivalry I am about to describe are not strictly erotic, Sedgwick's use of the term *homosocial desire* conveys the extent to which such relationships inspire passions that displace heterosexual desires in Chinese as well as English texts. In particular, the following discussion is indebted to Gayle Rubin's account of "the traffic in women," which is based on Claude Lévi-Strauss's formulation: "The total relationship of exchange which constitutes marriage is not established between a man and a woman, but between two groups of men, and the woman figures only as one of the objects in the exchange, not as one of the partners" (Lévi-Strauss, *Structures,* 115; qtd. in Rubin, "Traffic," 174, and Sedgwick, *Men,* 25–26).

In *Tripmaster Monkey,* Wittman the playwright narrates or restages most of the key episodes from the classic Chinese novel (and opera) *Three Kingdoms.* The leading female character in *Three Kingdoms* is Lady Sun, whose marriage to Liu Bei, the hero, marks a major turn in his fortunes. Kingston's feminist revision of this incident tacitly criticizes the original, but ultimately it respects the story's framing ideological assumptions about gender and heroism. Kingston has Wittman tell the story of Lady Sun and Liu Bei to his own newlywed bride, Tana de Weese, to whom he offers the role of Lady Sun in his play. His version goes like this: Lady Sun, a war-loving princess from the southland, proposes to Liu, a famous general who has recently been widowed. On their wedding night, Liu, who suspects a plot against his life, is horrified to find her bedchamber decked with arms and her maids armed. "Afraid of a few swords after half a lifetime of slaughter?" she laughs, and sends the maids away. During the happy year of marriage that follows, the couple fence together and compare their horsemanship, riding into the city together to the acclaim of the people. At last, at the New Year's season, the couple determines to flee from the city, which is controlled by Liu's enemies, Lady Sun's kin. Trapped on the road by hostile soldiers from his wife's country, Liu "faces the utter paranoia of marriage" and throws himself upon his wife's mercy. She takes his hand and, walking out among the soldiers sent by her own family, bullies and confuses the men into letting them go. Pursued again by others, she sends him on, again intimidates the pursuers, and rejoins him just in time to be rescued by his man (Kingston, *Tripmaster,* 172–75).

Turning to Moss Roberts's 1991 translation of Luo Guanzhong's *Three Kingdoms,* we find that half the story—the arms in the bedroom, the couple's flight, and the princess's fidelity, courage, and intelligence—is true to tradition (Luo, 409–20). By editing out the narrative frame of the incident, however, Kingston has obscured the fact that in the original Lady Sun is merely a pawn between two of the factions, or "kingdoms," competing for dominance in China, one headed by Liu Pei and his legendary military advisor, Zhuge Liang, and the other headed by Lady Sun's brother, Sun Quan. Sun proposes the match between his sister and Liu in order to lure Liu to Nanxu, a city where Sun can capture him. But, forewarned by his adviser, Liu arrives in Nanxu with a highly visible "wedding party" of five hundred armed men, thereby compelling Sun to give his sister away in fact. Lady Sun is neither consulted nor present during these prenuptial maneuvers; twenty years Liu's junior, she only appears on the wedding day to fulfill a role predetermined by others.

There is little romance for Lady Sun in Luo's narrative, which clearly subordinates the marriage to two homosocial relationships, Liu's rivalry with Sun Quan and his homosocial bond with his adviser, Zhuge Liang. Luo's Liu neither courts nor is courted by Lady Sun before marriage but gains her as a windfall of his competition with Sun Quan. In Luo's account, it is the brother, not the sister, whose horsemanship and new alliance with Liu are popularly acclaimed. Though Lady Sun is supposedly the most important woman in *Three Kingdoms,* she has no part in the action once this wedding episode ends. Not only is she a "medium of exchange" between her husband and her brother, but she is a prize awarded to Liu by his adviser Zhuge. It is Zhuge whose strategy forces Sun to fulfill the engagement, who masterminds the couple's escape, who anticipates the moment when Liu will need to throw himself on his wife's mercy, and who arrives with the getaway transportation. Before this episode, the adviser has been arduously sought and courted by Liu; once persuaded to join Liu's failing cause, Zhuge has guided his leader from obscurity to preeminence. Later, it will be the adviser, not the wife, who is the most trusted and beloved figure at Liu's deathbed in a famous scene in which Liu, now emperor, even considers turning the imperial succession over to Zhuge's son instead of his own. "Through you alone the imperial quest was achieved," gasps Liu, as both men weep. "My heir is an inconsequential weakling, and so I must entrust you with my cause" (Luo, *Three Kingdoms*, 646, chap. 85; Kingston, *Tripmaster*, 284). Zhuge, of course, begs to be excused from this dangerous "honor," once more confirming both his political acumen and his undying loyalty.

Clearly, Kingston's omission of Sun's and Zhuge's marital machinations is meant to restore Lady Sun's agency, to supplant the homosocial plots with a heterosexual romance plot, and to reaffirm marriage as a relationship between loving individuals rather than a strategic feint between warring clans. Yet the underlying logic linking women with betrayal and relegating them to outsider status remains intact. Given the enmity of her husband and brother and the Chinese custom that marks wives as the unconditional subjects of their husbands, Lady Sun is bound to become a rebel and an exile from her family and homeland, precisely *by fulfilling her duty as a woman*. The Chinese text also sanctions Lady Sun's switch to her husband's side on the grounds that her brother is mistreating her; Liu ostensibly is not. Thus, the bride's choice of husband over brother dramatizes both her obedience and Liu's personal attractiveness and supposedly superior virtue, but it also marks the prescribed limits of female loyalty. In loving the husband chosen for her, Lady Sun obeys her brother's public command (to marry Liu), yet she also deliberately undermines his private design (to murder Liu). Hence, the episode is an extreme but telling example of the patriarchal logic that views women as outsiders, born traitors to their birth families. In this story, both Sun Quan and Liu Bei behave deceitfully toward each other, but politically speaking neither is a traitor because each embodies his own cause: they don't betray themselves. But for Lady Sun, the medium of their mutual deceits, loyalty to one *requires* betrayal of the other. Indeed, the contradiction between Sun's word and his intent poses a koanlike contradiction that Lady Sun must solve at her own and her husband's peril: her very obedience to her brother requires her to rebel against him.

This "divided duty," and the double bind it poses, governs these medieval texts' attitudes toward women, who are consistently associated with betrayal, ruses, and moral ambiguity even when they are overtly presented as proper and virtuous (cf. *Othello*, 1.3.181). If the standard for heroism is integrity, its opposite is duplicity, and women operating in these men's texts are linked with doubleness not only because they must marry but because they are privy to and bound by different ethical and behavioral codes than men. But, rather than acknowledging the subaltern skills women must develop in order to negotiate between male and female codes or seriously considering the moral complexity that results, these texts generally view women as inherently deceptive and unreliable outsiders.

Hence, these martial texts virtually supplant patriarchies, which they consider the norm, with fraternities because the best and purest clan is an all-male clan: an army. This is why Liu on his deathbed has the impulse to favor Zhuge Liang over his own son and why the most important social unit in Luo's *Three Kingdoms* is a homosocial "ménage-à-trois," the sworn brotherhood of Liu Bei, Guan Yu (called Gwan Goong by Kingston), and Zhang Fei. The entire trajectory of *Three Kingdoms* is shaped by the famous Peach Orchard Oath in which Liu, Guan, and Zhang adopt each other as "brothers" and pledge to die on the same day—that is, to take immediate vengeance to the death against each others' enemies. Of course, neither Liu nor any other hero worth his soy sauce ever extends such a pledge to his wife or any other woman, though a good wife commits herself absolutely to her husband. When Zhang Fei, thinking he has lost Liu's land and family, offers his own life in atonement, Liu consoles him by explaining the fundamental priorities of their world: "A brother is a limb. Wives and children are but clothes, which torn can be mended. But who can restore a broken limb? We linked our destinies in the Peach Garden when we vowed to die as one. My land, my family, I can spare, but not you, midway in our course" (Roberts, "Introduction," xxiii). In short, Kingston's feminist "critique through revision" of the episode is suggestive but incomplete because the story's patriarchal assumptions are too deeply embedded in its plot. Taken alone, Kingston's romantic, modern treatment of the heroic couple as an independent unit does not address the larger feminist problem of these texts' fundamental mistrust and marginalization of women and their idealization of fraternities defined by their exclusion of the feminine. To understand one way Kingston transcends this impasse, we must turn to *The Journey to the West*.

The Empty Scrolls and the Writerly Text

At the risk of oversimplification, I have so far characterized Chin as a textual fundamentalist who seeks to vest authority in more or less univocal classical texts and to replace hegemonic mainstream narratives about Asians with his own, equally hegemonic narrative separating Asian Americans and their cultural productions into two groups, the heroic "real" and the self-abasing "fake." By contrast, I argue, Kingston has always taken the postmodern stance of celebrating rather than denying or attacking the importance and complexity of the interpretive process; her work tends to affirm the authority of individual readers, interpretive communities, and contemporary authors to engage dialogically with traditional texts. In *Tripmaster Monkey* and other texts, she portrays literary composition as a process enriched rather than threatened by dialogue, whether between a text and its predecessors or between an author and her audience. Like many postmodern fiction writers, Kingston understands history and culture as complex, multivocal, social constructs, yet she does not deny the existence or importance of specific past events, specific literary texts, or the history of anti-Asian racism in this country. Indeed, racism is a central subject or subtext for all three of her major books.

Like other postmodern writers, Kingston uses the postmodern techniques of parody and revision, not to distort or obliterate our understanding of Chinese American history and culture, as Chin charges, but to focus our attention on the process of constructing that culture, and the subjectivities it underwrites, through texts. For Kingston, in short, the complexity of those textual webs through which we know culture and history is an invitation to explore texts, not through rote learning and repetition but by entering imaginatively and actively "writing" texts in an effort to understand, and in some cases update or contest, their essences. But, for Kingston, to alter a text, to transplant it or otherwise struggle with it, is not an act of erasure or disrespect; rather, it is a way of affirming and exploring the power and resilience of the original and reinscribing it into her own American vision. This is nowhere more clearly illustrated than in her treatment of the episode of the blank texts, which is taken from Wu Ch'eng-en's *Journey to the West,* a classic Chinese novel ignored in Chin's initial account of the Chinese heroic tradition.

In claiming *Journey* as a classical source for Chinese American culture, Kingston critiques Chin's insistence that Chinese American conciousness be defined by martial virtues. *Journey* is a text whose central action is not one of war or conquest but a quest for Buddhist scriptures to be transplanted from India ("the West") to China in an act of cross-cultural insemination. *Journey*'s scripture pilgrims, of which Monkey is the most important, all mature and experience inner transformation as a result of their efforts throughout the journey. Though Monkey is widely beloved by audiences for his combativeness and martial prowess, his actions in the story are monitored, and if necessary disciplined, by the character of Kuan-yin, the goddess of mercy. Like an author or narrator, Kuan-yin also instigates and watches over the pilgrimage. As a result of her discipline, Monkey gradually learns the Buddhist virtues of humility and detachment and becomes less quarrelsome, ultimately attaining enlightenment by shedding his attachment to his mortal self (or ego). *Journey*'s overall emphasis on spiritual enlightenment provides a powerful alternative to the more overtly martial texts *Three Kingdoms* and *Water Margin,* which Frank Chin has chosen as the keynotes for Asian American character. Indeed, by linking Wittman to Monkey, Kingston hints that the former, like her combative rival Chin, also needs lessons in humility and detachment. Kingston herself, figured by the typist in the epigraph, seems closely identifiable with her novel's narrator, a distinctly feminist, maternal voice that evaluates and manages Wittman in a clear analogue to Kuan-yin's direction of Monkey and his progress.

Directly after hearing the rival typist and shutting out the implied possibility of dialogue, Wittman is shown vainly trying to grasp the culminating episode—that of the empty scrolls—from *Journey.* Clearly, this scene is a direct comment on the two writers' shared project of transporting Chinese classics into the American literary landscape. *Journey,* unlike Chin's chosen "heroic" texts, both revels in martial heroism and views it with playful irony, as Kingston's novel does. Of course, Wittman, the monkey and "tripmaster" of Kingston's title, is closely identified with the quarrelsome but brilliant hero of *Journey,* Monkey. But the pilgrims, who bring "sacred" texts from a tutelary culture to enrich their own, can be seen, surprisingly, as legendary Chinese archetypes for both Chin and Kingston, both of whom call upon Chinese texts as touchstones for portraying and transforming Chinese American and American culture. What is involved in such an act of transplantation and translation? Kingston's retelling of the empty scrolls episode suggests a key difference between her views and Chin's.

After many adventures (Kingston tells us), "Monkey and his friends" arrive safely in India, where they are cordially received and given scrolls to take back to China. But on the way home they discover that all the scrolls are blank. Feeling cheated, they return, demand an exchange, and obtain scrolls with words. "But," Kingston concludes, "the empty scrolls had been the right ones all along" (*Tripmaster Monkey,* 42). This highly compressed version both captures the essence of the original and is tellingly altered. For one thing, she suppresses almost all indications that this is a religious quest: for her, the scrolls are not sacred. Moreover, she elides a basic hierarchy built into the Chinese story in which one culture possesses truths set in texts that the other must learn. These assumptions are challenged in the original, however, by the blank scriptures themselves. In Anthony C. Yu's translation of *Journey,* the Buddhists explain that the blank scriptures were initially selected in response to the pilgrims' failure to provide an "offering" or bribe to the monks who were to select their scriptures; when the pilgrims return and offer an alms bowl, they are rewarded with what they desire, scriptures with words. Amused rather than provoked, the Buddhist patriarchs comment that those people in the East (the Chinese) are "so stupid and blind" and "so foolish and unenlightened" that they will be unable to use or appreciate these "true, wordless scriptures," which are "just as good as those with words" (Wu, *Journey,* 4:391, 393). These lines, though seemingly aimed at the Chinese, really invite all readers to question their preferences for orthodox truths in fixed forms. Kingston, in essence, makes the same point more succinctly: "But the empty scrolls had been the right ones all along."

In other words, the blank scriptures embody the essence of the higher wisdom that scriptures are supposed to teach, the wisdom that recognizes that "the real form is that form which has no form." Hence, the Buddhist disciple must learn to distinguish outward forms from the essence of truth, which has no form or body in itself but can be outwardly "like ten thousand things" (Wu, *Journey,* 2:297). Not only must individual desires, status, and achievements be seen as ultimately insignificant to the whole of reality, but verbal texts, like individual bodies, must be understood as shells, outward forms of understanding rather than its essence. In this sense, to focus one's learning on individual texts that are isolated from the broader teaching or practice of a community may be seen as a clumsy, second-hand practice. This is why the blank texts are "the right ones" and why the Buddhists in the story treat the two sets of scrolls as readily fungible.

In the context of Kingston and Chin's debate about the use and authority of classical texts, Chin's search for an authentic heroic tradition, and broader debates about the construction, or deconstruction, of literary canons, the lighthearted Buddhists of *Journey* are distinctly refreshing. The Chinese pilgrims have traveled for many years and braved many dangers to bring home a body of sacred texts for the emperor's scholars to study. Whereas the three brothers of *Three Kingdoms* seek to found a new Chinese dynasty, the pilgrims are in effect commissioned to bring the founding texts that, presumably will influence the direction of Buddhism in China for all posterity. Yet the canon they receive is arbitrary, its final selection contingent upon a single alms bowl. If the pilgrims had offered a different gift, would they have been given a different set of scrolls, a different founding canon? And, if American-born writers choose to invoke stories from the Chinese classics as the foundation, or an enriching source, for a Chinese American literary tradition, how will we decide whose stories, whose choices and interpretations, are the "true" ones?

In book after book, Kingston inscribes the struggles of the artist, an outlaw interpreter, to challenge and transform institutionalized texts and orthodox readings of those texts, including, in *Tripmaster Monkey,* Frank

Chin's reading of Chinese literature as a heroic tradition that defines Chinese American experience in martial terms. In her writing, Kingston celebrates the transience of oral storytelling and the possibility of endless invention, endless variations; for her, variability and ambiguity are both enjoyable and edifying. The author is not an authority or a solo creator but a producer or director who gives voice and shape to a collective artistic effort, which in turn defines an interpretive community. The interaction between the artist and his other community is central to the creative process.

In 1970, Roland Barthes introduced the idea of the "writerly" text, a text that is perpetually being created by the reader, and hence vests writerly authority in the reader; its opposite is the "readerly" text, the "classic," well-made text whose predetermined meanings force the reader into a passive posture of readerly consumption. Wrote Barthes:

> Why is the writerly our value? Because the goal of literary work (of literature as work) is to make the reader no longer a consumer, but a producer of the text. Our literature is characterized by the pitiless divorce which the literary institution maintains between the producer of the text and its user, between its owner and its customer, between its author and its reader. This reader is thereby plunged into a kind of idleness . . . instead of functioning himself, instead of gaining access to the magic of the signifier, to the pleasure of writing, he is left with no more than the poor freedom either to accept or reject the text; reading is nothing more than a *referendum.* (*S/Z,* 4)

Kingston's hero, Wittman, is confounded by the story of the empty scrolls; her colleague, Chin, might not be, but he has clearly voiced his preference for the Chinese classics as readerly texts with foreclosed or self-evident meanings (even though his actual readings are more complex than his rhetoric might suggest). For Kingston, the ideal text is writerly, not readerly. The Chinese heroic tradition is a rich source, but it is hardly a ready-made medium for her ideas. The empty scrolls may symbolize her preference for a Chinese tradition whose greatest worth comes from its refusal of texts as authorities, its questioning the very aim of the scripture pilgrimage. The empty scrolls — no longer scriptures — overtly return writerly authority to the reader. For Kingston, a Chinese American feminist reading and re-inscribing the Chinese heroic tradition, they are the right ones.

Rethinking Asian American Bildung

I have argued that Asian American rescriptions of the bildungsroman serve to create new paradigms for the process of self-formation, which this literature conceives as a process of reconciling Americanization with ethnic self-definition. Whereas Anglo-American bildungsromane often use heterosexual courtship plots to symbolize the subject's moral progress and marriage as the trope for the subject's constitution as a citizen, Asian Americans displace this paradigm with other figures. In male narratives, the immigrant romance constitutes triangular narratives of desire in which white women signify the dream of Americanization while Asian women represent the men's ambivalent attitudes toward their home or ancestral cultures. In the absence of legitimizing recognition by Asian American or white fathers, Asian American sons may adopt the trope of self-fathering, seeking to claim Americanness by constituting themselves as literal and literary fathers, or they may seek to prove their Americanness by demonstrating their expertise in deploying the discourses of American democracy. These strategies, derived from existing critical standards privileging certain values and subjects as definitive of the American spirit while marginalizing others, provide a range of paradigms for modeling the formation of Asian American subjects after the paradigms for white male American literary heroism, paradigms inherently hostile to the construction of American subject formation in feminine terms.

In contrast to such male paradigms, the narrative strategies of Asian American women may be divided into critical commentary on male perspectives, female appropriation of such models, and the creation of uniquely feminine paradigms, as suggested by my analysis of the first Chinese American woman writer, Edith Maude Eaton, and a contemporary immigrant who claims North American immigration as her subject matter, the Indian writer Bharati Mukherjee. Eaton's work includes stories that implicitly criticize the triangular structure of the male immigrant romance as well as the racial and sexual politics of the *Madama Butterfly* story popularized during her lifetime. In her introduction of a mother-daughter version of the immigrant romance, Eaton both recasts herself as a struggling author-hero in the mold later described by Nina Baym and appropriated by Asian American males and introduces a fresh paradigm for future Asian American women writers. Her constructions of Chinese American women as bourgeois sentimental heroines work implicitly to counter white stereotypes that confound Chinese femininity with moral, intellectual, and economic inferiority such as the stereotypes of Chinese women as prostitutes or thick-skinned peasants. Mukherjee, too, works to rewrite the immigrant romance from a female perspective; to interrogate orientalist perceptions of Asian women as exotic, tractable others; and to reclaim for her Asian heroine the familiar signs of feminine subjectivity encoded in the bildungsroman's privileging of domestic womanhood.

The mixed critical reception of Mukherjee's novel reveals a crucial difference between English and American perspectives on self-formation.

Whereas English novels typically celebrate fidelity to one's origins as a crucial aspect of the subject's authenticity, Mukherjee's *Jasmine* follows many American precedents in celebrating the heroine's perpetual reinvention of herself as definitively American. (Similar metamorphoses are attempted or achieved, for instance, by such disparate American characters as Mark Twain's Duke and Dauphin, Kate Chopin's Edna Pontellier, Theodore Dreiser's Sister Carrie, and Ralph Ellison's Invisible Man.) But, while the departure from one's origins is often recognized as a necessary step in American bildung, in Asian American culture this departure carries strongly mixed connotations. When placed within this literature, numerous moments in *Jasmine* become clearly readable as criticizing American culture for requiring the denial or containment of the immigrant's past, particularly if that past includes victimization, criminality, exposure to American racism, or postcolonial memory. Jasmine survives, but she irritates with her willing and eager compliance with this requirement, which is symbolized by her shedding of past names and her prim disapproval of less favored immigrants and immigrant communities who seek to hold onto their pasts. She calls them "nostalgic" and "immured," as if racism and economic inequities could be dissolved by corrections in immigrants' attitudes. Through Jyoti/Jasmine/Jane's flawed suturing of her assimilable and unassimilable selves, the novel resonates with the themes of cultural extinction, abjection, and amnesia found in the works of writers from Eaton to Mura, themes that return us insistently to the problem of American amnesia about Asian American pasts.

It is this problem that links my discussions of Chinese American ethnicity with my analysis of Americanization narratives. If the *Aiiieeeee* editors' attacks on writers who "fake" Asian American culture (including Amy Tan and Maxine Hong Kingston) are recognized as a defining moment in the formation of Asian American culture, then the recovery, or more properly the construction, of Asian American pasts is at the very heart of this literature, and the argument for fluid parameters in this task needs to go beyond a conventional dichomotization between authenticity and poetic license or the labeling of texts as orientalist or politically correct. For this reason, I have revisited these issues in Amy Tan's most visible novel and in the ongoing debate about authorship and the Chinese literary tradition between Maxine Hong Kingston and Frank Chin.

I have argued that Tan's writing of the mother-daughter romance serves multiple ideological functions in her construction of Asian American ideology. While Tan's novel invokes Chinese history as a ground for Chinese American character formation and assimilation, it also obscures and ignores the very historical narratives (such as those of Chinese nationalism, modernization, and feminism) that would have explained the successful

Americanization of the Chinese mothers, who are instead placed amid a familiar cast of types (abusive husbands and mothers-in-law, pitiful wives and concubines, gossipy servants, refugees, soldiers, and peasant entrepreneurs) in the novel's Chinese scenes. Thus, the novel's construction of Asian American subjectivity as the basis for, and result of, mother-daughter bonding requires it to contain its engagement with Chinese historical narratives in ways that characteristically subordinate Chinese to American perceptions.

Is such a containment of Chinese history (or culture) necessarily evil, or even a necessary evil? In this chapter, I have described Chin's invention of the Chinese heroic tradition as just that—a creative, polemical gesture (reminiscent of the quixotic father quests conducted by his early play protagonists), a cultural opening, rather than an authoritative act of cultural retrieval to whose authority and fidelity others should defer. In casting Kingston's postmodernist revision of Chinese cultural history as both sympathetic and resistant to Chin's masculinization of Chinese American culture, I argue that Kingston's vision of Asian American culture as dialogic, inclusive, adaptive, and alive wins—by underwriting the more vibrant art—over Chin's rhetorical critical model of Asian American culture as pure, male, fixed, embattled, and dying. While Tan and Chin appear to gesture toward a classical Chinese past as a guarantor of present-day ethnic authenticity, Kingston boldly claims the Chinese opera in America as an *American* tradition ("This is the journey *in* the west"). Her fidelity to the Chinese *American* past makes explicit the difficulty for her, as an American, of attempting to speak of Chinese history and subjectivity, categories she has generally presented as mediated for her by American culture and parental and community informants. At the same time, her novel gestures toward the next moment in Asian American literature, a moment when Asian American subjects and their stories will be read as "American," when the histories now laboriously or didactically asserted will be gracefully integrated into a wider American consciousness, and when both literary traditions and American political arenas will be transformed to include both new and longtime subjects. At such a moment, Asian American stories that are not about identity, assimilation, exclusion, or internment—in a word, race—will be both accepted and understood, and the need to construct Asian American culture as a liminal site, a place of political resistance and critique, will be obsolete.

Coda: "What We Should Become, What We Were"

———

You were supposed to be a poet. You were supposed to tell us what we should become, what we were. I would have been a king, I would have been anything if you
had shown me how. It is you who have betrayed us. You betrayed yourself because
you became something else. — Vikram Chandra, *Red Earth and Pouring Rain*

Vikram Chandra's novel is not obviously an Asian American bildungsroman, but it traces the careers of three Anglo-Indian brothers who ultimately lose their way in life because, as men of mixed blood, they are
claimed by neither the Indians nor the British during India's struggles for
nationhood. Like the authors and protagonists of Asian American literature, they had thought their race would not matter, that as Anglo-Indians
they belonged in both worlds, only to find themselves claimed by neither
side. As the bard of his generation, Sanjay is charged by his brother with
failing to provide the necessary narratives that would have given them and
their kind a history of their own, envisioning them as subjects in their own
right.

In a far less grandiose way, the creators of Asian American literature take
up the call simply to say who they are, to make a place within the American national literature where their stories belong. I've described how Asian
American revisions of the bildungsroman have served in a general broadening of the idea of America and some sites where that work is still going
on. Many Asian American writers, however, are moving past the assimilation narratives I have described. The interracial couple who relish difference
without inequity in Kingston's *Tripmaster Monkey,* Cynthia Kadohata's rewriting of race as an unmentioned subtext rather than the primary concern
of characters in *The Floating World,* and Shawn Wong's casting of Asian

Americans as cultural mentors to each other and to whites in *American Knees* all signal the prospect of Asian American subjects' true interpellation into the nation and a corresponding broadening of the subjects about which one may write. Such recent publications raise the questions, which I also pose for myself: when will Asian Americans write as assimilated subjects, and when we do, what will it mean to write as an Asian American?

The moment I quote in Chandra's novel gives me pleasure, partly because it invokes a traditional explanation for the centrality of literature and history, an explanation I first heard from my father, a Chinese historian: that we can only know what we are to become by understanding what we have been. This is the claim that each cohort of Asian American writers has recognized as it has sought to depict its perceptions to a public of non–Asian American readers, the claim that links the projects of literature and history in this field, and that lends, as I've argued, a certain urgency to their and my shared projects. Indeed, Chandra's brothers don't distinguish between poetry and truth; they think the best poetry has something to say not only about identity but about power and their place in the larger world. For Sanjay's heroic, warrior brother, "I could have been a king" is not an idle lament.

Red Earth's poet-hero, Sanjay, is accused of betraying his brothers and himself because he has been false to his *art*. Frustrated with the political limitations of his poetry, he has renounced his art for power (literally, in a magical-realist bargain with Yama, the god of death), only to find that without understanding he can attain vengeance but not a new social order. Already dehumanized by his hatred, he is then literally transformed into a monkey. In this guise, he regains his humanity only through the healing and redemptive labor of literary narration, an act that enables him, at last, to understand and communicate the meaning of his life. For Sanjay, as for the Asian American writers I have studied and for those of us seeking to understand the full complexity of American identity, the development and scrutiny of our particular voices and stories are not an extravagance but a necessity for survival.[1] It is through such writing that we find not only what we were but what we should become.

Notes

Introduction: "A City of Words"

1 Maxine Hong Kingston, *The Woman Warrior: Memoirs of a Girlhood Among Ghosts* (1975; New York: Vintage–Random House, 1989); *China Men* (1980; New York: Vintage–Random House, 1989).

2 Chang-rae Lee, *Native Speaker* (New York: Riverhead, 1995).

3 The idea that cultural texts offer symbolic reconciliations of social contradictions is borrowed from Fredric Jameson, *The Political Unconscious: Narrative as a Socially Symbolic Act* (Ithaca: Cornell UP, 1981), 74–102.

4 Here Chang-rae Lee seems deliberately to rewrite Louis Althusser's reading of citizens as "subjects" created by the state. See Louis Althusser, "Ideology and Ideological State Apparatuses (Notes Towards an Investigation)," in *Lenin and Philosophy and Other Essays*, trans. Ben Brewster (New York: Monthly Review Press, 1971), 127–86, esp. 127. In the Marxist theorist's first example, the subject recognizes the state's authority over him by responding to the "hailing" of the policeman. Lee's closing conveys his recognition that this process is accomplished more sweetly and pervasively through the school system — which Althusser would describe as an ideological state apparatus.

5 Virginia Woolf, *A Room of One's Own* (New York: Harcourt Brace Jovanovich, 1957).

6 Christine So, "Delivering the Punch Line: Racial Combat as Comedy in Gus Lee's *China Boy*." *MELUS* 21, no. 4 (winter 1996): 143.

7 According to Frank Chin, Daniel Okimoto was the first Asian American sociologist to apply the term *dual personality* to describe Asian American identity issues. My reference is to this Asian American context. See Frank Chin, "Come All Ye Asian American Writers, the Real and the Fake," in *The Big Aiiieeeee! An Anthology of Chinese American and Japanese American Literature,* ed. Jeffrey Paul Chan et al. (New York: Meridian-Penguin, 1991), 51. The dual personality model may be contrasted with two similar terms, *double consciousness* (W. E. B. Du Bois, *The Souls of Black Folk: W. E. B. Du Bois, Writings* [New York: Library of America, 1986], 357–547) and *marginal man* (Everett V. Stonequist, *The Marginal Man: A Study in Personality and Culture Conflict* [1937; New York: Russell and Russell, 1961]; Robert E. Park, *Race and Culture* [New York: Free Press, 1950], 345–92).

8   Because I believe that pan-Asian ethnicity is at times an appropriate and strategically
    useful concept, but also that specific subcultures and histories need to be examined in
    their own right before broader paradigms are imposed upon them, my two final chap-
    ters focus solely on constructions of Chinese Americans. My choice of this group is due
    to several factors. First, Chinese Americans have the oldest and arguably most significant
    presence in the mainstream American imagination of the various Asian American groups.
    Second, there is a strongly developed primary and critical literature by and about Chinese
    Americans. Finally, because I myself am Chinese American, I am most invested in under-
    standing discursive representations of this particular ethnicity. However, my intent is not
    to suggest that Chinese American texts can substitute for those of other Asian American
    ethnicities but rather to argue, by examining specific rhetorical moves made by Chinese
    American authors to construct their ethnicity, that any American ethnic subjectivity is the
    product of such conscious discursive efforts rather than a "natural" or preexisting "real"
    category that can be transparently and neutrally described.

9   Robert E. Park and Ernest W. Burgess, *Introduction to the Science of Sociology* (Chicago:
    U of Chicago P, 1921); Stow Persons, *Ethnic Studies at Chicago, 1905-45* (Urbana: U of
    Illinois P, 1987), 60–97.

10 Milton Gordon contrasts the melting pot connotation of mutual transformation, or amal-
    gamation, with Anglo-conformity as models for assimilation, but he acknowledges that
    the metallic metaphor has been linked with both ideas. He traces amalgamation imagery
    through Israel Zangwill's 1909 play *The Melting Pot*, Fredrick Jackson Turner, and Ralph
    Waldo Emerson back to J. Hector St. John Crevecoeur, who uses it to describe America's
    distinctive character. Eileen H. Tamura notes this usage but emphasizes the melting pot's
    association with the ideal of Anglo-conformity, which I believe is the dominant current
    connotation (*Americanization, Acculturation, and Ethnic Identity: The Nisei Generation in
    Hawaii* [Urbana: U of Illinois P, 1994], 49–50). See Milton Gordon, *Assimilation in Ameri-
    can Life: The Role of Race, Religion, and National Origins* (New York: Oxford UP, 1964),
    115–22. On melting pots in these and other cultural texts, see Werner Sollors, *Beyond Eth-
    nicity: Consent and Descent in American Culture* (New York: Oxford UP, 1986), 66–102.

11 Michael Omi and Howard Winant, *Racial Formation in the United States: From the 1960s
    to the 1980s* (New York: Routledge, 1986), 17.

12 Gordon, *Assimilation*, 68–78. The other variables are marital assimilation/amalgamation
    (large-scale intermarriage), identificational assimilation (identifying exclusively with the
    host society), attitude receptional assimilation (absence of prejudice), behavior recep-
    tional assimilation (absence of discrimination), and civic assimilation (absence of value
    and power conflict). Is it a sign of ethnicity school optimism that Gordon, writing in 1964,
    thought blacks had achieved "civic assimilation" (76)?

13 Gordon's policy recommendations, however, expressed ambivalence about government
    remedies for racial discrimination, advocating "desegregation" (in public facilities and in
    the government) but resisting government enforcement of "integration" on the level of
    primary group relationships and organizational affiliations. For instance, he inveighed
    against constraining employers' preferences through affirmative action or racial quotas
    or seeking to eliminate de facto segregation (ibid., 245–51).

14 Horace M. Kallen, *Culture and Democracy in the United States* (1924; New York: Arno,
    1970). On ethnic persistence and evolution, see Stephen S. Fugita and David J. O'Brien,
    Japanese American Ethnicity: The Persistence of Community (Seattle: U of Washington P,
    1991), 14–28; Tamura, *Americanization*, 49–52; and Sollors, *Ethnicity*, 20–39. My reading
    of Maxine Hong Kingston suggests how essential the idea of cultural evolution is to the
    continued vitality of an emerging Asian American literary culture.

15 See, for instance, Nathan Glazer and Daniel P. Moynihan's discussion of "ethnic group norms" in their introduction to Nathan Glazer and Daniel P. Moynihan, eds., *Ethnicity: Theory and Experience* (Cambridge: Harvard UP, 1975), 7, qtd. in Omi and Winant, *Formation*, 22.

16 Edward W. Said coined the term *orientalism* to describe the othering of nonwhite peoples as a justification for their colonial subjugation in *Orientalism* (New York: Random House, 1979); Lisa Lowe argues for the scrutiny of diverse orientalisms in *Critical Terrains: French and British Orientalisms* (Ithaca: Cornell UP, 1991). For arguments linking anti-Asian racism in America with European orientalism(s) and discrimination against other races, see Gary Y. Okihiro, *Margins and Mainstreams: Asians in American History and Culture* (Seattle: U of Washington P, 1994), 3–63, 118–47; and Ronald Takaki, *Iron Cages: Race and Culture in Nineteenth Century America* (New York: Oxford UP, 1990). Literary studies supporting or developing this thesis include Elaine H. Kim, *Asian American Literature: An Introduction to the Writings and Their Social Context* (Philadelphia: Temple UP, 1982); James S. Moy, *Marginal Sights: Staging the Chinese in America* (Iowa City: U of Iowa P, 1993); Sau-ling Cynthia Wong, *Reading Asian American Literature: From Necessity to Extravagance* (Princeton: Princeton UP, 1993), esp. 1–17; and E. San Juan Jr., *Racial Formations/Critical Transformations: Articulations of Power in Ethnic and Racial Studies in the United States* (Atlantic Highlands, N.J.: Humanities Press, 1992). Wong cogently demonstrates that Asian American literature, though ethnically heterogeneous, is united by a common group of tropes and themes, concerns that become evident when Asian American literary texts are read intertextually and with knowledge of the various ethnic cultures and the common history of Asian Americans.

17 For concise analyses and a chronology, see Sucheng Chan, *Asian Americans: An Interpretive History* (Boston: Twayne, 1991), esp. 45–62, 81–102, and 192–99; and Lisa Lowe, *Immigrant Acts: On Asian American Cultural Politics* (Durham: Duke UP, 1996), 1–36.

18 In *Acts*, Lisa Lowe summarizes the thesis of this argument: "Though Congress never enacted a law that specifically named 'Asians' or 'Orientals' as an Asiatic racial category, legal theorist Neil Gotanda has argued that the sequence of laws in 1882, 1917, 1924, and 1934 that excluded immigrants from China, Japan, India, and the Philippines, combined with the series of repeal acts overturning these exclusions, construct a common racial categorization for Asians that depended on consistently racializing each national-origin group as 'nonwhite.' . . . Through the [subsequent] enfranchisement of specific Asian ethnic groups as *exceptions* to the whites-only classification, the status of Asians as *nonwhite* is legally restated and reestablished" (19–20). See also Neil Gotanda, "Towards Repeal of Asian Exclusion . . ." in *Asian Americans in Congress: A Documentary History*, ed. Hyung Chan Kim (Westport, Conn.: Greenwood, 1995), 309–28; and "A Critique of 'Our Constitution Is Colorblind.'" *Stanford Law Review* 44, no. 1 (November 1991): 1–68.

19 Vincent Chin was a Chinese American draftsman unknown to the murderers, Ronald Ebens and Michael Nitz. The murderers' unemployment could be explained as a result of structural adjustments following years of mismanagement by the American auto industry, but many Americans blamed the layoffs on Japanese competition. Chin's murder must have been viewed sympathetically by the judge, who sentenced the confessed killers to only three years' probation and a fine of three thousand dollars plus court fees. This incident, and contemporary patterns of anti-Asian violence, are analyzed by Sucheng Chan in *Asian Americans* (176–79). The Los Angeles riots were sparked by the acquittal of police officers whose beating of Rodney King, an unarmed black man, had been documented on videotape. Although these particular events (the beating and the acquittal) were white-on-black injustices, the multiracial mob turned their rage heavily against

Korean businesses. For analyses of the "racial formations" contributing to and resulting from the event, see Lowe, *Acts,* 84–96; Bruce Cumings, *Korea's Place in the Sun: A Modern History* (New York: Norton, 1997), 447–50; and *Sa-I-Gu,* prod. Christine Choy, Elaine Kim, and Dai Sil Kim-Gibson, Cross Current Media, 1993, video.

20 Numerous cultural critics have argued for the underlying utility to the state of liberal and literary education in producing amenable citizens and workers, just as Althusser describes. Gauri Viswanathan, for instance, has found that the study of English as a discipline was invented by colonial administrators in India "for the ideological pacification and reformation of a potentially rebellious Indian population," to borrow Edward W. Said's concise formulation. Her finding resonates with historian Gary Y. Okihiro's scathing account of the segregated school system in interwar Hawaii, which sought to "Americanize" second-generation Japanese Americans by molding nonwhite pupils into docile and diligent workers while training whites for leadership, and suggests a fitting parallel between English colonialism and the American version practiced in Hawaii, where racist education and employment practices were thinly veiled by a rhetoric of inclusion. In "The Rise of English," in Terry Eagleton, *Literary Theory: An Introduction* (Minneapolis: U of Minnesota P, 1983), the Marxist critic Terry Eagleton records that formal literary study was introduced into higher education in England as a means of offering a transcendent value system, more accessible to working-class pupils and women (who were likewise shut out of elite schooling) than that staple of elite male training, the classics. Congruent with Benedict Anderson's observation that the idea of the nation replaced religion as a transcendent concept offering meaning and continuity in people's imaginations, Eagleton finds that the creation of a national literature served to represent an ideal of national identity and culture with which all were encouraged to identify, with the effect of reducing some pupils' appetites for political activism while fueling others to carry on the work of empire building "secure in a sense of their national identity, and able to display that cultural superiority to the envying colonial peoples" (Eagleton, 22–39). This point, made succinctly in Eagleton's essay, is developed in more depth by Edward W. Said in *Culture and Imperialism,* as well as by Anderson. The latter describes the predicament of colonial bureaucrats, schooled to identify with and serve the colonizing culture but ultimately shut out from its ruling classes. As an example, he recites the (1832) grievance of the Indian magistrate Bipin Chandra Pal, who finds himself and his fellow colonial jurists forever relegated to subordinate positions in the British Empire, despite consciously alienating themselves from their own communities in order to become more British (Benedict Anderson, *Imagined Communities: Reflections on the Origin and Spread of Nationalism,* rev. ed. [London: Verso, 1991], 92–93).

See also Gauri Viswanathan, *Masks of Conquest: Literary Study and British Rule in India* (New York, Columbia UP, 1989); Edward W. Said, *Culture and Imperialism* (New York: Vintage, 1993), 12; Gary Y. Okihiro, *Cane Fires: The Anti-Japanese Movement in Hawaii, 1865–1945* (Philadelphia: Temple UP, 1991), 129–62; and Terry Eagleton, *Literary Theory,* 17–53.

21 Such a view is voiced, for instance, by Paul Lauter in a 1984 article commemorating the progress of the Modern Language Association (MLA), the nation's largest organization of postsecondary instructors of language and literature. Commissioned to write about the impact of society on this profession over the previous twenty-five years, Lauter describes scholars of American literature in the 1920s (when it was a new field struggling for academic respectability) as claiming that their subject was "vital to understanding the character of an emerging world power" (17). Moreover, he says that the MLA's executive secretary portrayed the profession in 1958 as "playing a critical role in preparing

Americans to speak, think, and work effectively in other languages and cultures and thus enabling them to carry out the international roles of the United States" (17). Additional tasks were to prepare students "for participation in a complex democratic society" and to transmit "the cultural heritage upon which that society is founded" (17). Without endorsing the imperialist mission implied by his predecessor of 1958, Lauter reaffirms the belief that literary study "can be significant in shaping consciousness and even behavior and, more fundamentally, that the importance of what we do derives from the social values we help to foster" and invokes his own experience of teaching Richard Wright to young black students in Mississippi in the 1960s (as part of his work in the civil rights movement) and Frederick Douglass's account of the moment when he identifies literacy and critical thinking as "the pathway from slavery to freedom" (19). For Douglass, Lauter's students, and Lauter himself, the shared presumption is that literary training yields access to others' accounts, not only of the mainstream's preeminence or right to rule but of the struggles of individuals to survive in, or resist, oppressive public narratives. The article, in short, explains why we need to reconstruct the American literary canon. See Paul Lauter, "Society and the Profession, 1958–83," in *Canons and Contexts* (New York: Oxford UP, 1991), 3–21 (revision of an article published in *PMLA* 99 [May 1984]: 414–26).

22 Priscilla Wald, *Constituting Americans: Cultural Anxiety and Narrative Form* (Durham: Duke UP, 1995), 4.

23 Underlying Wald's method is a poststructuralist (Lacanian) model of subject formation. This model describes the subject as defined and necessarily divided by his entry into language. To recognize himself as a subject, a young child must learn not only to differentiate "I" from "you," but also to recognize himself in a range of seemingly contradictory subject positions ("he" or "she," "the baby," and so on) and to construct his or her subjectivity from this matrix of subject positions. Moreover, in learning to speak and formulate desires into verbal demands, a child renounces (represses) that which cannot be spoken, a process that divides the self and creates the unconscious. Thus, the self's division is postulated as the prerequisite for communication and socialization. In addition, subjectivity is constructed across a range of discourses in which the subject participates. These discourses construct the Althusserian subject "in ideology" while also creating a division within. In seeking to reconcile these contradictions, even as discursive social formations continually shift, the subject is perpetually under construction, and this state of being always in process leaves room for change. See Catherine Belsey, "Constructing the Subject: Deconstructing the Text," in *Feminist Criticism and Social Change: Sex, Class, and Race in Literature and Culture,* ed. Judith Newton and Deborah Rosenfelt (New York: Methuen, 1985), 45–64, esp. 47–50.

24 See, for instance, Takaki, *Cages,* 214–87; and Omi and Winant, *Formation.* Takaki demonstrates that blacks, Indians, Mexicans, and Asians served different rhetorical functions in nineteenth-century accounts that construct the "lovely white" as definitive of Americanness, while Omi and Winant examine the marking of Americans by race and class (racialization) for political purposes in recent decades. In addition to race-based exclusions from immigration and citizenship (see n. 18), Takaki shows that the Chinese were excluded from testifying in court by being classed as "nonwhites" and hence were analogous to the explicitly excluded races of blacks, mulattoes, and Indians (220).

25 Ernest Renan argues that the crucial consent of a people to live as a nation is founded on an agreement to forget the violence that generally occurs at the founding of a nation: "Forgetting, I would even go so far as to say historical error, is a crucial factor in the creation of a nation, which is why progress in historical studies often constitutes a danger for [the principle of] nationality. Indeed, historical enquiry brings to light deeds of

violence which took place at the origin of all political formations, even of those whose consequences have been altogether beneficial. Unity is always effected by means of brutality..." ("What Is a Nation?" trans. Martin Thom, in *Nation and Narration*, ed. Homi K. Bhabha [New York: Routledge, 1990], 8–22, esp. 11).

Homi Bhabha reformulates Renan's "consent" as "an obligation to forget" that "performs the problematic totalization of the national will." In his words: "To be obliged to forget—in the construction of the national present—is not a question of historical memory; it is the construction of a discourse on society that *performs* the problematic totalization of the national will. ... Being obliged to forget becomes the basis for remembering the nation, peopling it anew, imagining the possibility of other contending and liberating forms of cultural identification" ("DissemiNation: Time, Narrative, and the Margins of the Modern Nation," in Bhabha, *Nation*, 291–322, esp. 311). The discussion of literary assimilation that follows is indebted to these passages.

26 See Julia Kristeva, *Powers of Horror: An Essay on Abjection*, trans. Leon S. Roudiez (1980; New York: Columbia UP, 1982); Judith Butler, *Bodies That Matter: On the Discursive Limits of "Sex"* (New York: Routledge, 1993); and Anne McClintock, *Imperial Leather: Race, Gender and Sexuality in the Colonial Contest* (New York: Routledge, 1995).

27 Ethnographic documents may be a misnomer, as I realize that ethnographers can be highly self-conscious about their interpretation of their source materials. I have in mind literal readings of Asian American literary texts as transparent factual accounts. Such readings obscure Asian American cultural sophistication by treating literary texts as "artless" reminiscences rather than products of creative writers' labor, skill, and invention.

28 Lowe, *Acts*, 98.

29 James Hardin, introduction to *Reflection and Action: Essays on the Bildungsroman* (Columbia: U of South Carolina P, 1991), ix–xxvii. For other descriptions of this genre and its alter ego, the *kunstlerroman*, see Jeffrey L. Sammons, "The Bildungsroman for Nonspecialists: An Attempt at a Clarification," in Hardin, *Reflection*, 26–45; Marianne Hirsch, "The Novel of Formation as Genre: Between Great Expectations and Lost Illusions," *Genre* 12, no. 3 (fall 1979): 293–12; Franco Moretti, *The Way of the World: The Bildungsroman in European Culture* (London: Verso–New Left, 1987); and Maurice Beebe, *Ivory Towers and Sacred Founts: The Artist as Hero in Fiction from Goethe to Joyce* (New York: New York UP, 1964).

On novels, nations, and narrative, see Bhabha, "DissemiNation"; Bhabha, *Nation*; Timothy Brennan, "The National Longing for Form," in Bhabha, *Nation*, 44–70; Peter Brooks, *Reading for the Plot: Design and Intention in Narrative* (New York: Knopf, 1984); Jameson, *Unconscious;* and Ian Watt, *The Rise of the Novel: Studies in Defoe, Richardson, and Fielding* (Berkeley: U of California P, 1959). For feminist studies in these categories, see note 40.

On ethnic American bildung, the following works have been particularly useful: William Q. Boelhower, "The Immigrant Novel as Genre," *MELUS* 8, no. 1 (spring 1981): 3–13; William Boelhower, "The Brave New World of Immigrant Autobiography," *MELUS* 9, no. 2 (summer 1982): 5–24; William Boelhower, "Ethnic Trilogies: A Genealogical and Generational Poetics," in Sollors, *Ethnicity*, 5–24; King-kok Cheung, *Articulate Silences: Hisaye Yamamoto, Maxine Hong Kingston, Joy Kogawa* (Ithaca: Cornell UP, 1993); Mary Dearborn, *Pocohantas's Daughters: Gender and Ethnicity in American Culture* (New York: Oxford UP, 1986); Thomas J. Ferraro, *Ethnic Passages: Literary Immigrants in Twentieth-Century America* (Chicago: U of Chicago P, 1993); Elaine H. Kim, *Asian American Literature: An Introduction to the Writings and Their Social Context* (Philadelphia: Temple UP, 1982); Amy Ling, *Between Worlds: Women Writers of Chinese Ancestry* (New York: Pergamon, 1990); Stephen H. Sumida, *And the View From the Shore: Literary Traditions of*

Hawai'i (Seattle: U of Washington P, 1991); Bonnie TuSmith, *All My Relatives: Community in Contemporary Ethnic American Literatures* (Ann Arbor: U of Michigan P, 1994); and Sau-ling Cynthia Wong, *Reading Asian American Literature: From Necessity to Extravagance* (Princeton: Princeton UP, 1993).

30 Lukács is arguably best known for his study of the realist novel's representations of historical processes, *The Historical Novel,* trans. Hannah Mitchell and Stanley Mitchell (1962; Lincoln: U of Nebraska P, 1983). The classic novel is described by Roland Barthes as a text in which conflicting signifying codes are clearly hierarchized so that it is clear to the reader which levels of meaning to pay more attention to and how he or she must position himself or herself to enjoy the most coherent reading (*S/Z: An Essay,* trans. Richard Miller [1970; New York: Hill and Wang, 1974]).

31 These theses appear in Michael Peled Ginsburg, "Truth and Persuasion: The Language of Realism and of Ideology in *Oliver Twist,*" *Novel: A Forum on Fiction* 20, no. 3 (spring 1987): 220–36; Said, *Culture,* 62–80; and McClintock, *Leather.* In addition, Catherine Belsey uses the Sherlock Holmes stories to foreground realist fiction's affinities toward rationalism and scientific positivism and the failures of such discourses to account for or adequately represent sexuality, passion, and female subjectivities ("Constructing," 58–63). Finally, Toni Morrison and others have argued that in the United States the presence and contribution of blacks form an unacknowledged but essential frame of reference in a literature that has until recently placed white experience at its center. See *Playing in the Dark: Whiteness and the Literary Imagination* (New York: Vintage-Random House, 1993).

32 See Nancy Armstrong, *Desire and Domestic Fiction: A Political History of the Novel* (New York: Oxford UP, 1987), 108–34. The radical nature of the shift may be sensed through the seeming absurdity of the plot: after imprisoning Pamela, his fifteen-year-old serving maid, asserting at great length his right to her body, and seizing her in her bed, Mr. B. unexpectedly refrains from raping her; henceforth, he plots to read her diaries (Samuel Richardson, *Pamela, or Virtue Rewarded* [1740; New York: Norton, 1958], 212–17). If this marks a shift from external to internal surveillance, it also marks the replacement of external coercion and command by an intersubjective relationship that culminates in marriage.

33 Jane P. Tompkins's defense of the sentimental novel in America both anticipates Armstrong's account of the "rise" of the domestic woman and argues that this genre established women as the exemplary national subjects. Citing the best-selling, deeply influential *Uncle Tom's Cabin* as the premiere example of its genre, Tompkins asserts: "It is the *summa theologica* of nineteenth-century America's religion of domesticity, a brilliant redaction of the culture's favorite story about itself: the story of salvation through motherly love. Out of the ideological materials they had at their disposal, the sentimental novelists elaborated a myth that gave women the central position of power and authority in the culture" ("Sentimental Power: *Uncle Tom's Cabin* and the Politics of Literary History" [1978], in *Feminist Criticism: Essays on Women, Literature, and Theory,* ed. Elaine Showalter [New York: Pantheon, 1985], 81–104). See also Jane P. Tompkins, *Sensational Designs: The Cultural Work of American Fiction, 1790–1860* (New York: Oxford UP, 1985).

34 I have been tracing a lineage of the subject of Anglo-American bildungsroman as an articulate, sensitive, ethical, middle-class subject through the arguments of Watt, Armstrong, Tompkins, and Rachel Blau DuPlessis (*Writing beyond the Ending: Narrative Strategies of Twentieth Century Women Writers* [Bloomington: Indiana UP, 1985]). These critics focus on the female bildungsroman. In England, the preeminent practitioners of the male bildungsroman at midcentury, Charles Dickens and William Makepeace Thackeray, registered both discomfort with and loyalty to the genre's bourgeois domestic values;

the domestic woman does hold as the exemplary subject for the whole culture's middle-brow fiction. In America, alternate lineages defining male bildung as an antidomestic process, and female bildung as a more or less domestic one, came to be canonized, though Gillian Brown takes the construction of these competing canons as the basis for a discussion of their common grounds (Lauter, *Canons,* 22–47; Nina Baym, "Melodramas of Beset Manhood: How Theories of American Fiction Exclude Women Authors," in Elaine Showalter, ed., *The New Feminist Criticism: Essays on Women, Literature, and Theory* [New York: Pantheon–Random House, 1985], 63–80; Gillian Brown, *Domestic Individualism: Imagining Self in Nineteenth Century America* [Berkeley: U of California P, 1990]). Later I describe the responses of Frank Chin, David Mura, and Maxine Hong Kingston to the male lineage.

35 Of course, some Asian American writers prefer to challenge or expose the codes of the classic realist novel, combining modernist or postmodernist techniques with the specific, politically self-conscious project of challenging the realist novel's hegemonic construction of a unified national consciousness. Critical readings emphasizing this metafictional aspect of Asian American literary texts appear, for instance, in Linda Hutcheon's work on historiographic metafiction (see *A Poetics of Postmodernism: History, Theory, Fiction* [London: Routledge, 1988] and *The Politics of Postmodernism* [London: Routledge, 1989]. See also Elaine H. Kim and Norma Alarcon, eds., *Writing Self, Writing Nation* (Berkeley: Third Woman Press, 1994); Lowe, *Acts;* and E. San Juan Jr., introduction to Carlos Bulosan, *On Becoming Filipino: Selected Writings of Carlos Bulosan,* ed. E. San Juan Jr. (Philadelphia: Temple UP, 1995), 1–44, though this is not an exhaustive list. A few literary texts analyzed in this way include Bulosan's *America,* Kingston's *China Men* and *The Woman Warrior,* Joy Kogawa's *Obasan,* Jessica Hagedorn's *Dogeaters,* and Theresa Cha's *Dictée.* Much more work with metafictional and other literary genres needs to be done. In reading Asian American literary texts as bildungsromane that assume or manipulate realist fictional conventions, I do not mean to suggest that ethnic writers are limited to conventional forms but rather to emphasize that knowledge of this genre informs their choices as authors. My personal choice to emphasize realist modes of writing and reading these texts is meant to work in dialogue with the antirealist approaches of other critics in the field.

36 See Charlotte Brontë, *Shirley* (Oxford: Oxford UP, 1979); or Elizabeth Gaskell, *North and South* (New York: Penguin, 1970).

37 See Renny Christopher, *The Viet Nam War/The American War: Images and Representations in Euro-American and Vietnamese Exile Narratives* (Amherst: U of Massachusetts P, 1995), for more on such texts.

38 Consider, for instance, the enormous success and critical attention accorded Maxine Hong Kingston's *The Woman Warrior* versus the tepid critical response to her subsequent books *China Men* and *Tripmaster Monkey: His Fake Book* (New York: Vintage–Random House, 1989). The first book focuses most closely on the bildung of a single person, the narrator, while the others are more diffuse; the theme of racism is, in my view, more central to the latter two books.

39 Several birth dates appear in the Bulosan critical literature, including 1911, 1913, and 1914; it seems that Bulosan himself was an inconsistent source. See Bulosan, 3, 215, and Paul Lauter, gen. ed., *The Heath Anthology of American Literature,* 3d ed. (Boston: Houghton Mifflin, 1998), 2124.

40 The following summary is indebted to Elizabeth Abel, Marianne Hirsch, and Elizabeth Langland, eds., *The Voyage In: Fictions of Female Development* (Hanover: UP of New England, 1983), 12–19, for their brisk overview of relevant thematic and formal innovations.

In addition, my work is informed by Armstrong, *Desire;* DuPlessis, *Writing;* Sandra M. Gilbert and Susan Gubar, *The Madwoman in the Attic: The Woman Writer and the Nine-teenth-Century Imagination* (New Haven: Yale UP, 1984); Marianne Hirsch, *The Mother/Daughter Plot: Narrative, Psychoanalysis, Feminism* (Bloomington: Indiana UP, 1989); Tompkins, *Designs;* and additional sources cited in Laura Sue Fuderer, *The Female Bil-dungsroman in English: An Annotated Bibliography of Criticism* (New York: Modern Language Association, 1990).

41 On Asian and Western definitions of self and resulting differences in psychology, see Alan Roland, *Cultural Pluralism and Psychoanalysis: The Asian and North American Experience* (New York: Routledge, 1996), esp. 1–20.

42 For a study of this theme in the literatures of four ethnic groups, see TuSmith, *Relatives.* I do not wish to suggest that Asian cultures are inimical to individual autonomy and de-velopment, or that American culture is hostile to family, community, and connection. Rather, I suggest that this formulation is useful but must also be compared to claims that other ethnic Americans of both genders, as well as women in general, also define them-selves intersubjectively. However, the appearance of similar themes and literary forms in female and Asian American narratives of formation suggests that Asian American efforts to reconcile and inhabit contradictory discourses of self-definition strongly resemble the work done by women in reconciling the discourse of autonomy and self-development and the discourse of femininity.

43 The centrality of marriage as a signifier for subject formation in the genre serves also to inscribe heterosexuality as a narrative norm, a norm generally accepted by the authors I will discuss.

44 In their literary studies of American ethnicity and race, Werner Sollors and Mary Dear-born cite stories in which white romantic partners function both as symbols for America and as agents for (white, Jewish) ethnic subjects' Americanization. These studies do not foreground a distinction between ethnicity and race, but by comparing these cases with the white-black and white-Indian love stories they describe one can conclude that the more tragic outcomes dominating the *interracial* stories imply the culture's greater re-sistance to the full integration of subjects perceived as racial others. See Sollors, *Beyond Ethnicity;* and Dearborn, *Daughters.*

45 The tasks undertaken by Eaton anticipate, and may be compared to, Maxine Hong Kings-ton's "courageous daughtering," described in Thomas J. Ferraro, "Changing the Rituals: Courageous Daughtering and the Mystique of the Woman Warrior," in *Passages,* 154–90.

46 Chin's reply, in his utopian bildungsroman *Donald Duk* (Minneapolis: Coffee House Press, 1991), seems to signify concurrence with Kingston's postmodernist use of Chinese texts, but, tellingly, it reinscribes the centrality of the male author-hero and the margin-ality of women in his vision of Asian America.

1 America in the Heart

1 Younghill Kang, *East Goes West: The Making of an Oriental Yankee* (New York: Scribners, 1937); Daniel Okimoto, *An American in Disguise* (New York: Walter-Weatherhill, 1971).

2 Annette Kolodny, *The Lay of the Land: Metaphor as Experience and History in American Life and Letters* (Chapel Hill: U of North Carolina P, 1975).

3 According to Sucheng Chan, the Constitution stated that only "free white persons" could be naturalized. In 1870, the privilege was extended to "aliens of African nativity and to persons of African descent." The 1878 case *In re Ah Yup* and the 1882 law singling out Chi-nese for immigration exclusion closed remaining loopholes allowing Chinese to be natu-

ralized. *In Re Saito* (1894) held that Japanese were ineligible; *In re Knight* (1909) barred a person of partly Japanese, partly Chinese, and half English descent; *Takao Ozawa v. United States* (1922) decisively barred Japanese naturalization on the basis of racial origins; Koreans were barred in two state cases; and Asian Indians and Filipinos received inconsistent rulings due to their ambiguous racial categorization. But in *United States v. Bhugat Singh Thind* (1923) the U.S. Supreme Court ruled that Thind, though already naturalized, could be stripped of his citizenship because Asian Indians, albeit "Aryan," were not "white" enough to be naturalized (*Asian Americans: An Interpretive History* [Boston: Twayne, 1991], 47, 92–94).

4 Sucheng Chan emphasizes the strictness of restrictions against Chinese women and its effects on the Chinese in America. Between 1876 and 1882, Chan notes, more than 100,000 Chinese men entered the United States but only 1,340 Chinese women. The male/female ratio reached its nadir in 1890, fifteen years after passage of the Page Law restricting female immigration to twenty-seven to one. Japanese, Koreans, Filipinos, and Asian Indians also faced sexual segregation to differing degrees. Japanese picture brides (women emigrating to the United States to join husbands they had not met but with whom they had exchanged pictures and had legally married before emigrating) could enter the United States until 1920, and Korean picture brides until 1924, resulting in communities with more families in which the women's labor helped to establish the immigrants economically. Filipinos were more likely to be single men; Chan records a mainland sex ratio of nineteen to one for this group in 1920. Fewer than a dozen Asian Indian women entered the United States before World War II, but several hundred Asian Indian men married Mexican women in Southern California.

5 It appears that thirty-eight states had antimiscegenation laws at some point, but it is unclear which states applied such laws to Asians desiring to marry non-Asians. Chan suggests that the interpretation of such laws was a local, and therefore inconsistent, matter, but the fact that such laws were applied to Asians in California is significant due to the high concentration of Asians in that state.

6 If the American wife was of Asian descent, she could not regain her citizenship, even if widowed or divorced, from 1922 through 1931. American women of other races were not excluded to this degree.

7 Kang, *East Goes West.*

8 Carlos Bulosan, *America Is in the Heart: A Personal History* (1946; Seattle: U of Washington P, 1973). Elaine H. Kim notes that Bulosan's background is slightly different from that of his protagonist. "The son of a small farmer in central Luzon, Bulosan had almost completed secondary school in the Philippines" before he emigrated; he "had already shown interest and ability in writing in high school, where he worked on the school literary journal" (*Literature*, 46–47).

9 The Immigration Act of 1924 barred "aliens ineligible to citizenship," a category that described most Asian immigrants. Filipinos, who were "wards" or "nationals," were barred on other grounds. Korean emigration had already been largely curbed by the Japanese except for an estimated five hundred nationalists who entered the United States between 1910 and 1924, some of whom petitioned to enter as political refugees. This "trickle" of immigration ended in 1924. See Sucheng Chan, *Asian Americans*, 54–57.

10 On the occupation, see Cumings, *Korea's Place*, 139–84.

11 This also seems to be an indirect reference to Joyce's *Ulysses* (New York: Modern Library, 1934), an appropriate literary antecedent for Kang's novel of racial marginality and homelessness in a modern urban landscape. Joyce's novel, published after a decade-long struggle with obscenity charges, preceded Kang's book in New York by just a few years and

Joyce is one of numerous modernist writers cited in Kang's novel. Kang's representation of Han as an isolated modern but also a specifically racialized person may be compared and contrasted with Kingston's injection of these themes into a *Ulysses*-like narrative structure self-consciously revised to focus on the Chinese American love of community in *Tripmaster Monkey*. My point is not that citing Western classics increases ethnic texts' literary merit but that Asian American writers share the project of transforming the Anglo-American literary tradition.

12   This may be compared with Maxine Hong Kingston's enchantment myth, "The Ghost-mate," which King-kok Cheung has read as a commentary on America's elusive promises to the Chinese male sojourners. See Kingston, *China Men;* and Cheung, *Silences.* Kingston, like Kang, is known for adapting both Western and Eastern sources.

13   See Stuart Creighton Miller, *The Unwelcome Immigrant: The American Image of the Chinese, 1785–1882* (Berkeley: U of California P, 1969), 198.

14   The book is subtitled "A Personal History" but is usually read as a fictionalized one. Carey McWilliams thinks that Bulosan includes others' experiences as those of "Carlos" (Bulosan, *America,* vii). Marilyn Alquizola identifies Carlos as a fictive narrator whose experiences are based on those of the author and other Filipinos in America ("The Fictive Narrator of *America Is in the Heart,*" in *Frontiers of Asian American Studies,* ed. Gail M. Nomura et al. [Pullman: Washington State UP, 1989]: 211–17); and E. San Juan Jr. calls the book a "novelistic synthesis of Filipino lives" and identifies "Allos, the youthful protagonist" as "Bulosan's persona" (Introduction, 9–10).

15   Shawn Wong, *Asian American Literature* (New York: HarperCollins, 1996) 103.

16   For more on Bulosan's relations with white women, see Susan Evangelista, *Carlos Bulosan and His Poetry: A Biography and an Anthology* (Seattle: U of Washington P, 1985); and his own "Letters to an American Woman," in Bulosan, *Becoming,* 185–214.

17   For a few narratives about actual Filipina lives, see Dorothy Cordova, "Voices from the Past: Why They Came," in *Making Waves: An Anthology of Writings by and about Asian American Women,* ed. Asian Women United of California (Boston: Beacon, 1989), 42–49; and Yen Le Espiritu, *Filipino American Lives* (Philadelphia: Temple UP, 1995).

18   For my purposes here, the "quest" is a plot that traces an individual's search for achievement and happiness. I borrow the term from Rachel Blau DuPlessis, who uses it to contrast with the romance plot of sexual success or failure. Blau's paradigm for women's bildungsromane here is useful in distinguishing between Carlos, who is about to pursue a quest for the values he identifies with America, and the nameless prostitute, a stand-in for the sisters of the immigrant Filipino boys, whose quest gets subordinated to a story of sexual success (if married) or failure (if seduced or fallen into prostitution). Carlos's married brothers can also be seen as having subordinated the quest plots of their lives to what is seen as a deadening romance plot. Paradoxically, for these men sexual success in traditional terms—a marriage appropriate to their class—is tantamount to failure.

      I believe Carlos's physical liberty to go to the United States, and then to flee whenever he gets in trouble, is preferable to the stasis of his family members at home. My celebration of his "mobility" is tempered, however, by the recognition that Asian Americans have a different symbolic relation to the American landscape than European Americans do. As Sau-ling Wong has shown, tropes of mobility have a double edge for Asian American men. The American ideals of vertical social mobility and horizontal spatial mobility as aspects of individual liberty are rewritten in a text such as Bulosan's, where vertical mobility is foreclosed by various forms of racism, and horizontal mobility is the sign of compulsory homelessness and exile for the migrant Filipino workers (*Reading,* 119–65, esp. 119–24, 128–36).

19 McClintock, *Leather,* 71–74.

20 As Oscar Campomanes has ruefully pointed out, the official invisibility of the U.S. colonial (1898–46) and postcolonial history in the Philippines, and indeed of Filipinos, to American cultural studies (or is it just to Americans?) is so concerted that "the forgotten Filipino" is becoming a cliché of the scholarship. This invisibility serves to ensure "the invisibility of American imperialism to itself," in Amy Kaplan's words (letter to Oscar Campomanes, October 10, 1989, cited in Oscar V. Campomanes, "Filipinos in the United States and Their Literature of Exile," in Lim and Ling, *Reading,* 49–78, esp. 52–54).

21 Baym, "Melodramas."

22 My summary is indebted to Stephen H. Sumida's reading of this novel, in which he persuasively questions the equation of the parents' interpretation of "filial piety" with purely Asian beliefs and customs, arguing that the parents, having come to Hawaii when young and accepted the word of the failed Grandfather Oyama, may perhaps be perpetuating a self-interested abuse of Confucian ideals that actually supports and is supported by American capitalism at its worst (*View,* 112–37). Though Sumida's reading loosens the homology equating the parents' values with Japaneseness and the sons' with Americanness, it nonetheless equates the mother with the discredited ideology and constructs the sons as the more skillful interpreters of Asian American reality.

23 This paragraph grew out of a conversation with Stephen Sumida that took place around 1988 and his references to the unreliable narrator in "Japanese American Moral Dilemmas in John Okada's *No-No Boy* and Milton Murayama's *All I Asking for Is My Body*" (in Nomura et al., *Frontiers,* 222–33).

24 Gayle K. Fujita Suto, "Momataro's Exile: John Okada's *No-No Boy*," in Lim and Ling, *Reading,* 239–58.

25 Similarly, one can read the death of the deliberately self-destructive no-no boy Freddy as a symbolic purging of the shame that Ichiro has taken on as the pariah (abjected being) of the Japanese American community and the death of Kenji to prove that there is something lethal about accepting the charge of winning American identity through redoubled patriotism (with being "200% American") when this patriotism is divorced from the right to question one's government.

2 *Authoring Subjects*

1 A representative sample of these essays includes Chin, "Come All"; Frank Chin, "This is Not an Autobiography," *Genre* 18, no. 2 (1985): 109–30; Frank Chin et al., Preface to *Aiiieeeee! An Anthology of Asian American Writers,* ed. Frank Chin et al. (1974; New York: Mentor-Penguin, 1991); and Frank Chin et al., "An Introduction to Chinese and Japanese American Literature," in Chin et al., *Aiiieeeee!* These essays, and the two *Aiiieeeee* anthologies, are Chin's principal critical contribution to Asian American studies. His critical work is well known but is considered controversial within Asian American studies; the 1974 anthology and essays may be considered a formative influence on Asian American literary studies.

2 Eric J. Sundquist, in *Home as Found: Authority and Genealogy in Nineteenth-Century American Literature* (Baltimore: Johns Hopkins UP, 1977) has proposed genealogy as a central concern of American authors:

> I want to . . . propose that for each of four nineteenth-century American writers [Cooper, Thoreau, Hawthorne, and Melville], the source of satisfaction found wanting [i.e., the source of the desire that drives the narrative] is tied in an urgent way to his family or genealogy, which by virtue of either their instability or their unwanted

pressure act as surrogates for a more abstractly envisioned "past," and to this extent stimulate the writer's *desire* to find in the family a model for the social and political constructs still so much in question for a recently conceived nation. Whether that act takes the form of idealization or criticism, calm veneration or violent attack, what is at issue is the authority generated by dependence upon, or independence of, a genealogy; and it is precisely in the very personal terms of such a question that authorship may find its own power. (xii)

3 Edward W. Said originally used the term *orientalism* to describe colonialist European attitudes toward Middle Eastern cultures under which European knowledge of other peoples was used to exert and justify control of these others, who are stereotyped as nonrational, childlike, primitive, exotic objects of European knowledge and natural inferiors (*Orientalism* [New York: Random House, 1979]). The term has since been extended to include Western attitudes toward various Asian countries and peoples. By American orientalism, I refer to analogous American attitudes toward Asian Pacific people and cultures, which are understood in Asian American studies to describe much American interaction with Asian immigrants and their American-born offspring. As Lisa Lowe has pointed out, orientalism is not a monolithic structure or ideology but an ideological mode that takes different forms in different contexts; the specific content (stereotypes, ideological rationales, and policy decisions) associated with orientalism must be analyzed in terms of each local context in order to build a sufficiently complex and nuanced account of this constantly evolving system of ideas (*Terrains,* 5–8).

4 Strictly speaking, Chin and his colleagues criticized *The Woman Warrior*'s misrepresentations of Chinese culture first, before publicly celebrating the Chinese heroic texts. Chin announced the newly discovered centrality of the Chinese heroic tradition to all *real* Asian Americans—with a couple of Japanese texts included—in his essay "This Is Not an Autobiography" (1985). According to this essay, the definitive texts of Chinese culture, and by extension other Confucian cultures as well, were *The Art of War* (Sun Tzu); *Three Kingdoms* (Luo Guanzhong); *The Water Margin* (Shih Nai'an and Luo Guanzhong); and *Chusingura* (Takeda Izumo, Miyoshi Shoraku, and Namiki Senryu; the main Japanese text). Later, after Kingston published a novel celebrating the folk hero Monkey from *Journey to the West* (by Wu Ch'eng-en), Chin included this text in his canon. He excluded an entire tradition of equally central and beloved nonmartial texts such as *The Dream of the Red Chamber* (Tsao Hsueh-chin), which clashed with his ideological objectives. The essay disqualifies Asian North Americans unfamiliar with these texts, or not setting their watches by them, as nonrepresentative cultural incompetents, but it admits that Chin himself "came late" to these texts.

5 Baym, "Melodramas."

6 See, for instance, Nina Baym, *Woman's Fiction: A Guide to Novels by and about Women in America, 1820–70* (1978; Urbana: U of Illinois P, 1993); and Ling, *Worlds.*

7 Mike Masaoka was a nisei who led the Japanese American Citizens' League during the internment era. Both Masaoka and the JACL sought to prove Japanese American loyalty by encouraging the community to cooperate with the American government and in some cases attempted to stifle and isolate Japanese Americans who took another line. The latter group included James Omura, whose resistant activities included the publication of a small nisei paper, and the nisei draft resisters held at the internment camp in Heart Mountain, Wyoming. For a contemporary synthesis of the internment history that assesses these and other Japanese Americans' motives, acts, and options in more detail, and with a stronger sense of the feelings of that period, see Roger Daniels, *Asian America: Chinese and Japanese in the United States since 1850* (Seattle: U of Washington P, 1988),

186–282. See also Michi Weglyn, *Years of Infamy: The Untold Story of America's Concentration Camps* (New York: Morrow, 1976).

8 Tam's "milk of amnesia" may be a second-generation allusion to processes of amnesia and abjection like those discussed earlier, but, whereas Carlos Bulosan uses distancing techniques to manage unruly emotions toward a mother(land) he still claims fondly and proudly, Tam is engaged in a process of overt disavowal.

9 In "The Post-colonial Critic," Spivak is asked to explicate her idea, "negotiating with the structures of violence," in terms of the negotiations the questioners (members of the subaltern studies group in India) must undertake in their work and lives. In response, she says: "As far as I can understand, in order to intervene one must negotiate. . . . The more vulnerable your position, the more you have to negotiate. . . . I guess all I mean by negotiation here is that one tries to change something that one is obliged to inhabit, since one is not working from the outside. In order to keep one's effectiveness, one must also preserve those structures — not cut them down completely. And that, as far as I can understand, is negotiation. You inhabit the structures of violence and violation, here defined by you as Western liberalism" (72). See Gayatri Chakravorty Spivak, "The Post-colonial Critic," in *The Postcolonial Critic*, ed. Sarah Harasym (New York: Routledge, 1990), 67–74.

10 In fiction, the sense of the Japanese Americans' constricted possibilities in and after the World War II era is most poignantly conveyed in Velina Hasu Houston's play *Tea*, Cynthia Kadohata's *The Floating World*, Joy Kogawa's *Obasan*, John Okada's *No-No Boy*, Hisaye Yamamoto's collection *Seventeen Syllables and Other Stories*, and Wakako Yamauchi's collection *Songs My Mother Never Taught Me*. Also relevant, but less thematically focused on the theme of lowered expectations, are Jeanne Wakatsuki Houston's memoir *A Farewell to Manzanar*, Milton Murayama's comic novel *All I Asking for Is My Body*, Monica Sone's memoir *Nisei Daughter*, and Steward D. Ikeda's novel *What the Scarecrow Said*.

11 Although David thinks of his father as denying David's birthright, "the throne," the Muras' naming of David, their firstborn son, seems to convey the opposite feeling. Not only does the name mean beloved, which he clearly is in their eyes, but the biblical David, a poet and a king, is honored as a founding father by both Jews and Christians.

12 This ghost, the invisible "Asian" self that comes and goes, is one version of what Sauling Wong has called "the racial shadow" (*Reading*, 77–92). Mura's lyric representation contrasts with the usual connotations of the racial shadow as the embodiment of qualities that are dreaded, despised, and associated with Asia by the Asian American subject. Wong does not use the term *abjection* but clearly describes the racial shadow as possessing qualities that are both cast out (abjected) by the Asian American subject and definitive of his or her subjectivity. Although Mura avoids replicating the Okada political problem of portraying Japaneseness as something to be viewed negatively, this example nonetheless resonates with the motif of Asian maternal abjection. Note that the "Japanese self" is once again identified with the issei mother, in contrast to her assimilating son.

13 See, for instance, the Japanese American works cited in note 10. As we have seen, the themes of cultural and personal erasure and extinction are central to the works of Asian American males. On the motif of experience in excess of official narratives thematized in Asian American women's texts, see Lowe, *Acts*, 97–127, and Patricia Chu, " 'The Invisible World the Emigrants Built': Cultural Self-Inscription and the Anti-Romantic Plots of *The Woman Warrior*," *Diaspora: A Journal of Transnational Studies* 2, no. 1 (1992): 95–116.

1   This paradigm, I suggest, appears in the works of writers of various ethnic origins writing in various decades. The particular texts examined were selected in part to suggest a range of historical moments, from Younghill Kang's *East Goes West* (1937) to David Mura's *Where the Body Meets Memory* (1996). The intervening texts discussed included Carlos Bulosan's *America Is in the Heart* (1946), John Okada's *No-No Boy* (1957), Milton Murayama's *All I Asking for Is My Body* (copyrighted 1959, 1968, and 1975), and Frank Chin's play *The Year of the Dragon* (premiered in 1974, published in 1981). In the 1980s, the most important literary text on issues of race, gender, and subject construction by an Asian American male author is arguably David Henry Hwang's hit play *M. Butterfly,* which premiered in 1988, but it does not include an Asian American character. Although American attitudes and policies toward the various groups do change during these decades, my claim here is that the male authors in this emerging tradition all see and position themselves and their literary protagonists as outsiders marginalized due to race and the narratives they devise about this perception have the common structure I've described.

2   This view is indebted to Nancy Chodorow's account of female gender formation in *The Reproduction of Mothering: Psychoanalysis and the Sociology of Gender* (Berkeley: U of California P, 1978).

3   See, for example, China Mama in Chin's *The Year of the Dragon* or Mura's "To H.N.," in *The Colors of Desire* (New York: Anchor-Doubleday, 1995), 21–22. The latter is a poem addressed to a Vietnamese immigrant, a former girlfriend, whose initials are H. N.

4   Classic studies of female authorship include Virginia Woolf's *A Room of One's Own,* Sandra M. Gilbert and Susan Gubar's *The Madwoman in the Attic,* and Joanna Russ's *How to Suppress Women's Writing* (Austin: U of Texas P, 1983).

5   "FOB" in David Henry Hwang, *FOB and Other Plays* (New York: Plume-Penguin, 1990).

6   Marian's sacrifice may be compared with that of a character in *Chusingura,* a classical Japanese puppet play celebrated by Frank Chin as definitive of Asian American culture. Central to this tragedy is an episode wherein a young woman is willingly sold by her parents into a five-year contract as a prostitute in order to raise funds to help her husband recover his *honor.* Everyone in the play agrees that the sacrifice is extraordinary but appropriate because it is in the service of her husband's lord. Of course, this must be understood as part of a traditional Confucian culture that has been much criticized by modern Asians. However, in "Come All Ye Asian American Writers of the Real and the Fake," Frank Chin implies that traditional Chinese and Japanese cultures are not "really" oppressive to women and that writers who claim they are are pandering to white stereotypes. In the same essay, he also insists that *Chusingura* is one of a few texts that define a Confucian heroic tradition that is important to "real" Asian Americans. Whether the resemblance between *America*'s and *Chusingura*'s honoring of female sacrifice is purely coincidental, whether Bulosan's direct and Chin's indirect celebration of these episodes suggests the lingering of Confucian ideals about female sacrifice in the Asian American male imagination, or whether Carlos Bulosan and Frank Chin just didn't notice anything wrong with these stories, I leave to my readers. See Takeda Izumu et al., *Chusingura* (New York: Columbia UP, 1971); and Frank Chin, "Come," in Chan et al., *The Big Aiiieeeee!* 1–92, esp. 1–10, 36–37.

7   Jade Snow Wong, *Fifth Chinese Daughter* (New York: Harper and Row, 1945); Jeanne Wakatsuki Houston and James D. Houston, *Farewell to Manzanar* (Boston: Houghton Mifflin, 1973); Kim, *Literature,* 71–84.

8   Hisaye Yamamoto, *Seventeen Syllables and Other Stories* (Latham, N.Y.: Kitchen Table/

Women of Color Press, 1988). Wakako Yamauchi, *The Music Lessons,* "The Handkerchief," "Charted Lives," and "The Coward," in Wakako Yamauchi, *Songs My Mother Taught Me: Stories, Plays, and Memoir,* ed. Garrett Hongo (New York: Feminist Press, 1994).

9 Notice the revision of the "melting pot" marriage plot here: the untrustworthy offer of assimilation through artistic patronage linked with sexual exploitation is figured as adultery and refused by the nisei narrator. Her suspicion of the white man's paternalism seems informed by the Japanese American disillusionment with the American promise of assimilation in exchange for submission.

10 The author's own life includes elements of artistic self-denial and literary mediation. During the early years of her marriage, she put her husband through college and kept house, putting her literary and artistic ambitions on hold and at one point painting shower curtains for a living. She returned to literary publication when she persuaded the editor of the Los Angeles *Rafu Shimpo* to publish her stories as a condition of gaining her services as a graphic artist; the negotiating idea came from her husband, then a caterer. Later, her work was stimulated by the interest of younger ethnic writers and dramatic artists (Garrett Hongo, Introduction to Yamauchi, *Songs*).

11 The most recent incarnation of Eaton's work is, in keeping with Dearborn's observations, mediated by the expert research and editorial efforts of Annette White-Parks and Amy Ling. In her critical study of Sui Sin Far's career, White-Parks builds her case for the author's importance by using many of the legitimating tropes discussed here. See Sui Sin Far, *Mrs. Spring Fragrance and Other Writings,* ed. Amy Ling and Annette White-Parks (Urbana: U of Illinois P, 1995) and Annette White-Parks, *Sui Sin Far/Edith Maude Eaton: A Literary Biography* (Urbana: U of Illinois P, 1975).

12 See, for instance, Cecilia Mangerra Brainard, *When the Rainbow Goddess Wept* (New York: Penguin, 1995), a "domestic" novel about Filipinos in World War Two, not strictly Asian American except in its questioning of Philippine-American relations; Chitra Banerjee Divakaruni, *Arranged Marriage* (New York: Anchor-Doubleday, 1995), short stories; Winnifred Eaton, *Me: A Book of Remembrance* (1915; Jackson: UP of Mississippi, 1997); Hagedorn, *Dogeaters,* which also questions U.S. cultural hegemony in the Phillipines and hence is not about Asian American subjects per se; Velina Hasu Houston, *Tea,* in *Unbroken Thread: An Anthology of Plays by Asian American Women,* ed. Roberta Uno (Amherst: U of Massachusetts P, 1993), one of a cycle of domestic plays; Cynthia Kadohata, *The Floating World* (New York: Ballantine–Random House, 1989); Kogawa, *Obasan,* a novel about Japanese Canadians; Sky Lee, *The Disappearing Moon Cafe* (1990; Seattle: Seal Press, 1991), a novel about Chinese Canadians; Kirin Narayan, *Love, Stars, and All That* (New York: Pocket Books, 1994); Fae Myenne Ng, *Bone* (New York: HarperCollins, 1993); Kim Ronyoung, *Clay Walls* (Sag Harbor, N.Y.: Permanent Press, n.d.); Bapsi Sidhwa, *An American Brat* (Minneapolis: Milkweed, 1993); and Lois-Ann Yamanaka, *Blu's Hanging* (New York: Avon, 1997). This is not an exhaustive list. These texts draw on other traditions linking domestic women with nationalism, and the use of bildungsroman conventions varies greatly; but in the large, heterogeneous category of Asian American women's writing these are some of the texts in which domestic femininity or marriage plots figure prominently as a means of constructing women as national subjects.

13 I refer to Edith Eaton by her English name to emphasize that Sui Sin Far was her literary construct; appropriately enough, this pseudonym does not include a conventional Chinese surname: as a Chinese person, Sui Sin Far is self-authored.

14 On Eaton's negotiations between radical content and conventional form, see Ling, *Worlds;* Elizabeth Ammons, "Audacious Words: Sui Sin Far's *Mrs. Spring Fragrance,*" in *Conflicting Stories: American Women Writers at the Turn into the Twentieth Century* (New York:

Oxford UP, 1991); and Annette White-Parks, *Sui Sin Far/Edith Maude Eaton: A Literary Biography* (Urbana: U of Illinois P, 1995).

15   See, for instance, "Chinese Food," in Sui Sin Far, *Mrs. Spring Fragrance and Other Writings,* ed. Amy Ling and Annette White-Parks (Urbana: U of Illinois P, 1995), 255–57. Though this example is one of many early articles in which Eaton positions herself as a non-Chinese, perhaps masking more intimate knowledge of the culture, there are no counterbalancing selections in which Eaton presents Chinese cooking as part of her own family culture. Not even the intimate, ethnically revelatory "Leaves" mentions Chinese cooking, instead citing Eaton's arguably British love of tea and rice as her means of bonding with Chinese women.

16   Mrs. Eaton also used the name Lotus Blossom, which unfortunately has since come to signify the orientalist stereotype of a submissive Asian woman. To avoid foregrounding that connotation here, I use her other names.

17   Eaton's 1912 debut, the short story collection *Mrs. Spring Fragrance,* is not to be confused with Ling and White-Parks's scholarly selection of representative pieces from her oeuvre, *Mrs. Spring Fragrance and Other Writings,* published in 1995.

18   Regrettably, the conjunction of *bays* and *ancestors* evokes a Jack Londonish image of racial atavism, with Man You regressing to a wolfish Chineseness reminiscent of "South of the Slot," a tale of class atavism (1909), and its canine equivalent, *The Call of the Wild* (1903). Since Chinese were not usually portrayed as wolves, particularly in Eaton's work, the verb is otherwise inexplicable. While this may strike the modern reader as racist, when taken in context this seeming lapse suggests that London's racist portrayals of Asians were among those Eaton sought to counteract. Man You's instinctive baying foreshadows but contrasts with Pan's voluntary reclamation of Chinese identity at the story's end.

19   In this regard, the story's equation of whiteness with amnesiac faithlessness, and Chineseness with remembrance and fidelity, evokes a similar coding in Eaton's "Pat and Pan," a story in which a white boy, raised first by Chinese parents then taken away to be raised by whites as a white American, becomes "white" by learning to deny his faithful (and smarter) Chinese sister, also named Pan (160–66).

20   According to David Mesher, Giacomo Puccini's opera premiered at La Scala in 1904 and in America at the New York Metropolitan Opera in 1907, but it was based on a play by David Belasco produced in 1900 and published in 1917. Belasco's version was derived from Pierre Loti's popular novel of 1887, *Madame Chrysantheme,* of which Mesher notes, "The popularity of *Madame Chrysantheme* in the United States, published at the height of an Orientalist rage in Europe and America that was prompted as much by western economic and territorial colonization of the Far East as by any cultural appreciation, was sufficient to assure it a place, as late as 1920, among the first hundred volumes reprinted in the Modern Library series" (5). See David Mesher, "Metamorphosis of a Butterfly," *San Jose Studies* 17, no. 3 (fall 1991): 4–21.

It seems likelier that Edith knew this story, given that her sister Winifred's social circle in New York included David Belasco (Ling, *Worlds,* 29). It would be intriguing to compare the different uses made by Edith and Winifred of this theme. In Winifred's autobiographical novel *Me,* the plot is driven by a wealthy married man's attempts to secure the narrator, a young woman frankly in love with him, as his mistress, but as this was originally published as an autobiographical novel under the name "Nora Ascough," and the narrator's ethnicity is disguised, the effects of racial difference in the story are also masked.

The repulsively knowing officer who fails to entice the author in "Leaves" (226) is another Pinkerton figure; clearly Eaton was acquainted with the Pinkerton mentality, whether or not she knew the Madame Butterfly story.

21 On reporting with a vengeance, see *The Woman Warrior,* 53; and Chu, " 'Invisible World.' " Mark's exposure of community secrets can be compared, too, to Kingston's telling of family secrets in *The Woman Warrior,* which aptly has been likened by Thomas J. Ferraro to a Sicilian-American's betrayal of *omerta,* the code that links silence with family honor in Mafia narratives by Mario Puzo and others (*Passages,* 66).

22 As noted earlier, *racial shadow* is Sau-ling Wong's term for Asian American "doubles," who embody negative qualities coded as Asian that are rejected by Asian American protagonists but return to haunt them in the form of these figures (*Reading Asian American Literature,* 77–117). Wong doesn't use the concept of abjection, but the twofold movement of casting out (abjecting) the unwanted, Asianized traits and symbolically bringing them back in the form of the double links her concept to mine. However, Wong's examples emphasize doubles who uncannily *resemble* the protagonists in gender and age, whereas in my model the abjected other (the Asian mother) overtly *contrasts* with the subject (the Asian American son) and helps to constitute his limits. It is possible that Wong's racial shadow represents an entity produced by repression, a process that contrasts with abjection in the psychoanalytical literature. In both cases, the formation of the self depends upon the constitution of an other who is both inside and outside the psyche.

23 The irony with which Eaton refers to westernization as the "wisdom of the new" may be surmised by her choice of the name Wou Sankwei for the character of the husband. In Chinese history, Wu San-kuei (1612–1678) has the distinction of betraying two dynasties. As a Ming dynasty general, Wu joined forces with the Manchu invaders and abandoned the capital city of Beijing to them in 1644. Wu then served the Manchu (Ch'ing or Qing) dynasty for thirty years and achieved the rank of *Ch'in-wang,* or prince, of the blood of the first degree. However, in 1673 he revolted against the Manchu emperor as well, setting up his own dynasty (Chou) and declaring his intent to restore the Ming regime. He died only five-and-a-half months after declaring himself emperor (in March of 1678), and the rebellion ended with the suicide of his son and heir in 1681. See Fang Chao-ying, "Wu San-kuei," in *Eminent Chinese of the Ch'ing Period (1644–1912),* vol. 2, ed. Arthur W. Hummel (Washington: United States Government Printing Office, 1944), 877–80.

24 Marlon K. Hom writes: " 'Full moon' is a literary allusion for the reunion of lovers, family members, or friends" (*Songs of Gold Mountain: Cantonese Rhymes from San Francisco Chinatown* [Berkeley: U of California P, 1987], 128 n.). In his collection of poems by Cantonese sojourners, the moon is often associated with longing for a speaker's absent spouse, or with homesickness, as in poem no. 92 (174):

> Months and years, like a current, flow along.
> Counting on my fingers, I realize it's now the middle of the eighth month.
> Tonight is marvelous, moonlight at the doorsteps;
> The moon, crystal-clear, so round and full.
> I view the moon.
> But seeing the moon arouses my sorrow.
> The moon makes me long for home, so far away.
> Leaning by the rail before the full, round moon, all in vain.

Hom's translation, the simple diction, the evocative, elliptical syntax, and the presumed self-evidence of the moon's significance are typical of the poems in his anthology. In Eaton's story, by contrast, the translated chant is fairly unintelligible — and its relevance to the story baffling — partly because of the elaborate, very un-Chinese diction ("disburtheneth me") and style chosen by Eaton; it's as if she's obscured the gist of some actual performance she may have witnessed through the labor of some act of transcription and adaptation. By comparison, the symbolic resonance of the moon in "Its Wavering Image" seems closer to that in Hom's examples, while both the songs in "Image" and "Americanizing" are more effectively voiced.

25 Gayatri Chakravorti Spivak, "Can the Subaltern Speak?" in *Marxism and the Interpretation of Culture,* ed. Cary Nelson and Lawrence Grossberg (Urbana: Univ. of Illinois Press, 1988), 296. This famous essay poses a question central to the work of Asian American writers seeking to imagine and give fictional voice to figures who in some way represent the experiences of their ancestors. Eaton's early embrace of this task with respect to the Chinese American communities of her time (who stand in her own mind for "her mother's people"), puts her at the beginning of the entire tradition of Asian American literature. Her specific interest in Chinese women, who I believe mediate her desire to understand and pay tribute to her mother, anticipates the mother-daughter narratives of current Asian American women writers.

The Spivak essay does not, of course, address Asian American literature directly, but it raises questions about the work of the intellectual who wants to speak for the subaltern. It examines the difficulty of locating the subaltern woman's consciousness and advocates critical scrutiny of the intellectual's positioning of herself in relation to that subject. The essay cautions against presuming the intellectual's transparency and neutrality or nostalgically invoking the subaltern subject's "authenticity." As Spivak puts it: "In seeking to learn to speak to (rather than listen to or speak for) the historically muted subject of the subaltern woman, the postcolonial intellectual *systematically* 'unlearns' female privilege. This systematic unlearning involves learning to critique post-colonial discourse with the best tools it can provide and not simply substituting the lost figures of the colonized" (295). It's in this spirit that I suggest these stories have mixed ideological effects and specifically suggest that Eaton's critical representations of well-meaning white women reflect her own process of "unlearning" her own kind of privilege.

The social institution Spivak interrogates in response to her title question is the Hindu institution of *sati,* in which Indian widows commit suicide by throwing themselves on the funeral pyres of their husbands. After comparing various British and Indian representations of sati, Spivak concludes that in this instance the subaltern cannot speak: none of the written accounts provides access or insight into the widows' motivations or subjective experiences; only various ideologies, apparently all voiced by male writers, are represented. In this context, "White men are saving brown women from brown men," a phrase that symbolizes the colonizers' justifications for ruling India, is a cautionary example of how feminist and humane concerns can be linked with paternal interference. In these stories, Eaton seems to address similar concerns about white interventions in Chinese family life. As Annette White-Parks notes in *Sui Sin Far/Edith Maude Eaton,* criticism of white intervention is more direct in stories like "A Chinese Boy-Girl," in which a teacher mistakenly tries to remove a child from his father's care; "The Land of the Free," wherein immigration officials separate an infant from his parents; and "The Sugar Cane Baby," in which white missionaries mistakenly try to "protect" a Jamaican baby from its supposedly neglectful parents.

Spivak's essay ends with the cautionary example of Bhuvaneswari Bhudari, a young woman nationalist whose politically motivated suicide was, according to Spivak, intended as "an emphatic, ad hoc, subaltern rewriting of the social text of *sati*-suicide" because it expressed radical Indian nationalism rather than sexual disgrace or wifely grief. Since no one in her community has recognized the suicide as an expression of nationalism, however, Spivak concludes that even this subaltern could not speak.

My reading of "Wisdom," and of Eaton's political agendas, continually returns me to this vexed scene of the would-be interpreter gazing at the silent woman's body. In "Wisdom," Eaton shrewdly and sympathetically suggests that Pau Lin is silenced by Chinese custom (she is said to have been trained in China to be quiet in her husband's presence), American ignorance of Chinese, and her husband's refusal to listen to her. Despite the well-meant intervention of Adah, who stands structurally for the author as "postcolonial intellectual" and even voices Pau Lin's position in relation to Sankwei, he cannot hear his wife speak or "read" her protest until she resorts to murder.

26 Fluent, articulate letter writing about one's inner life is particularly identified with the origins of the English novel's unique portrayal of subjectivity — and its privileging of middle-class female subjectivity — by Ian Watt (*Rise,* 189–96).

27 In "Wisdom," not only is Adah Charlton, like Edith Eaton, an artist and a friend to Chinese, but her names even sound like Eaton's. Ada is also the name Winifred Eaton gave to the eldest sister, Edith's fictional surrogate, in her fictionalized family memoir *Marion: The Story of an Artist's Model* (White-Parks, *Sui,* 27–28). In addition, the husband's association of Adah with "a pure water-flower — a lily" in "Wisdom" may be an intentional reference to Eaton's pen name, which in Chinese means narcissus or water lily (Far, "Wisdom," 51). Is Eaton playfully identifying Adah with herself?

28 Pau Lin's passionate need for consideration and intimacy, if not love, beyond the call of duty may be the first exploration of a theme central to this literature, the tension between "necessity" and "extravagance." As Sau-ling Wong has persuasively demonstrated (in *Reading*), Asian American texts repeatedly seem to align the immigrant generation with conformity to the laws of necessity and survival and their offspring with the longing for extravagance, additional pleasures that nourish the spirit only to demonstrate again and again that, even for the most self-denying, disciplined immigrants, a measure of extravagance is also essential to survival.

29 This is a translated selection of poems culled from two collections published by Tai Quong Co., a noted bookseller and publisher in San Francisco's Chinatown. The collections, *Jinshan ge ji* and *Jinshan ge erji,* were published in 1911 and 1915 respectively. See Marlon K. Hom, introduction to *Songs of Gold Mountain* by Marlon K. Hom, 53–54.

30 If nothing else, *Jasmine* suggests why a woman of a certain class could not become a "self-made man" in America due to the obvious barriers of gender, race, education, and class.

30 See also Rachel Blau DuPlessis's account of the quest and romance plots that compete in many nineteenth-century Anglo-American women's bildungsromane, including *Jane Eyre.* Briefly, *quest* signifies the female protagonist's drive for meaning through independence and achievement, and *romance* signifies a heterosexual plot in which she may succeed by marrying appropriately or fail by losing her sexual honor outside of marriage. DuPlessis argues that romance trumps quest in defining the endings of these novels. Hence, sexual success or failure is definitive of the novels' outcomes and the protagonists' characters (*Writing*).

31 Mukherjee's earlier novel, *Wife,* describes more scrupulously the severe limits encountered by a young woman of limited means and education who comes to the United States within the constraints set by marriage to a fellow immigrant who expects her to remain home alone all day. The protagonist of *Wife* begins with a better situation, but fails to adapt to her isolated American existence or to find a viable escape from it. Unfortunately, the novel's action shares the sense of stasis and confinement experienced by its protagonist, a stasis that we are asked to imagine leads her to commit a violent murder. *Jasmine* revisits this technical problem (justifying an entire novel about someone who in "real life" would be leading an outwardly repetitive, predictable existence) and solves it by giving the protagonist more mobility and outward experience than her predecessor. I feel more inclined to grant Mukherjee some poetic license to give Jasmine implausible adventures,

given that she had already tried her hand at a novel focused on an immigrant's interior life in *Wife*.

4 "That Was China, That Was Their Fate"

1 Matrilineal Asian North American narratives of note include Cynthia Kadohata's *The Floating World*, Julie Shikeguni's *A Bridge between Us*, Sky Lee's *The Disappearing Moon Cafe*, and the texts cited in note 3. For an analysis of Tan's popular success, see Sau-ling Cynthia Wong, " 'Sugar Sisterhood': Situating the Amy Tan Phenomenon," in *The Ethnic Canon: Histories, Institutions, and Interventions*, ed. David Palumbo-Liu (Minneapolis: U of Minnesota P, 1995), 174–210.

2 Melanie McAlister, "(Mis)Reading *The Joy Luck Club*," *Asian America: Journal of Culture and the Arts* 1 (winter 1992): 102–18.

3 My reading of Tan's treatment of this theme may be taken as a sequel to my study of daughterly self-formation in Maxine Hong Kingston's *The Woman Warrior*, which was in turn enriched by the mother-daughter studies cited therein. The mother-daughter plot may be read as a feminist alternative to the male immigration plots of romantic desire for white women and the abjection of Asian women. It may be placed in dialogue with oedipal male narratives such as Frank Chin's and David Mura's, in which American-born sons re-create themselves by separating and differentiating themselves from fathers perceived as deficient. It may also serve as a paradigm for reading Asian American men's narratives such as Gus Lee's *Honor and Duty*.

   Some of the most prominent and effective Asian American fictional examples include Kim Ronyoung's *Clay Walls*, Fae Myenne Ng's *Bone*, and Velina Hasu Houston's *Tea*. Biographical works structured by this plot include Denise Chong's *The Concubine's Daughter*, Lydia Minatoya's *Talking to High Monks in the Snow*, and, of course, Eaton's "Leaves."

4 *Myth* here denotes an archetypical plot that shapes numerous individual narratives defining the American sense of self and nation, both fictional and nonfictional. Although I have argued that Asians have often been portrayed and perceived as fundamentally un-American, Tan clearly invites crossracial identification by modeling her immigrant Chinese women after this myth of the immigrant as quintessential American self.

5 The idealism with which Chinese in particular have traditionally regarded America is embedded in their names for it: Beautiful Country and Gold Mountain.

6 A classic immigrant success story that largely incorporates this plot is Abraham Cahan's *The Rise of David Levinsky* (1917; New York: Penguin, 1993). Levinsky does not marry but considers this a deviation from the usual pattern of transferring one's aspirations to one's children. An orphan whose assimilation is linked with his commercial success as a cloak manufacturer, Levinsky claims agency primarily through his capacity for entrepreneurial initiative and risk taking. Levinsky's rise through his own "luck and pluck" in turn resonates with the formula for personal success popularized in Horatio Alger's stories for boys. See, for instance, Horatio Alger Jr., *Ragged Dick and Struggling Upward*, ed. Carl Bode (1868, 1890; New York: Penguin, 1985). For various reasons, such opportunities tend not to be the focus of female immigration narratives.

   In addition to these implicitly male paradigms, my account of the immigration myth draws upon my reading of Asian American immigration narratives and upon William Boelhower's multiethnic studies of immigration narratives. See his "Ethnic Trilogies" and "Brave New World."

7 Here James Joyce's fictional alter ego, Stephen Dedalus, announces his intention to create a new literary voice, which will be both modern and distinctly Irish. Dedalus differs from

Tan's June in his willingness to authorize *himself* in order to renounce traditional obligations, but he shares with her the objective of creating a literature for his community, his
"race." Dedalus's greater ambition, to create a literature that will define his community as
a people, goes beyond June's immediate aim, but it significantly resembles the collective
Asian American project of literary self-authoring.

8 Johannes Fabian, *Time and the Other: How Anthropology Makes Its Object* (New York:
Columbia UP, 1983), cited in Rey Chow, *Women and Chinese Modernity: the Politics of
Reading between West and East* (Minneapolis: U of Minnesota P, 1991).

Most of the Chinese episodes in Tan's novel occur between 1914 and 1946, the beginning
of World War I and the end of World War II from the Western point of view. However,
since the interwar period was one of continuous civil war and unrest for China, I use the
term *pre-Communist* to refer to the period between the fall of the Manchu dynasty (1911)
and the establishment of the People's Republic of China (1949), a time when China lacked
a strong central government.

9 Rey Chow, *Women and Chinese Modernity*, 30–31. See also Sau-ling Cynthia Wong's discussion of temporal distancing in Amy Tan's work ("Sugar-Sisterhood," 185–86). While I
concur with her analysis, my work is more concerned with how this allochronism enables
readers to overlook the problems raised by the novel's representations of female agency,
how it contributes to the erasure of modern Chinese subjectivities from the text, and how
it contributes to the construction of the mother-daughter romance as an immigration
narrative.

10 Melanie McAlister reads this as a moment when Ying-ying asserts that she must *change*
her relationship with Lena ("(Mis)Reading," 112). Her deft reading avoids crediting all
Chinese mothers with ancient folk wisdom; it does, however, accept a highly optimistic
view of Ying-ying's agency, the view that she could reverse the effects of a lifetime of
passivity and poor communication by speaking frankly with her daughter on this single
occasion.

11 Historian Jonathan Spence argues in *The Search for Modern China* (New York: Norton,
1990) that with the abdication of the last Ching emperor in 1912 the following decades of
social and political upheaval were also characterized by an ongoing search for new ideas
about how to govern China, with Western liberal democracies and the Russian socialist system emerging as the most significant foreign models. Significant histories of feminist movements in China, which may counter the notion of classical China as socially
unchanged for the first five decades of this century, are offered by Elisabeth Croll, *Feminism and Socialism in China* (London: Routledge, 1978); Kazuko Ono, *Chinese Women in
a Century of Revolution, 1850–1950*, trans. Kathryn Bernhardt et al., ed. Joshua A. Fogel
(1978; Stanford: Stanford UP, 1989); and Kay Ann Johnson, *Women, the Family, and Peasant Revolution in China* (Chicago: UP of Chicago, 1983). Such histories, combined with
the novel about to be discussed, confirm Tan's sense that Chinese women had few means
of resisting the sex-gender system characterized by arranged marriages, but they also provide a more complex and varied sense of how the Chinese inhabited this system and how
it could continue despite being a source of misery for so many.

12 On the experiences of Chinese women immigrants in America, see Judy Yung, *Unbound
Feet: A Social History of Chinese Women in San Francisco* (Berkeley: U of California P,
1995).

13 For instance, Ying-ying St. Clair is born in 1914. In the "Moon Lady," which takes place
in 1918, she depicts her father, "a dedicated scholar of ancient history and literature,"
emending ancient poetry with his gentleman guests while her mother, oblivious to the
literary discussion, discusses herbal cures for sore feet (an oblique reference to foot bind-

ing?) with other women (70–71). This tranquil scene, replete with traditionally gendered topics of instruction, contributes to the episode's allochronism. At the time, the country was embroiled in civil war, it lacked a stable central government, and it was confronting the outrage of Japan's twenty-one demands (Tse-tung Chow, 9–10). Tan's story does not evoke a peaceful interlude in a period of turmoil, an upper-class family wilfully denying events that might affect them or others, or the memories of a child registering but unable to interpret the troubles of her adult relatives; rather, it evokes an idealized classical China free of political or social tensions. If we take the American episodes to be "contemporary" in 1989, the year of publication, we should imagine the mothers as women in their seventies; Canning Woo is seventy-two in the novel's "present" (268).

14 Concepts of the self vary within cultures, but a useful starting point might be Alan Roland's discussion of the Western philosophical roots of psychoanalytic concepts of self, as contrasted with May Tung's account of Chinese concepts of the self. See Alan Roland, "How Universal Is the Psychoanalytic Self?" (3–21, esp. 3–13), and May Tung, "Insight-Oriented Therapy and the Chinese Patient" (175–86), both in Alan Roland, *Cultural Pluralism and Psychoanalysis: The Asian and North American Experience* (New York: Routledge, 1996).

15 Pa Chin, *Family,* trans. Sidney Shapiro (1931, 1972; Prospect Heights, Ill.: Waveland, 1989).

16 King-kok Cheung, "Re-viewing Asian American Literary Studies," in *An Interethnic Companion to Asian American Literature,* ed. King-kok Cheung (Boston: Cambridge UP, 1997), 30, n. 16.

17 In his 1918 satire, "The Diary of a Madman," Lu's mad diarist writes: "I take a look at history; it is not a record of time but on each page are confusedly written the characters 'benevolence, righteousness, and morals' " and "Desperately unsleeping, I carefully look it over again and again for half the night, and at last find betwen the lines that it is full of the same word 'cannibalism!' " He goes on: "Having unconsciously practiced cannibalism for four thousand years, I am awakening now and feel ashamed to face a genuine human being!" See Lu Hsun, "The Diary of a Madman," *New Youth* 4, no. 5 (May 15, 1918): 414–24 (trans. and qtd. in Chow Tse-tung, 308).

18 The novel's ending replicates the author's permanent departure from Chengdu in 1923. His studies and literary work led him to Shanghai, Nanjing, and Paris, but he returned to Shanghai in 1928. He chose to remain in China for the rest of his life, and his novel reflects a commitment to the need for and possibility of change within China that is, understandably, absent from Tan's.

5 Tripmaster Monkey, *Frank Chin, and the Chinese Heroic Tradition*

1 Among many publications referring to this debate, five particularly useful essays are King-kok Cheung, "The Woman Warrior versus the Chinaman Pacific: Must a Chinese American Critic Choose between Feminism and Heroism?" in *Conflicts in Feminism,* ed. Marianne Hirsch and Evelyn Fox Keller (New York: Routledge, 1990), 234–51; Elaine H. Kim, " 'Such Opposite Creatures': Men and Women in Asian American Literature," *Michigan Quarterly Review* 29, no. 1 (winter, 1990): 68–92; Robert G. Lee, "The Woman Warrior as an Intervention in Asian American Historiography," in *Approaches to Teaching Maxine Hong Kingston's* The Woman Warrior, ed. Shirley Geok-lin Lim (New York: Modern Language Association, 1991), 52–63; Sau-ling Cynthia Wong, "Autobiography as Guided Chinatown Tour? Maxine Hong Kingston's *The Woman Warrior* and the Chinese American Autobiographical Controversy," in *Multicultural Autobiography,* ed. James Robert Payne (Knoxville: U of Tennessee P, 1992), 248–79; and Deborah Woo, "Maxine Hong

Kingston: The Ethnic Writer and the Burden of Dual Authenticity," *Amerasia* 16, no. 1 (1990): 173–200.

2 For a summarizing footnote, see chapter two, n. 1. In 1984, Chin also published a hostile parody of *The Woman Warrior* and its defenders, "The Most Popular Book in China" (Reprinted as the Afterword to Frank Chin, *The Chinaman Pacific and Frisco R.R. Co.* [Minneapolis: Coffee House Press, 1988]). As noted earlier, excessively successful female authors are roundly scolded for appealing to mainstream readers.

3 See, for instance, Kim, *Literature;* Moy, *Sights;* and Chan, *Asian Americans.*

4 *Postmodern parody* is a term borrowed from Linda Hutcheon (*Politics,* 93–117). For analyses of Kingston's revisions of traditional plots, see Cheung, *Silences;* Chu, "Invisible World"; David Leiwei Li, "*China Men:* Maxine Hong Kingston and the American Canon," *ALH* 2, no. 3 (1990): 483–502; and Shu-mei Shih, "Exile and Intertextuality in Maxine Hong Kingston's *China Men,*" in *The Literature of Emigration and Exile,* ed. James Whitlark and Wendell Aycock (Lubbock: Texas Tech UP, 1992).

5 The term *myth* conveniently glosses over the fact that many of the classic Chinese novels cited combined historical sources with the embellishments of storytellers. As Debra Shostak points out, both the oral and written versions of these stories were viewed as "popular history" by the Chinese, who did not traditionally consider literature and history as distinct as we now do ("Maxine Hong Kingston's Fake Books," in *Memory, Narrative, and Identity: New Essays in Ethnic American Literatures,* ed. Amritjit Singh, Joseph T. Skerrett Jr., and Robert E. Hogan [Boston: Northeastern UP, 1994], 235–36). See also note 6.

6 In fact, the textual scholarship for these Chinese classics points to a collaborative process of composition similar to the process Kingston describes and Chin attacks; Kingston makes this creative process the central action of *Tripmaster Monkey.*

The scholarship tells us that the ancient Chinese novelists combined official histories, promptbooks, and popular legends with their own inventions to produce these "original" works. Translator Moss Roberts provides a thorough introduction to the textual history of *Three Kingdoms* in his afterword to *Three Kingdoms: A Historical Novel* [Luo Guanzhong?], trans. Moss Roberts (Berkeley: U of California P, 1991), 937–86. Translator Anthony C. Yu provides a similar survey for *Journey* in his introduction to *The Journey to the West,* [Wu Ch'eng-en?] (Chicago: U of Chicago P, 1977–83), 1–21. For *Water Margin,* translator Sidney Shapiro merely notes, "Since its original publication, [this novel] has appeared in numerous editions ranging from seventy to 124 chapters, the denouement sometimes changing with the political temper of the ruling monarch" (translator's note to *Outlaws of the Marsh,* vol. 1, attributed to Shi Nai'an and Luo Guanzhong, trans. Sidney Shapiro [Beijing: Foreign Languages P, 1988]: n.p.). More complete textual histories of all three novels are provided, however, by Lu Hsun and C. T. Hsia in their authoritative surveys of Chinese fiction. On *Water Margin,* see Lu Hsun, *A Brief History of Chinese Fiction,* trans. Yang Hsien-Yi and Gladys Yang (Westport: Hyperion P, 1973), 180–97; and C. T. Hsia, *The Classic Chinese Novel: A Critical Introduction* (New York: Columbia UP, 1968), 75–82.

The Art of War, an older, nonnarrative text, has been more visibly transformed by its readers; centuries of commentary have been incorporated into the text itself.

7 "Horatio Algiers Wong" is an allusion to Chin's attacks on Jade Snow Wong, author of *Fifth Chinese Daughter,* who has been criticized for presenting herself as a model minority author. On another note, critic Sau-ling Cynthia Wong has identified accommodationist genres as "food pornography," which she finds is a central trope of Frank Chin's writing. Both tropes, prostitution and pornography, convey Chin's feeling that packaging and selling one's ethnicity can be analogous to sexual commodification (*Reading,* 55).

8 In light of Chin's critical arguments, it must be recalled that these texts were all written centuries ago under circumstances that are now matters of scholarly conjecture. For these texts and Wu Ch'eng-en's *Journey,* the authorship is disputed but traditionally attributed to these figures. Without delving deeply into Chinese history, a rough survey of these texts' estimated dates of origin will support my argument that the texts convey feudal social values (both Buddhist and Confucian) from ancient China and are therefore problematic for the project of defining contemporary Chinese American culture and character.

According to Bruce Cleary, *The Art of War* (*Sun-tzu ping fa*) is believed to have originated in the Warring States period (ca. 403–221 B.C.), with commentaries added by readers through the Sung dynasty (ca. 960–1279 A.D.). See Bruce Cleary, translator's introduction to *The Art of War* by Sun Tzu, trans. Bruce Cleary (Boston: Shambala, 1988), 1–38. The period designations are cited on pages 27–33. Moss Roberts's unabridged (1991) translation of *Three Kingdoms* (*San kuo chih yen i*) is based on the Mao Zonggang edition, believed to have been published in the mid-1660s based on a text from ca. 1522. Sidney Shapiro's translation of *Water Margin* (*Shui hu zhuan*), which he calls *Outlaws of the Marsh,* does not explicitly identify the two versions he used, but in *Chinese Novel* C. T. Hsia offers approximate dates for two editions influential in this novel's development, the Kuo Hsun version (ca. 1550) and the Chin Sheng-t'an edition (ca. 1628–43). Anthony C. Yu's translation of *Journey* (*Hsi yu chi*) uses a version based on a text from ca. 1592.

A full discussion of the three texts' *differences* in ethical standards is impossible here, but Hsia, *Chinese Novel,* gives a good idea of the contrast between the tragically idealistic ethical standards of the brothers in *Three Kingdoms* and the "gang morality" of the sadistic outlaws in *Water Margin.* My argument will follow Chin's "Autobiography" in grouping *The Art of War, Three Kingdoms,* and *Water Margin* together as a heroic tradition, which I contrast with the more spiritual *Journey.*

After the publication of *Tripmaster Monkey,* Frank Chin published another essay insisting on the centrality of "the three classics of the heroic tradition" ("Come All," 34), but he cited three *different* classics. Without acknowledging Kingston's influence directly, he substituted *Journey* for *The Art of War.* Thus, the Chinese heroic tradition improved greatly between 1985 and 1991.

Coda

1 I'm indebted to Sau-ling Cynthia Wong for these terms. See *Reading.*

Bibliography

Abel, Elizabeth, Marianne Hirsch, and Elizabeth Langland, eds. *The Voyage In: Fictions of Female Development.* Hanover: UP of New England, 1983.

Alger Jr., Horatio. *Ragged Dick and Struggling Upward,* ed. Carl Bode. 1868, 1890. New York: Penguin, 1985.

Alquizola, Marilyn. "The Fictive Narrator of *America Is in the Heart.*" In Nomura et al., *Frontiers,* 211–17.

———. "Subversion or Affirmation: The Text and Subtext of *America Is in the Heart.* In *Asian Americans: Comparative and Global Perspectives,* ed. Shirley Hune, Hyung-chan Kim, Stephen S. Fugita, and Amy Ling, 199–210. Pullman: Washington State UP, 1991.

Althusser, Louis. "Ideology and Ideological State Apparatuses." In *Lenin and Philosophy and Other Essays,* trans. Ben Brewster, 127–86. New York: Monthly Review Press, 1971.

Ammons, Elizabeth. "Audacious Words: Sui Sin Far's *Mrs. Spring Fragrance.*" In *Conflicting Stories: American Women Writers at the Turn into the Twentieth Century,* 105–20. New York: Oxford UP, 1991.

Anderson, Benedict. *Imagined Communities. Reflections on the Origin and Spread of Nationalism.* 1983. Rev. ed. London: Verso, 1991.

Armstrong, Nancy. *Desire and Domestic Fiction: A Political History of the Novel.* New York: Oxford UP, 1987.

Austen, Jane. *Pride and Prejudice,* ed. Donald Gray. 1913. New York: Norton, 1993.

Babcock, Winifred Eaton. *Marion: The Story of an Artist's Model.* New York: W. J. Watt, 1916.

Banerjee, Debjani. " 'In the Presence of History': The Representation of Past and Present Indias in Bharati Mukherjee's Fiction." In Nelson, *Bharati,* 161–79.

Barthes, Roland. *S/Z: An Essay,* trans. Richard Miller. 1970. New York: Hill and Wang, 1974.

Baym, Nina. "Melodramas of Beset Manhood: How Theories of American Fiction Exclude Women Authors." *American Quarterly* 33 (1981): 123–39. Rpt. in Showalter, *Criticism,* 63–80.

———. *Woman's Fiction: A Guide to Novels by and about Women in America, 1820–70.* 1978. Urbana: U of Illinois P, 1993.

Beebe, Maurice. *Ivory Towers and Sacred Founts: The Artist as Hero in Fiction from Goethe to Joyce.* New York: New York UP, 1964.

Belsey, Catherine. "Constructing the Subject: Deconstructing the Text." In *Feminist Criticism and Social Change: Sex, Class and Race in Literature and Culture,* ed. Judith Newton and Deborah Rosenfelt, 45–64. New York: Methuen, 1985.

Beruch, Claire Hoffman. "The Feminine Bildungsroman: Education through Marriage." *Massachusetts Review* 22 (1981): 335–57.

Bhabha, Homi K. "DissemiNation: Time, Narrative, and the Margins of the Modern Nation." In Bhabha, *Nation,* 291–322.

———, ed. *Nation and Narration.* New York: Routledge, 1990.

Blaise, Clark, and Bharati Mukherjee. *Days and Nights in Calcutta.* 1977. St. Paul: Hungry Mind Press, 1995.

Boelhower, William. "The Brave New World of Immigrant Autobiography." *MELUS* 9, no. 2 (summer 1982): 5–24.

———. "Ethnic Trilogies: A Genealogical and Generational Poetics." In *The Invention of Ethnicity,* ed. Werner Sollors, 158–75. New York: Oxford UP, 1989.

———. "The Immigrant Novel as Genre." *MELUS* 8, no. 1 (1981): 3–13.

Braendlin, Bonnie Hoover. "*Bildung* in Ethnic Women Writers." *Denver Quarterly* 17, no. 4 (1983): 58–74.

Brainard, Cecilia Mangerra. *When the Rainbow Goddess Wept.* New York: Penguin, 1995.

Brennan, Timothy. "The National Longing for Form." In Bhabha, *Nation,* 44–70.

Brontë, Charlotte. *Jane Eyre,* ed. Q. D. Leavis. 1847. New York: Penguin, 1966.

———. *Shirley.* 1849. Oxford: Oxford UP, 1979.

Brooks, Peter. *Reading for the Plot: Design and Intention in Narrative.* New York: Knopf, 1984.

Brown, Gillian. *Domestic Individualism: Imagining Self in Nineteenth Century America.* Berkeley: U of California P, 1990.

Buckley, Jerome Hamilton. *Season of Youth: The Bildungsroman from Dickens to Golding.* Cambridge: Harvard UP, 1974.

Bulosan, Carlos. *America Is in the Heart.* 1946. Seattle: U of Washington P, 1973.

———. *On Becoming Filipino: Selected Writings of Carlos Bulosan,* ed. E. San Juan Jr. Philadelphia: Temple UP, 1995.

———. *The Cry and the Dedication,* ed. E. San Juan Jr. Philadelphia: Temple UP, 1995.

———. "As Long as the Grass Shall Grow." 1949. In Bulosan, *Becoming,* 38–43.

———. "Passage into Life." In Bulosan, *Becoming,* 47–59.

Butler, Judith. *Bodies That Matter: On the Discursive Limits of "Sex."* New York: Routledge, 1993.

Cahan, Abraham. *The Rise of David Levinsky.* 1917. New York: Penguin, 1993.

Campomanes, Oscar V. "Filipinos in the United States and Their Literature of Exile." In Lim and Ling, *Reading,* 49–78.

Cha, Theresa. *Dictée.* New York: Tanam P, 1982.

Chakrabarty, Dipesh. "Post-coloniality and the Artifice of History: Who Speaks for 'Indian' Pasts?" *Representations* 37 (1992): 1–26.

Chan, Jeffrey Paul, Frank Chin, Lawson Fusao Inada, and Shawn Wong, eds. *The Big Aiiieeeee! An Anthology of Chinese American and Japanese American Literature.* New York: Meridian-Penguin, 1991.

Chan, Sucheng. *Asian Americans: An Interpretive History.* Boston: Twayne, 1991.

Chandra, Vikram. *Red Earth and Pouring Rain.* Boston: Little, Brown, 1996.

Cheung, King-kok. *Articulate Silences: Hisaye Yamamoto, Maxine Hong Kingston, Joy Kogawa.* Ithaca: Cornell UP, 1993.

———. "Re-viewing Asian American Literary Studies." In *An Interethnic Companion to Asian American Literature,* ed. King-kok Cheung, 1–36. Boston: Cambridge UP, 1997.

———. "The Woman Warrior versus the Chinaman Pacific: Must a Chinese American Critic

Choose between Feminism and Heroism?" In *Conflicts in Feminism,* ed. Marianne Hirsch and Evelyn Fox Keller, 234–51. New York: Routledge, 1990.

Chin, Frank. Afterword to Chin, *Chinaman Pacific* i–v. Rpt. of "The Most Popular Book in China." *Quilt* 4 (1984): 6–10.

———. "Backtalk." In *Counterpoint: Perspectives on Asian America,* ed. Emma Gee, 556–57. Los Angeles: Asian American Center, 1976.

———. *The Chickencoop Chinaman and The Year of the Dragon.* Seattle: U of Washington P, 1981.

———. *The Chinaman Pacific & Frisco R.R. Co.* Minneapolis: Coffee House Press, 1988.

———. "Come All Ye Asian American Writers, the Real and the Fake." In Chan et al., *The Big Aiiieeeee!* 1–92.

———. *Donald Duk.* Minneapolis: Coffee House Press, 1991.

———. *Gunga Din Highway.* Minneapolis: Coffee House Press, 1994.

———. "This Is Not an Autobiography." *Genre* 18, no. 2 (1985): 109–30.

Chin, Frank, Jeffrey Paul Chan, Lawson Fusao Inada, and Shawn Wong, eds. *Aiiieeeee! An Anthology of Asian American Writers.* 1974. New York: Mentor-Penguin, 1991.

———. "An Introduction to Chinese and Japanese American Literature." In Chin et al., *Aiiieeeee!* 3–38.

———. Preface to Chin et al., *Aiiieeeee!* xii–xxii.

Chodorow, Nancy. *The Reproduction of Mothering: Psychoanalysis and the Sociology of Gender.* Berkeley: U of California P, 1978.

Chong, Denise. *The Concubine's Children.* New York: Viking, 1994.

Chow, Rey. *Women and Chinese Modernity: The Politics of Reading between West and East.* Minneapolis: U of Minnesota P, 1991.

———. *Writing Diaspora: Tactics of Intervention in Contemporary Cultural Studies.* Bloomington: Indiana UP, 1993.

Chow Tse-tung. *The May Fourth Movement: Intellectual Revolution in Modern China.* Cambridge: Harvard UP, 1960.

Choy, Christine, Elaine Kim, and Dai Sil Kim-Gibson. *Sa-I-Gu.* Cross Current Media, 1993. Video.

Christopher, Renny. *The Viet Nam War/The American War: Images and Representations in Euro-American and Vietnamese Exile Narratives.* Amherst: U of Massachusetts P, 1995.

Chu, Patricia. " 'The Invisible World the Emigrants Built': Cultural Self-Inscription and the Anti-Romantic Plots of *The Woman Warrior.*" *Diaspora: A Journal of Transnational Studies* 2, no. 1 (1992): 95–116.

Chua, C. L. "Passages from India: Migrating to America in the Fiction of V. S. Naipaul and Bharati Mukherjee." In *Reworlding: The Literature of the Indian Diaspora,* ed. Emmanuel S. Nelson. New York: Greenwood Press, 1992.

Cleary, Bruce. Translator's introduction to *The Art of War* by Sun Tzu, trans. Bruce Cleary, 1–38. Boston: Shambala, 1988.

Cleaver, Eldridge. *Soul on Ice.* New York: Dell, 1970.

Cordova, Dorothy. "Voices from the Past: Why They Came." In *Making Waves: An Anthology of Writings by and about Asian American Women,* ed. Asian Women United of California, 42–49. Boston: Beacon, 1989.

Croll, Elisabeth. *Feminism and Socialism in China.* London: Routledge, 1978.

Cumings, Bruce. *Korea's Place in the Sun: A Modern History.* New York: Norton, 1997.

Daniels, Roger. *Asian America: Chinese and Japanese in the United States since 1850,* 186–282. Seattle: U of Washington P, 1988.

Dearborn, Mary. *Pocahontas's Daughters: Gender and Ethnicity in American Culture.* New York: Oxford UP, 1986.

Dickens, Charles. *David Copperfield*, ed. Nina Burgis. 1850. New York: Oxford UP, 1986.

————. *Great Expectations*. 1861. New York: Holt, Rinehart, 1961.

Divakaruni, Chitra Banerjee. *Arranged Marriage*. New York: Anchor-Doubleday, 1995.

Du Bois, W. E. B. *The Souls of Black Folk: W. E. B. Du Bois, Writings*. New York: Library of America, 1986.

DuPlessis, Rachel Blau. *Writing beyond the Ending: Narrative Strategies of Twentieth Century Women Writers*. Bloomington: Indiana UP, 1985.

Eagleton, Terry. *Literary Theory: An Introduction*. Minneapolis: U of Minnesota P, 1983.

Eaton, Winnifred. *Me: A Book of Remembrance*. 1915. Jackson: UP of Mississippi, 1997.

Emi, Frank. "Resistance: The Heart Mountain Fair Play Committee's Fight for Justice." *Amerasia* 17, no. 1 (1991): 47–51.

Espiritu, Yen Le. *Filipino American Lives*. Philadelphia: Temple UP, 1995.

Evangelista, Susan. *Carlos Bulosan and His Poetry: A Biography and an Anthology*. Seattle: U of Washington P, 1985.

Fabian, Johannes. *Time and the Other: How Anthropology Makes Its Object*. New York: Columbia UP, 1983.

Fang Chao-ying, "Wu San-kuei." In Hummel, *Eminent Chinese*, vol. 2, 877–80.

Fanon, Frantz. *Black Skin, White Masks*, trans. Charles Lam Markmann. 1952. New York: Grove Weidenfeld, 1967.

Far, Sui Sin (Edith Maude Eaton). "The Americanizing of Pau Tzu." In Far, *Spring*, 83–92.

————. "The Inferior Woman." In Far, *Spring*, 28–41.

————. " 'Its Wavering Image.' " In Far, *Spring*, 61–68.

————. "Leaves from the Mental Portfolio of an Eurasian." In Far, *Spring*, 218–30.

————. "Mrs. Spring Fragrance." In Far, *Spring*, 17–27.

————. *Mrs. Spring Fragrance and Other Writings*, ed. Amy Ling and Annette White-Parks. Urbana: U of Illinois P, 1995.

————. "Pat and Pan." In Far, *Spring*, 160–168.

————. "The Wisdom of the New." In Far, *Spring*, 42–60.

Ferguson, Mary Anne. "The Female Novel of Development and the Myth of Psyche." *Denver Quarterly* 17, no. 4 (1983): 58–74.

Ferraro, Thomas J. "Changing the Rituals: Courageous Daughtering and the Mystique of the Woman Warrior." In Ferraro, *Passages*, 154–90.

————. *Ethnic Passages: Literary Immigrants in Twentieth-Century America*. Chicago: U of Chicago P, 1993.

Freud, Sigmund. *Totem and Taboo*. New York: Norton, 1950.

Fuderer, Laura Sue. *The Female Bildungsroman in English: An Annotated Bibliography of Criticism*. New York: Modern Language Association, 1990.

Fujita, Stephen S., and David J. O'Brien. *Japanese American Ethnicity: The Persistence of Community*. Seattle: U of Washington P, 1991.

Gaskell, Elizabeth. *North and South*. 1855. New York: Penguin, 1970.

Gilbert, Sandra M., and Susan Gubar. *The Madwoman in the Attic: The Woman Writer and the Nineteenth-Century Imagination*. New Haven: Yale UP, 1984.

Ginsburg, Michal Peled. "Truth and Persuasion: The Language of Realism and of Ideology in *Oliver Twist*." *Novel: A Forum on Fiction* 20, no. 3 (spring 1987): 220–36.

Glazer, Nathan, and Daniel P. Moynihan, eds. *Ethnicity: Theory and Experience*. Cambridge: Harvard UP, 1975.

Gordon, Milton. *Assimilation in American Life: The Role of Race, Religion, and National Origins*. New York: Oxford UP, 1964.

Gotanda, Neil. "A Critique of 'Our Constitution is Colorblind.' " *Stanford Law Review* 44, no. 1 (November 1991): 1–68.

————. "Towards Repeal of Asian Exclusion . . ." In *Asian Americans in Congress: A Documentary History*, ed. Hyung Chan Kim, 309–28. Westport, Conn.: Greenwood, 1995.

Grewal, Gurleen. "Born Again American: The Immigrant Consciousness in *Jasmine*." In Nelson, *Bharati*, 181–96.

Hagedorn, Jessica. *Dogeaters*. New York: Penguin, 1990.

Hardin, James, ed. *Reflection and Action: Essays on the Bildungsroman*. Columbia: U of South Carolina P, 1991.

Hartman, Edward George. *The Movement to Americanize the Immigrant*. New York: AMS, 1967.

Heung, Marina. "Daughter-Text/Mother-Text: Matrilineage in Amy Tan's *Joy Luck Club*." *Feminist Studies* 19, no. 3 (1993): 597–616.

Higham, John. *Strangers in the Land: Patterns of American Nativism*. New Brunswick: Rutgers UP, 1955.

Hirsch, Marianne. *The Mother/Daughter Plot: Narrative, Psychoanalysis, Feminism*. Bloomington: Indiana UP, 1989.

————. "The Novel of Formation as Genre: Between Great Expectations and Lost Illusions." *Genre* 12, no. 3 (fall 1979): 293–312.

Hom, Marlon K. *Songs of Gold Mountain: Cantonese Rhymes from San Francisco Chinatown*. Berkeley: U of California P, 1987.

Hongo, Garrett. Introduction to *Songs My Mother Taught Me: Stories, Plays, and Memoir* by Wakako Yamauchi, ed. Garrett Hongo. New York: Feminist Press, 1994.

Houston, Jeanne Wakatsuki, and James D. Houston. *Farewell to Manzanar*. Boston: Houghton Mifflin, 1973.

Houston, Velina Hasu. *Tea*. In *Unbroken Thread: An Anthology of Plays by Asian American Women*, ed. Roberta Uno, 155–200. Amherst: U of Massachusetts P, 1993.

Hsia, C. T. *The Classic Chinese Novel: A Critical Introduction*. New York: Columbia UP, 1968.

Hummel, Arthur W., ed. *Eminent Chinese of the Ch'ing Period (1644–1912)*, vol. 2. Washington: United States Government Printing Office, 1944.

Hutcheon, Linda. *A Poetics of Postmodernism: History, Theory, Fiction*. London: Routledge, 1988.

————. *The Politics of Postmodernism*. London: Routledge, 1989.

Hwang, David Henry. "Family Devotions." In *FOB and Other Plays*, 87–146. New York: Plume-Penguin, 1990.

————. "FOB." In Hwang, *FOB and Other Plays*, 1–50.

————. *M. Butterfly*. New York: Plume-Penguin, 1988.

Ikeda, Stewart D. *What the Scarecrow Said: A Novel*. New York: HarperCollins, 1996.

Izumo, Takeda, Miyoshi Shoraku, and Namiki Senryu. *Chusingura (The Treasury of Loyal Retainers)*, trans. Donald Keene. New York: Columbia UP, 1971. Translation of *Kanadehon Chusingura* (1748).

Jameson, Fredric. *The Political Unconscious: Narrative as a Socially Symbolic Act*. Ithaca: Cornell UP, 1981.

Johnson, Kay Ann. *Women, the Family, and Peasant Revolution in China*. Chicago: U of Chicago P, 1983.

Joyce, James. *A Portrait of the Artist as a Young Man*, ed. Seamus Deane. 1916. New York: Viking-Penguin, 1976.

————. *Ulysses*. New York: Modern Library, 1934.

Kadohata, Cynthia. *The Floating World*. New York: Ballantine–Random House, 1989.

Kallen, Horace M. *Culture and Democracy in the United States*. 1924. New York: Arno, 1970.

Kang, Younghill. *East Goes West: The Making of an Oriental Yankee*. New York: Scribners, 1937.

Kaplan, Amy. Letter to Oscar Campomanes. October 10, 1989.

Kim, Elaine H. *Asian American Literature: An Introduction to the Writings and Their Social Context.* Philadelphia: Temple UP, 1982.

———. " 'Such Opposite Creatures': Men and Women in Asian American Literature." *Michigan Quarterly Review* 29, no. 1 (winter 1990): 68–92.

Kim, Elaine H., and Norma Alarcon, eds. *Writing Self, Writing Nation.* Berkeley: Third Woman Press, 1994.

Kim Ronyoung. See Ronyoung, Kim.

Kingston, Maxine Hong. *China Men.* 1980. New York: Vintage–Random House, 1989.

———. "Cultural Mis-readings by American Reviewers." *Asian and Western Writers in Dialogue,* ed. Guy Amirthanayagam, 55–65. London: Macmillan, 1982.

———. *Tripmaster Monkey: His Fake Book.* 1989. New York: Vintage–Random House, 1990.

———. *The Woman Warrior: Memoirs of a Girlhood Among Ghosts.* 1975. New York: Vintage–Random House, 1989.

Knippling, Alpana Sharma. "Toward an Investigation of the Subaltern in Bharati Mukherjee's *The Middleman and Other Stories* and *Jasmine.*" In Nelson, *Bharati,* 143–59.

Kogawa, Joy. *Obasan.* 1981. New York: Anchor-Doubleday, 1994.

Kolodny, Annette. *The Lay of the Land: Metaphor as Experience and History in American Life and Letters.* Chapel Hill: U of North Carolina P, 1975.

Kornfeld, Eve, and Susan Jackson. "The Female Bildungsroman in Nineteenth-Century America: Parameters of a Vision." *Journal of American Culture* 104 (1987): 69–75.

Kristeva, Julia. *Powers of Horror: An Essay on Abjection,* trans. Leon S. Roudiez. 1980. New York: Columbia UP, 1982.

Lang, Olga. Introduction to Pa Chin, *Family,* vii–xxvi.

Lauter, Paul. *Canons and Contexts.* New York: Oxford UP, 1991.

———, gen. ed. *The Heath Anthology of American Literature,* 3d ed. Boston: Houghton Mifflin, 1998.

———. "Society and the Profession, 1958–83." In Lauter, *Canons and Contexts,* 3–21.

Lee, Chang-rae. *Native Speaker.* New York: Riverhead, 1995.

Lee, Gus. *China Boy.* 1991. New York: Signet-Penguin, 1992.

———. *Honor and Duty.* New York: Ivy-Random House, 1994.

Lee, Robert G. "The Woman Warrior as an Intervention in Asian American Historiography." In *Approaches to Teaching Maxine Hong Kingston's* The Woman Warrior, ed. Shirley Geok-lin Lim, 52–63. New York: Modern Language Association, 1991.

Lee, Sky. *The Disappearing Moon Cafe.* 1990. Seattle: Seal Press, 1991.

LeSeur, Geta. "One Mother, Two Daughters: The Afro-American and the Afro-Caribbean Female *Bildungsroman.*" *The Black Scholar* (March-April 1986): 26–33.

Lévi-Strauss, Claude. *The Elementary Structures of Kinship.* Boston: Beacon, 1969.

Li, David Leiwei. "*China Men:* Maxine Hong Kingston and the American Canon," *ALH* 2, no. 3 (1990): 483–502.

Lim, Shirley Geok-lin, and Amy Ling, eds. *Reading the Literatures of Asian America.* Philadelphia: Temple UP, 1992.

Ling, Amy. *Between Worlds: Women Writers of Chinese Ancestry.* New York: Pergamon, 1990.

———. Introduction to part one of Far, *Mrs. Spring Fragrance and Other Stories,* 11–16.

Ling, Amy, and Annette White-Parks. Introduction to Far, *Mrs. Spring Fragrance and Other Stories,* 1–8.

London, Jack. *The Call of the Wild.* 1903. New York: Dover, 1990.

———. "South of the Slot." In *The Heath Anthology of American Literature,* ed. Paul Lauter et al., 2d ed., 2 vols., 2:744–55. 1909. Lexington: D. C. Heath, 1994.

Lowe, Lisa. *Critical Terrains: French and British Orientalisms.* Ithaca: Cornell UP, 1991.

————. *Immigrant Acts: On Asian American Cultural Politics.* Durham: Duke UP, 1996.

Lowe, Pardee. *Father and Glorious Descendant.* Boston: Little, Brown, 1943.

Lu Hsun, *A Brief History of Chinese Fiction,* trans. Yang Hsien-Yi and Gladys Yang, 180–97. Westport: Hyperion P, 1973,

————. "The Diary of a Madman." *New Youth* 4, no. 5 (May 15, 1918): 414–24.

Lukács, Georg. *The Historical Novel,* trans. Hannah Mitchell and Stanley Mitchell. 1962. Lincoln: U of Nebraska P, 1983.

Luo Guanzhong. *Three Kingdoms: A Historical Novel,* trans. Moss Roberts. Berkeley: U of California P, 1991.

McAlister, Melanie. "(Mis)Reading *The Joy Luck Club.*" *Asian America: Journal of Culture and the Arts* 1 (winter 1992): 102–18.

McClintock, Anne. *Imperial Leather: Race, Gender, and Sexuality in the Colonial Contest.* New York: Routledge, 1995.

McWilliams, Carey. Introduction to Bulosan, *America,* vii–xxiv.

Mesher, David. "Metamorphosis of a Butterfly." *San Jose Studies* 17, no. 3 (fall 1991): 4–21.

Miller, Stuart Creighton. *The Unwelcome Immigrant: The American Image of the Chinese, 1785–1882.* Berkeley: U of California P, 1969.

Minatoya, Lydia. *Talking to High Monks in the Snow.* New York: HarperCollins, 1992.

Mohanty, Chandra. "Under Western Eyes: Feminist Scholarship and Colonial Discourses." *Feminist Review* (autumn 1988): 61–88.

Moretti, Franco. *The Way of the World: The Bildungsroman in European Culture.* London: Verso–New Left, 1987.

Morrison, Toni. *Playing in the Dark: Whiteness and the Literary Imagination.* New York: Vintage–Random House, 1993.

Moy, James S. *Marginal Sights: Staging the Chinese in America.* Iowa City: U of Iowa P, 1993.

Mukherjee, Bharati. *Darkness.* New York: Fawcett Crest–Random House, 1985.

————. "A Four-Hundred-Year-Old Woman." In *Critical Fictions: The Politics of Imaginative Writing,* ed. Philomena Mariani. Seattle: Bay Press, 1991.

————. *Holder of the World.* New York: Fawcett Crest–Random House, 1993.

————. *Jasmine.* New York: Fawcett Crest–Random House, 1989.

————. *The Middleman and Other Stories.* New York: Fawcett Crest–Random House, 1988.

————. *The Tiger's Daughter.* Fawcett Crest–Random House, 1971.

————. *Wife.* New York: Fawcett Crest–Random House, 1975.

Mura, David. *After We Lost Our Way.* New York: Dutton, 1989.

————. *The Colors of Desire.* New York: Anchor-Doubleday, 1995.

————. *A Male Grief: Notes on Pornography and Addiction.* Minneapolis: Milkweed Editions, 1987.

————. "Strangers in the Village." In *The Graywolf Annual Five: Multi-Cultural Literacy,* ed. Rich Simonson and Scott Walker. Saint Paul, Minn.: Graywolf Press, 1988. 135–53.

————. *Turning Japanese: Memoirs of a Sansei.* New York: Anchor-Doubleday, 1991.

————. *Where the Body Meets Memory: An Odyssey of Race, Sexuality, and Identity.* New York: Anchor-Doubleday, 1996.

Murayama, Milton. *All I Asking for Is My Body.* 1975. Honolulu: U of Hawaii P, 1988.

————. *Five Years on a Rock.* Honolulu: U of Hawaii P, 1994.

Narayan, Kirin. *Love, Stars, and All That.* New York: Prospect Books, 1994.

Nelson, Emmanuel, ed. *Bharati Mukherjee: Critical Perspectives.* New York: Garland, 1993.

Ng, Fae Myenne. *Bone.* New York: HarperCollins, 1993.

Nomura, Gail M., et al., eds. *Frontiers of Asian American Studies.* Pullman: Washington State UP, 1989.

Oe, Kenzaburo. *A Personal Matter*, trans. John Nathan. New York: Grove-Atlantic, 1970.

Okada, John. *No-No Boy*. 1957. Seattle: U of Washington P, 1976.

Okihiro, Gary Y. *Cane Fires: The Anti-Japanese Movement in Hawaii, 1865–1945*. Philadelphia: Temple UP, 1991.

———. *Margins and Mainstreams: Asians in American History and Culture*. Seattle: U of Washington P, 1994.

Okimoto, Daniel. *An American in Disguise*. New York: Walter-Weatherhill, 1971.

Omi, Michael, and Howard Winant. *Racial Formation in the United States: From the 1960s to the 1980s*. New York: Routledge, 1986.

O'Neale, Sondra. "Race, Sex, and Self: Aspects of *Bildung* in Select Novels by Black American Women Novelists." *MELUS* 9, no. 4 (winter 1982): 25–37.

Ono Kazuko. *Chinese Women in a Century of Revolution, 1850–1950*, trans. Kathryn Bernhardt et al., ed. Joshua A. Fogel. 1978. Stanford: Stanford UP, 1989.

Pa Chin. *Family*, trans. Sidney Shapiro. 1931, 1972. Prospect Heights, Ill.: Waveland, 1989.

Palumbo-Liu, David. "Discourse and Dislocation: Rhetorical Strategies of Asian American Exclusion and Confinement." *LIT (Literature, Interpretation, Theory)* 2, no. 1 (July 1990): 1-7.

Park, Robert E. *Race and Culture*. New York: Free Press, 1950.

Park, Robert E., and Ernest W. Burgess. *Introduction to the Science of Sociology*. Chicago: U of Chicago P, 1921.

Persons, Stow. *Ethnic Studies at Chicago, 1905–45*. Urbana: U of Illinois P, 1987.

Rafael, Vicente. "White Love: Surveillance and Nationalist Resistance in the U.S. Colonization of the Philippines." In *Cultures of United States Imperialism*, ed. Amy Kaplan and Donald E. Pease, 185–218. Durham: Duke UP, 1993.

Rajan, Gita. "Bharati Mukherjee." In *Writers of the Indian Diaspora: A Bio-Bibliographical Critical Sourcebook*, ed. Emmanuel S. Nelson, Westport: Greenwood, 1993. 235–42.

Renan, Ernest. "What Is a Nation?" trans. Martin Thom. In Bhabha, *Nation*, 8–22.

Richardson, Samuel. *Pamela, or Virtue Rewarded*. 1740. New York: Norton, 1958.

Roberts, Moss. Afterword to *Three Kingdoms: A Historical Novel* [Luo Guanzhong?], trans. Moss Roberts, 937–86. Berkeley: U of California P, 1991.

———. Introduction to Lo Kuan-chung, *Three Kingdoms: China's Epic Drama*, xix–xxv. New York: Pantheon. 1976.

Roland, Alan. *Cultural Pluralism and Psychoanalysis: The Asian and North American Experience*. New York: Routledge, 1996.

———. "How Universal is the Psychoanalytic Self?" In Roland, *Cultural Pluralism*, 3–21.

Ronyoung, Kim. *Clay Walls*. Sag Harbor, N.Y.: Permanent Press, n.d.

Rubin, Gayle. "The Traffic in Women: Notes toward a Political Economy of Sex." In *Toward an Anthropology of Women*, ed. Rayna Reiter, 157–210. New York: Monthly Review Press, 1975.

Russ, Joanna. *How to Suppress Women's Writing*. Austin: U of Texas P, 1983.

Said, Edward W. *Culture and Imperialism*. New York: Vintage, 1993.

———. *Orientalism*. New York: Random House, 1979.

Sakurai, Patricia Ann. "Speaking of Identity: Naming, Experience, and Sexual Politics in Asian American Literature of the 1970s." Ph.D. diss., Department of English, SUNY-Stonybrook, 1995.

Sammons, Jeffrey L. "The Bildungsroman for Nonspecialists: An Attempt at a Clarification." In Hardin, *Reflection*, 26–45.

San Juan Jr., E. *Carlos Bulosan and the Imagination of the Class Struggle*. 1972. New York: Oriole Editions, 1976.

———. Introduction to Bulosan, *Becoming*, 1–44.

———. *Racial Formations: Critical Transformations: Articulations of Power in Ethnic and Racial Studies in the United States*. Atlantic Highlands, N.J.: Humanities Press, 1992.

Sato, Gayle K. Fujita. "Momataro's Exile: John Okada's *No-No Boy*." In Lim and Ling, *Reading*, 239–58.

Schear, Walter. "Generational Differences and the Diaspora in *The Joy Luck Club*." *Critique: Studies in Contemporary Fiction* 24, no. 3 (1993): 193–99.

Schueller, Malini Johar. "Theorizing Ethnicity and Subjectivity: Maxine Hong Kingston's *Tripmaster Monkey* and Amy Tan's *The Joy Luck Club*." *Genders* 15 (1992): 72–85.

Sedgwick, Eve Kosofsky. *Between Men: English Literature and Male Homosocial Desire*. New York: Columbia UP, 1985.

Shakespeare, William. *The Complete Works*, ed. Alfred Harbage. New York: Viking-Penguin, 1969.

Shapiro, Sidney. Translator's note to *Outlaws of the Marsh*, Vol. 1 [Shi Nai'an and Luo Guanzhong?], trans. by Sidney Shapiro, n.p. Beijing: Foreign Languages P, 1988.

Sharma, Maya Manju. "The Inner World of Bharati Mukherjee: From Expatriate to Immigrant." In Nelson, *Bharati*, 3–22.

Shaw, George Bernard. *Pygmalion*. 1913. New York: Penguin, 1977.

Shi Nai'an and Luo Guanzhong. *Outlaws of the Marsh*, trans. and ed. Sidney Shapiro. 4 vols. Beijing: Foreign Languages Press, 1988. Best known as *The Water Margin* in English.

Shih, Shu-mei. "Exile and Intertextuality in Maxine Hong Kingston's *China Men*." In *The Literature of Emigration and Exile*, ed. James Whitlark and Wendell Aycock, Lubbock: Texas Tech UP, 1992.

Shikeguni, Julie. *A Bridge between Us*. New York: Anchor-Doubleday, 1995.

Shostak, Debra. "Maxine Hong Kingston's Fake Books." In *Memory, Narrative, and Identity: New Essays in Ethnic American Literatures*, ed. Amritjit Singh, Joseph T. Skerrett Jr., and Robert E. Hogan, 233–60. Boston: Northeastern UP, 1994.

Showalter, Elaine, ed. *The New Feminist Criticism: Essays on Women, Literature, and Theory*. New York: Pantheon–Random House, 1985.

Sidhwa, Bapsi. *An American Brat*. Minneapolis: Milkweed, 1993.

So, Christine. "Delivering the Punch Line: Racial Combat as Comedy in Gus Lee's *China Boy*." *MELUS* 21, no. 4 (winter 1996): 141–55.

Sollors, Werner. *Beyond Ethnicity: Consent and Descent in American Culture*. New York: Oxford UP, 1986.

Sone, Monica. *Nisei Daughter*. 1953. Seattle: U of Washington P, 1979.

Spence, Jonathan. *The Search for Modern China*. New York: Norton, 1990.

Spivak, Gayatri Chakravorty. "Can the Subaltern Speak?" In *Marxism and the Interpretation of Culture*, ed. Cary Nelson and Lawrence Grossberg. Urbana: U of Illinois P, 1988.

———. "The Post-colonial Critic." In Gayatri Chakravorty Spivak, *The Postcolonial Critic*, ed. Sarah Harasym. New York: Routledge, 1990. 67–74.

Stewart, G. B. "Mother, Daughter, and the Birth of the Female Artist." *Women's Studies* 6 (1979): 127–45.

Stonequist, Everett V. *The Marginal Man: A Study in Personality and Culture Conflict*. 1937. New York: Russell and Russell, 1961.

Stowe, Harriet Beecher. *Uncle Tom's Cabin*, ed. Elizabeth Ammons. New York: Norton, 1993.

Sumida, Stephen H. "Japanese American Moral Dilemmas in John Okada's *No-No Boy* and Milton Murayama's *All I Asking for Is My Body*." In Nomura et al., *Frontiers*, 222–33.

———. *And the View from the Shore: Literary Traditions of Hawai'i*. Seattle: U of Washington P, 1991.

Sun Tzu. *The Art of War,* trans. Bruce Cleary. Boston: Shambala, 1988.

Sundquist, Eric J. *Home as Found: Authority and Genealogy in Nineteenth-Century American Literature.* Baltimore: Johns Hopkins UP, 1977.

Takaki, Ronald. *Iron Cages: Race and Culture in Nineteenth Century America.* New York: Oxford UP, 1990.

———. *Pau Hana: Plantation Life and Labor in Hawaii.* Honolulu: U of Hawaii P, 1983.

———. *Strangers from a Different Shore.* Boston: Little, Brown, 1989.

Tamura, Eileen H. *Americanization, Acculturation, and Ethnic Identity: The Nisei Generation in Hawaii.* Urbana: U of Illinois P, 1994.

Tan, Amy. *The Hundred Secret Senses.* 1995. New York: Vintage–Random House, 1998.

———. *The Joy Luck Club.* 1989. New York: Vintage–Random House, 1991.

———. *The Kitchen God's Wife.* 1992. New York: Vintage–Random House, 1993.

Teng, Emma Jinhua. "Miscegenation and the Critique of Patriarchy in Turn-of-the-Century Fiction." *Race, Gender, and Class: Asian American Voices* 4, no. 3 (1997): 69–87.

Tompkins, Jane P. *Sensational Designs: The Cultural Work of American Fiction, 1790–1860.* New York: Oxford UP, 1985.

———. "Sentimental Power: *Uncle Tom's Cabin* and the Politics of Literary History." In Showalter, *Criticism,* 81–104.

Tsao, Hsueh-chin. *Dream of the Red Chamber,* trans. Chi-Chen Wang. 1958. New York: Anchor-Doubleday, 1989.

Tung, May. "Insight-Oriented Therapy and the Chinese Patient." In Roland, *Cultural Pluralism,* 175–86.

TuSmith, Bonnie. *All My Relatives: Community in Contemporary Ethnic American Literature.* Ann Arbor: U of Michigan P, 1994.

Viswanathan, Gauri. *Masks of Conquest: Literary Study and British Rule in India.* New York: Columbia UP, 1989.

Voloshin, Beverly R. "The Limits of Domesticity: The Female *Bildungsroman* in America, 1820–1870." *Women's Studies* 10 (1984): 283–302.

Wald, Priscilla. *Constituting Americans: Cultural Anxiety and Narrative Form.* Durham: Duke UP, 1995.

Watt, Ian. *The Rise of the Novel: Studies in Defoe, Richardson, and Fielding.* Berkeley: U of California P, 1959.

Weglyn, Michi. *Years of Infamy: The Untold Story of America's Concentration Camps.* New York: Morrow, 1976.

White-Parks, Annette. Introduction to part two of Far, *Mrs. Spring Fragrance and Other Stories,* 169–77.

———. *Sui Sin Far/Edith Maude Eaton: A Literary Biography.* Urbana: U of Illinois P, 1995.

Whitman, Walt. *Leaves of Grass,* ed. Sculley Bradley and Harold W. Blodgett. New York: Norton, 1973.

Wolf, Margery. "Women and Suicide in China." In *Women in Chinese Society,* ed. Margery Wolf and Roxanne Witke, Stanford: Stanford UP, 1975. 111–41.

Wong, Jade Snow. *Fifth Chinese Daughter.* New York: Harper and Row, 1945.

Wong, Sau-ling Cynthia. "Autobiography as Guided Chinatown Tour? Maxine Hong Kingston's *The Woman Warrior* and the Chinese American Autobiographical Controversy." In *Multicultural Autobiography,* ed. James Robert Payne, 248–79. Knoxville: U of Tennessee P, 1992.

———. *Reading Asian American Literature: From Necessity to Extravagance.* Princeton: Princeton UP, 1993.

———. "'Sugar Sisterhood': Situating the Amy Tan Phenomenon." In *The Ethnic Canon: His-*

tories, Institutions, and Interventions, ed. David Palumbo-Liu, 174–210. Minneapolis: U of Minnesota P, 1995.

Wong, Shawn. *American Knees.* New York: Simon and Schuster, 1995.

———. *Asian American Literature.* New York: HarperCollins, 1996.

Woo, Deborah. "Maxine Hong Kingston: The Ethnic Writer and the Burden of Dual Authenticity." *Amerasia* 16, no. 1 (1990): 173–200.

Woolf, Virginia. *A Room of One's Own.* New York: Harcourt Brace Jovanovich, 1957.

[Wu Ch'eng-en?]. *The Journey to the West,* trans. and ed. Anthony C. Yu. 4 vols. Chicago: U of Chicago P, 1977–83.

Yamamoto, Hisaye. *Seventeen Syllables and Other Stories.* Latham, N.Y.: Kitchen Table/Women of Color Press, 1988.

Yamanaka, Lois-Ann. *Blu's Hanging.* New York: Avon, 1997.

Yamauchi, Wakako. *Songs My Mother Taught Me: Stories, Plays, and Memoir,* ed. Garrett Hongo. New York: Feminist Press, 1994.

Yeh, William. "To Belong or Not to Belong: The Liminality of John Okada's *No-No Boy.*" *Amerasia* 19, no. 1 (1993): 121–33.

Yin, Xiao-Huang. "Between the East and West: Sui Sin Far, the First Chinese-American Woman Writer." *Arizona Quarterly* 47, no. 4 (winter 1991): 49–84.

Yu, Anthony C. Introduction to *The Journey to the West,* trans. and ed. [Wu Ch'eng-en?], trans. Anthony C. Yu, 4 vols., 1:1–21. Chicago: U of Chicago P, 1977–83.

Yung, Judy. *Unbound Feet: A Social History of Chinese Women in San Francisco.* Berkeley: U of California P, 1995.

Index

Asian American bildungsroman: meta-fictional aspect of, 198 n.35; rethinking, 184–87; toward an, 15–17. *See also* Bildungsroman

Asian American ethnicity: as American, 187; claiming, 100–102; distinctions within, 21–22; women as embodiments of, 43, 54–60, 61, 90–91, 92, 100, 112–15

Asian American literary canon: as American, 187; Chinese American, 70, 170–84; and early Chinese male immigrant poetry, 123–28; the emerging, 20; Frank Chin's view of, 70–71, 169–73; gendering of the, 64–70; the male, 61–62, 67–71; and postmodern writing, 172–73, 181–84, 187, 214 n.4. *See also* American literary canon

Asian Americans: as Americans, 6–7, 122, 187; common racial history of, 9, 189

Asian countries. *See specific country names or ethnic groups*

Asian culture: Asian women and transmission of, 43, 93, 123; changing definitions of fake and real, 65–67, 70, 75, 170, 181, 186; Christian stereotype of, 65–66; containment or claiming of, 186–87; as feminized and inflexible, 93, 102, 112, 123, 127, 149, 170–71; gendered recognition and support within, 94–95, 157; as inferior, 115–16, 121, 148; negative images of, 166, 176; underestimation of, 159, 163. *See also* Stereotypes of Asians

Asian male characters: American-born sons, 54–60; brothers, 45–46; idealized fathers of sons, 44, 49. *See also* Father-son relationships; Male subjects, Asian American

Asian women characters: Chinese wife, 120–22; emancipated, 126–27; fallen, 48, 49; half-sisters in the homeland, 166–68; idealized mothers, 44, 45, 49; idealized sisters, 44, 46–47, 49; ideologically engaged with subjectivity, 60–61, 62–63; as mothers defining Asian values, 54–60, 61, 112; self-defining, 78–79, 126–27, 155, 158

Asian women in male Asian American texts: abjection of, 49–51, 54–60, 61, 85, 90–91, 208 n.22; and amnesia, 51; and filial nostalgia, 42–49; as full-fledged subjects, 61, 62–63; functions of, 20, 43, 51–52, 94–95; as retarding American socialization, 54–60; and the snare motif, 44–46, 49, 125

Assimilation: achievement of, 187; ambivalence toward, 57, 62; and amnesia, 51, 80–82, 186; Anglo-conformity as model for, 21, 192 n.10; bildungsroman's function in, 12, 18, 21, 89; cultural and structural, 8, 73–74, 187; as extinction of the ethnic American self, 87–88; and gender, 4–5, 6–7, 20–21, 50–51, 110–16, 136–37; and the immigrant analogy, 7–9; mother-daughter, 145; narratives moving beyond, 188–89; of readers and writers, 9–12, 171, 184; as a tantalizing goal, 6, 187; through cross-cultural understanding, 166–68; through English, 3, 10, 113; variables, 8. *See also* Americanness; Mobility, tropes of

Assimilation trophies. *See* White women in male Asian American texts

Austen, Jane, 131, 132

Authenticity thesis. *See* Chin, Frank, works by: "Come All Ye Asian American Writers"

Author-hero myth: Chin's Asian American, 70–71, 77; female Asian American, 185; the Kingston-Chin debate on, 169–73, 183–84; the white male American, 67–69, 185. *See also* Heroes

Authorship and authority, 64–89, 202 nn.1–13; as central trope for subject formation, 6, 19; difficulties facing women's, 93–97, 136–37; the importance of, 11; legitimization of female, 96–97; male and female differences in, 4–5, 20–21, 136–37; masculinization of, 20, 28, 42, 61–62, 69–70, 91, 187; and paternity, 69, 71; readerly, 181, 184; the struggle for, 2, 28, 93–95; women writers' claims to, 20–21; the writer's call to, 146. *See also* Fathering

Autobiographies. *See specific writer names*

Bachelors: Asian immigrant, 29–42; poetry by, 21, 93, 123–28, 208 n.24. *See also* Sexual segregation

Banerjee, Debjani, 129, 134

Barthes, Roland, 171, 184, 197 n.30

Bastard son metaphor, 83–85

Baym, Nina: "Melodramas of Beset Manhood," 54, 67–71, 76, 123, 185

Chinese classics (*continued*)
hero and, 177–80; feudal origins of, 214
n.8; "original," 214 nn.6, 8; as readerly
texts, 171–72, 181, 184; transplantation and
translation of, 182–84
Chinese ethnicity: constructions of, 22–
23; containment or claiming of, 186–87;
and exclusion, 29, 123–28; and sexual
segregation, 29, 123–28. *See also* Chinese
American ethnicity
Chinese Eurasian, construction as a, 100–102
Chinese heroic tradition. *See* Heroic tradition, Chinese
Chow, Rey, 148, 156
Chusingura (classical Japanese puppet play),
67, 205 n.6
Cinderella stories. *See* Romance plot
Citizenship: loss of, 29. *See also* Exclusion
era; Exclusion of Asians
Civil rights: internment era suspension of,
58, 66–67
Clan: the all-male army, 180; the Chinese
American community, 174
Class differences: and domestic novels, 14–
15, 16, 132–34; improbable discontinuities
in, 151–58; between writer and character,
129–30
Classic realism. *See* Realist novel
Classic texts, Chinese. *See* Chinese classics
Clinton, William Jefferson, 132
Colonialism: cultural legacy of, 133; the need
to forget, 53. *See also* Imperialism
Commodification of ethnicity, 214 n.7
Communal text, 173–77, 184
Countries of origin. *See* Homeland, the im-
migrant's; *specific country names or ethnic
groups*
Creative process: communal, 173–77, 184;
dialogic, 175–76, 181, 187
Cross-cultural understanding, 166–68, 181

Daughtering: courageous, 199 n.45; self-
formation, 211 n.3
Daughters, Chinese American: ethnicity of,
167–68; immaturity and orientalism of,
149–50; as representing America, 22, 167.
See also Mother-daughter plot
Dearborn, Mary: *Pocahontas's Daughters,* 19,
94, 199 n.44

Democratic rhetoric of inclusion, 1–4, 30,
173–74. *See also* Horatio Alger myth;
Mobility
Denial, themes of: of Chinese self, 158; of
immigrant pasts, 80–82, 186; of racism
after internment, 80–83. *See also* Abjec-
tion; Amnesia, themes of
Descent line: American, 64, 202 n.2; Asian
American, 64, 71. *See also* American literary canon; Asian American literary
canon
Desire: homosocial, 177–80. *See also* Political
desire
De Witt, John, 66
Discrimination against Asians, 29. *See also*
Exclusion; Racism
Disinheritance from American manhood, 85
Distance: emotional, 51, 80–81, 204 n.8;
temporal (allochronism), 148, 156, 159
Domestic novel, the, 14–15; and Asian
immigrant women, 21, 96–97, 123;
depoliticization of class conflict in, 16,
133; double-voiced rescription of, 136–
37; romantic triangles in, 110–22. *See also*
Novel
Doubles, Asian American. *See* Racial
shadow
Draft resistance: internment era, 55–56, 67,
70
The Dream of the Red Chamber, 118
Dream sequences, 31, 51
Dual personality model: Chin's criticism of,
66–67; of Japanese American psychology,
57–59
DuPlessis, Rachel Blau, 201 n.18, 210 n.30

Eagleton, Terry, 194 n.20
East Goes West. See Kang, Younghill
Eaton, Edith Maude. *See* Far, Sui Sin (Edith
Maude Eaton)
Eaton, Grace Trefusis (Lotus Blossom), 99,
102, 103, 104, 122
Eaton, Winifred, 98–99, 101–2, 207 n.20
Education: of elite Chinese women, 163–64;
functions of literary, 9–12; gendered stan-
dards for, 94; of the immigrant heroine,
134, 155–59
Education novels. *See* Domestic novel;
Romance plot

Emancipation of women, 126–27
Emasculation thesis, Chin's, 65
Empowerment: "just say grr" fable of, 155, 158. *See also* Agency
Empty scrolls and the writerly text, 180–84
English, learning, 3, 9–10, 113
English and American literature: the bildungsroman in, 12; and fidelity to origins, 186; and immigrant socialization, 10, 123; self-formation in, 132, 185–86. *See also* American literary canon; Bildungsroman; Domestic novel, the
Erasure, theme of. *See* Extinction, theme of cultural
Escape from homeland society: plausibility of, 152–55, 159
Ethnicity: and agency, 141–68; distinctions within Asian, 21–22; and intergenerational difference, 146–49; in *The Joy Luck Club,* 141–68, 211 nn.1-18; the Kingston-Chin debate on, 169–73. *See also specific country names or ethnic groups*
Ethnicity theory and assimilation, 7–9
Ethnographic documents, 196 n.27
Evolution, cultural, 192 n.14
Exclusion era: Chinese women's silence during, 122; male poetry, 21, 93, 123–28, 208 n.24
Exclusion of Asians: and Asian American sexuality, 28–29, 123–28; and assimilation, 4; cases of, 199 n.3; from discourse, the double, 11; extinction thesis and cultural, 64–65; and the immigrant romance, 27–42, 122; from immigration, 29, 122, 123–28, 193 n.18; legislative history of, 29, 66, 199 n.3. *See also* Abjection
Exclusion of women authors: from the literary canon, 67–68
Exotic: to be or not to be, 175
Extinction, theme of cultural, 186; Chin's, 64–65, 76, 171; dread of, 80, 85–86; Kang's, 35; or reinscription, 181

Fabian, Johannes, 148
Fake and real culture. *See* Asian culture
Fake books and musical improvisation, 173
Family (novel). *See* Pa Chin
Family life: escape from Asian homeland, 152–55, 159; and female loyalty, 179–80; as

feminized and private, 14–15, 54; multicultural, 103–4; novel attacking old Chinese, 160–65
Family narratives, Asian American: after internment, 79–80; of dissolution, 56–57; and intersubjective recognition, 76–77; of separation through emigration, 43–51
Fanon, Frantz, 86
Far, Sui Sin (Edith Maude Eaton), 17, 18, 98–105, 185; Chinese male views contemporary to, 123–28; feminist perspective of, 21; fictions of Americanization, 105–23; life of, 98–99; and Mukherjee, 136–38; the names of, 206 n.13, 207 n.16; public persona as an author, 99–102
Far, Sui Sin (Edith Maude Eaton), works by, 18; "The Americanizing of Pau Tzu," 110–11, 116–22; "The Inferior Woman," 107–8; "Its Wavering Image," 108–10; *Leaves from the Mental Portfolio of an Eurasian,* 21, 90, 98–105; *Mrs. Spring Fragrance,* 102, 107–8, 117, 127–28, 207 n.17; "Pat and Pan," 207 n.19; *The Wisdom of the New,* 110–16, 118–22, 209 n.25, 210 n.27
Fatherhood: acceptance by the white, 83–84, 185; and assimilation, 88–89; as literary metaphor, 20, 35, 42, 69
Fathering: literary offspring, 35, 38, 62, 86–87; a literary tradition, 20, 69–70, 91, 185; and promiscuity, 86–87. *See also* Authorship and authority
Father-son relationships, 49, 75–77, 81–84
Fat lady metaphor, 174–75
Fealty: and homosocial bonding, 177–80
Female hero: trope of, 177–80. *See also* Heroines
Female immigration restrictions, 200 n.4
Female sacrifice, 154–55, 161, 205 n.6; by men, 177–80
Female writers. *See* Women writers
Feminism and self-assertion, 150–51, 164
Feudal texts. *See* Chinese classics
Fiedler, Leslie, 68
Filial attitudes: of indignation, 83–84, 160; of piety, 160–63
Filipina lives, portrayals of, 44–48, 201 n.17
Filipino Americans: identity of, 35–37, 41; invisibility of, 36, 202 n.20; Pinoy migrant workers, 37–40, 47

First-world bias, 148; in immigrant novels, 129–30, 134

Folklore, immutable or improvised, 172

Food pornography, 74–76, 214 n.7

Fraternity: and homosocial bonding, 177–80

Gaskell, Elizabeth, 132

Gender bias, literary. *See* Asian American literary canon

Gender construction: and authorship, 4–5; by Chinese immigrant bachelors, 123–28; and division of cultural labor, 93, 123, 127; and marriage plots, 18–19, 97; and oppression, 47–48, 159–64, 177–80; as traditional or progressive, 53

Gender gap among Asian American writers: Kingston and Chin, 6, 176–77

Gendering Asianness: and abjection of women, 49–51, 54–60, 61, 85, 90–91, 208 n.22; and amnesia, 51; and filial/homeland nostalgia, 42–49

Gender-specific oppression: male authors on, 47–48, 159–64, 177–80

Genealogy: as a central concern of American authors, 64, 202 n.2; as theme, 6

Ghost: becoming a, 87

Ghost, the invisible "Asian" self. *See* Racial shadow

Ghosts, Memoirs of a Girlhood Among. See Kingston, Maxine Hong, works by

Gordon, Milton: *Assimilation in American Life,* 8, 192 nn.10, 12, 13

Gotanda, Neil, 193 n.18

Grewal, Gurleen, 129–30, 134

Hardin, James: on bildungsromane, 12–13

Harlequin romance novels, 132

Hawaii: plantation workers' life in, 55

Heroes: homosocial text and female, 177–80; the Kingston-Chin debate on, 169–73, 179–80; masculine Americanness of, 20, 28, 61–63; searching for, 72–73; well-married, 18–19, 88–89; the writer's literary, 88. *See also* Author-hero myth

Heroic tradition, Chinese, 169–87; and Chin's authenticity thesis, 65–66; definitive texts of, 203 n.4, 214 n.8; feudal origins of, 214 n.8; *Tripmaster Monkey* meditations on, 169–73, 177–80; usage by

Chin and Kingston, 23, 169–73, 187. *See also* Chinese classics

Heroines: archetypal English romance novel, 132–33; bildungsroman construction of women as, 97, 118, 132–33; the Chinese immigrant, 152–53; female hero trope, 177–80; and homosocial text, 177–80; self-reinvention by, 186. *See also* Women characters

Heterosexuality: as narrative norm, 199 n.43

Historical novels: Asian American difficulties with, 16; postcolonial, 128–30. *See also* Chinese classics

Hom, Marlon K. (ed.), *Songs of Gold Mountain,* 21, 93, 123–28, 208 n.24; "Ballads of the Libertines," 125–27; "Lamentations of Estranged Wives," 124–25; "Songs of Western Influence," 126

Homeland, the immigrant's: ambivalence toward, 57, 62; escape from, 151–55, 159; growing up in the, 44–46; as idealized and feminized, 53; immigrant mothers as personifying, 43, 54–60, 61, 90–91, 92, 100, 112–15; nostalgia for, 42–49; original discontent back in the, 152–53; return or visit to, 46–47, 119, 166–68; women left behind in, 28–29, 122, 124–25. *See also* China

Homelessness: theme of, 30–31

Homosocial text: female hero and, 177–80

Horatio Alger myth, 130

Houston, Jeanne Wakatsuki: *Farewell to Manzanar,* 95

Hutchinson, Linda, 172–73

Hwang, David Henry, 70, 94

Identity: the immigrant's search for, 35–37, 41, 71–79; and national literature, 10, 187, 194 n.20

Immigrant, myth of the: female paradigms, 185; male paradigms, 137, 185, 211 n.6; and the mother-daughter romance, 143–44, 165–68, 185; as the quintessential American self, 211 n.4

Immigrant analogy, 7–9

Immigrant romance: and Americanization, 19–21, 40–41, 90, 110–22, 185; by women writers, 91, 92–93, 98–105, 110–22, 128–38, 185; and exclusion, 27–42, 122; gender differences in, 20–21, 90–93, 185; and the *Jasmine* controversy, 128–38; and racism, 39–42. *See also* Mother-daughter plot

Immigration Act of 1924, 30, 200 n.9

Imperialism: abjection central to industrial, 50; invisibility of, 202 n.20; and literary education, 194 n.20; the need to forget national, 53. *See also* Colonialism

Inada, Lawson Fusao. *See* Chin, Frank, et al. (eds.)

Inclusiveness: political and cultural, 173–74

India: Buddhist pilgrimage to, 181–84

Individualism versus intersubjectivity: in the author-hero myth, 68–69; theme of, 17–18

Intergenerational difference. *See* Father-son relationships; Mother-daughter plot

Interiority: of Chinese women immigrants, 122, 157; in realist fiction, 14–15, 16

Internment of Japanese Americans, 4; abjections in literature of, 54–60; after-effects of, 79–82, 95–96; attitudes toward, 58, 66–67, 70, 203 n.7

Interracial romance plots, 19–21; ambivalence toward, 74, 76; gendered differences in, 20–21, 93; involving writers, 77–78; and the *Jasmine* controversy, 131–36; Korean American, 31–33. *See also* Assimilation; Marriage plots; Romance plot

Interwar period in China, 212 n.8

Invisibility themes: of becoming ghosts, 87; Filipino American, 36, 202 n.20; Japanese American, 84–85, 87, 89

Japanese American Citizens' League (JACL), 70, 203 n.7

Japanese American writing: in and after World War II, 204 n.10; Chin's criticism of, 66–67, 70; internment era (World War II), 54–60, 66–67, 95–96, 204 n.10

Jasmine controversy. *See* Mukherjee, Bharati, works by

Jazz improvisation: metaphor of, 173, 175–76

Journalism by a white reporter, 108–10

The Journey to the West. See Wu Ch'eng-en

Joyce, James: *Ulysses,* 200 n.11, 211 n.7

The Joy Luck Club. See Tan, Amy

Kadohata, Cynthia, 188

Kallen, Horace, 8

Kang, Younghill, 20, 41, 61–62; *East Goes West: The Making of an Oriental Yankee,* 27, 29, 30–35, 42, 92, 94

Kim, Elaine H.: *Asian American Literature,* 30, 95

King, Rodney, 193 n.19

Kingston, Maxine Hong: on communal text, 173–77, 184; contrast between Chin and, 6, 22–23, 70, 169–73; feminist revision of *Three Kingdoms* by, 177–80; life of, 213 n.1

Kingston, Maxine Hong, works by, 18, 169–87; *China Men,* 2; *Tripmaster Monkey: His Fake Book,* 169–73, 177–80, 198 n.38; *The Woman Warrior: Memoirs of a Girlhood Among Ghosts,* 1, 2, 95, 96, 198 n.38

Kinship, "in your bones" trope of, 141–43

Korean Americans: fictional treatments, 1–3, 30–35; and Los Angeles riots, 193 n.19

Labor, division of cultural, 93, 123, 127

Labor movement: Filipino American, 35–37

Lang, Olga, 160

Laundrymen, Chinese, 100, 103

Lauter, Paul, 194 n.21

Lee, Chang-rae: *Native Speaker,* 1, 2–3, 18

Letter writing: middle-class female, 210 n.26

Lévi-Strauss, Claude, 177

Liberal arts education: and ideology, 10

Literacy and Americanization, 40–41

Literary education and imperialism, 194 n.20. *See also* Education

Literary offspring. *See* Fathering

Literature: centrality of, 189; knowledge of Anglo-American, 33, 173

Literature, Asian American: as American, 187, 189; and common history, 9, 189; the double exclusion of, 11; immigrant knowledge of, 32–33; immutable or improvised, 172–73

London, Jack, 207 n.18

Los Angeles riots of 1992, 9, 193 n.19

Loti, Pierre: *Madame Chrysantheme,* 207 n.20

Lotus Blossom. *See* Eaton, Grace Trefusis

Lowe, Lisa, works by: *Critical Terrains,* 203 n.3; *Immigrant Acts: On Asian American Cultural Politics,* 12, 18–19, 193 n.18

Loyalty oath: internment era, 55–56, 58; Peach Orchard, 180

Lu Hsun, works by: "A Brief History of Chinese Fiction," 214 n.8; "The Diary of a Madman," 163, 213 n.17
Lukács, Georg, 13, 197 n.30
Luo Guanzhong: *Three Kingdoms: A Historical Novel,* 174, 177–80. *See also* Shi Nai'an and Luo Guanzhong

Madama Butterfly story, 185, 207 n.20
"Magpies" (in *The Joy Luck Club*), 153–55, 161
Mahjong club, the Joy Luck. *See* Tan, Amy, work by
Male subjects, Asian American: abjection of female Asians by, 11, 20, 49–51, 54–60, 85, 90–93; and ethnic heroism, 169–73, 176–77; identity search by, 71–79; literary fathers, 5, 35, 38, 62, 86–87; outlaws, 5, 67, 72–73; rebellious sons, 5, 55–60, 72. *See also* Author-hero myth; White women characters
Male writers, Asian American: narrative strategies of, 185; as subjects, 74–79, 84–85, 169–80. *See also* Fathering
Marginalization: of Asian American men by male writers, 20, 176; cultural and political, 42; of women, 179–80
Marriage: agency and liberation from, 150–51; arranged, 115–16, 160–63; entrapment into enforced, 45–46; and female loyalty, 178–80; loss of citizenship through, 29; as medium of exchange in homosocial relationships, 177–79; as signifier for subject formation, 18–19, 199 n.43; varied Chinese attitudes toward, 160–63
Marriage plots: and colonialism, 133; English domestic novel, 130–33; the missing, 18–19; within homosocial texts, 177–80; women writers' transformations of, 97, 134, 137. *See also* Interracial romance plots; Romance plot
Masaoka, Mike, 70, 203 n.7
Masculinity: and Asian American male authors, 28, 176, 187; cultural denigrations of Asian, 170–71
Matrilineal narratives, Asian American, 141, 168, 211 n.1. *See also* Mother-daughter plot, the
May Fourth Movement. *See* China

McAlister, Melanie, 212 n.10
McClintock, Anne, 50, 52–53
McWilliams, Carey, 41
Mediation: of ethnic female texts, 94, 95; intercultural, 94
Melting pot: connotations of, 7–8, 192 n.10, 206 n.9
Memoirs, Asian American: by Sui Sin Far, 21, 90, 98–105; by Maxine Hong Kingston, 1, 2, 95, 96, 198 n.38; by David Mura, 79–89; by Jeanne Wakatsuki, 95; by Jade Snow Wong, 95
Ménage-à-trois. *See* Triangular relationships
Mentorship and homosocial bonding, 178–79
Metafiction, 198 n.35
Middle class: in domestic and sentimental fiction, 14–15, 118, 185; entry into, 61–62, 71–72, 80, 135; forces mediating passage into, 155–56; as not Chinese, 74; WASP intellectual men of, 68, 72, 74, 75, 134. *See also* Assimilation
Minority groups: assimilation of, 7–8
Miscegenation: laws against, 29, 200 n.5; taboos, 103
Misogyny in male literary texts, 58, 126–27, 177
Mobility, tropes of: for Asian American men, 201 n.18; class (vertical and social), 72, 73–74, 78, 80, 130–32, 201 n.18; horizontal and geographic, 78, 201 n.18; and the *Jasmine* controversy, 128–38; overstated, 157–58; through marriage, 132–33; through sexual attraction, 135. *See also* Assimilation; Middle class
Model minority paradigm, 65
Modern Language Association, 194 n.21
Monkey's pilgrimage. *See* Wu Ch'eng-en
Moon allusions, 208 n.24
Mother-daughter plot, 143–44, 165–68, 211 n.3; and Chinese ethnicity, 22, 141–46, 186–87. *See also* Immigrant romance
Mother figures: abjection of, 54–60, 61, 90–91, 208 n.22; adapting well to change, 104–5; agency of Chinese American, 150–55; as both alien and familiar, 165–68; connection and continuity with, 91, 102–3; controlling, 54, 61, 149, 168; daughter's ignorance of, 146; disavowal of, 72,

76; immigrant, 98–105; remote, 80–81; unassimilable, 112–15

Mother-son relationships: separation and Americanness, 43, 54–60, 61, 90–91, 100, 112–15

Moyers, Bill, 82

Mukherjee, Bharati: and Far/Eaton, 136–38, 185; and the *Jasmine* controversy, 128–36, 185–86

Mukherjee, Bharati, works by, 18; *Jasmine*, 21, 90, 96, 97, 128–38, 185–86; *Wife*, 210 n.31

Mura, David: as author-hero, 20

Mura, David, works by: *Turning Japanese: Memoirs of a Sansei*, 79, 82, 84–85; *Where the Body Meets Memory*, 79–82, 83, 86, 87

Murayama, Milton, 20, 60–61; *All I Asking for Is My Body*, 54–55

Murder by a mother, 114–15, 121

Myths as immutable or open-ended, 172–73. *See also* Author-hero myth; Immigrant, myth of the

Nationalism narratives: gendered disjunction in, 52–53; and Japanese ethnicity, 55–60

National literature: and national identity, 10, 187, 194 n.20

Naturalization cases, 199 n.3

Necessity and extravagance: the tension between, 210 n.28

Negative images. *See* Stereotypes

Nisei generation. *See* Internment of Japanese Americans; *specific writer names*

No-No Boy. See Okada, John

Nonwhites: classifications of, 193 n.18, 195 n.24

Nostalgia: filial and homeland, 42–49

Novel: the classic Anglo-American, 33–34, 197 n.30, 200 n.11; the historical, 16, 174, 177–80, 197 n.30; the realist, 13, 14–15, 16, 96–97, 123, 197 nn.30, 31, 198 n.35; the sentimental, 14–15, 118, 185, 197 n.33. *See also* Bildungsroman; Chinese classics; Domestic novel

Oath, the Peach Orchard, 180

Oe, Kenzaburo: *A Personal Matter*, 88

Offspring. *See* Children

Okada, John, 20, 60–61, 70; themes of, 18

Okada, John, work by: *No-No Boy*, 55–60, 202 n.25

Okihiro, Gary Y., 194 n.20

Okimoto, Daniel, 191 n.7; Chin's criticism of, 66–67

Okimoto, Daniel, work by: *An American in Disguise*, 27, 28, 35

Omi, Michael, 8, 9

Omura, James, 70

Opera tradition: Chinese American, 174, 187

Oral narratives: immutable or improvised, 172

Orientalism: American anti-Asian, 193 n.16, 203 n.3; and Chinese alterity, 148–50, 159; and gendered polarization of American and Asian values, 102–3; racist love as, 65, 170–71; of white men toward Asian women, 135, 185, 207 n.20

Oriental Yankee. See Kang, Younghill

Ostrich metaphor, 82

Outlaws of the Marsh. See Shi Nai'an and Luo Guanzhong

Outsiders or others: construction of Asian Americans as, 9, 12, 20, 148; construction of women as, 179–80

Pa Chin: *Family*, 160–65, 213 n.18

"A Pair of Tickets" (in *The Joy Luck Club*), 167–68

Park, Robert E., 7–8

Parody: hostile, 214 n.2; postmodern, 172–73, 181, 214 n.4

Passing as white, 83, 101, 104–5

Paternity. *See* Fathering

Patriarchy: Chinese attitudes toward, 159–65; gendered recognition and support within, 94–95, 157; heroism and homosocial texts of, 177–80

Philippines, 44–46. *See also* Filipino Americans

Pilgrimage journey: Buddhist, 181–84

Pinoys. *See* Filipino Americans

Play: collective fashioning of a, 174–75

Plays: Chinese American, 71–79

Plots: Asian American authorship of, 19; interracial romance, 19–21; romantic triangle, 110–22; self-fathering, 71–79; well-married hero, 18–19, 88–89

Poetry: by a character, 33–34, 117–18; by Chinese immigrant bachelors, 21, 93, 123–28, 208 n.24

Political desire: and exclusion in the immigrant romance, 27–42; and gendering Asianness, 42–61; and male Americanization, 61–63

Political novels: Asian American difficulties with, 16

Politics: as peripheral in bildungsroman, 134; postcolonial Third World, 128–29

Pornography, food. See Food pornography

Postmodern writers: revision and parody by, 172–73, 181–84, 187, 214 n.4

Promiscuity: sexual, 48, 86–87, 125–26, 135

Pronouns: unclarity of we, they, and you, 3

Prostitution: of Asian women, 48, 125–26; of ethnicity, 214 n.7

Psychoanalysis and race, 83–84, 86

Puccini, Giacomo: Madama Butterfly, 185, 207 n.20

Quest plot, the: and filial nostalgia, 48–49; and romance plot, 201 n.18, 210 n.30

Racial conflict and the immigrant analogy, 7–9

Racial discrimination: and antifeminist feeling, 58; cultural history of, 9, 187; government remedies for, 192 n.13; internment era, 54–60, 66, 70; toward Asian Americans, 8–9

Racial formation, 8

Racial history of Asian Americans, 9, 187

Racial shadow, 204 n.12, 208 n.22

Racism: battles against, 103–4; as besetting Asian American males, 70, 170–71, 176; denial or repression of, 81–82, 186; heroic tradition response to, 170, 176, 187; indirect writing on, 16–17, 39; and literacy for Americanization, 40–41; ostrich metaphor denying, 82; and psychoanalysis, 83–84, 86

"Racist love" for Asian Americans. See Orientalism

Radway, Janice, 132

Readerly texts, 181; versus writerly texts, 171, 184

Readers: assimilation of, 9–12, 174, 184; interpellation of, 13

Realist fiction: and interpellation of reader, 13

Realist novel: the Anglo-American domestic, 15, 96–97, 123. See also Bildungsroman; Novel

Reconciliation: symbolic American-Chinese, 166–67

"The Red Candle" (in The Joy Luck Club), 151–53, 155–59

Relativism, cultural, 163

Renan, Ernest, 53, 195 n.25

Repressed or untold stories, 10–11

Return to homeland: theme of, 46–47, 114–15, 119, 166–68

Reviewers: misreadings by, 175

Richardson, Samuel, 15, 132, 197 n.32

Rivalry: and homosocial bonding, 177–80

Roberts, Moss (trans.). See Luo Guanzhong

Romance plot: and American success myths, 130, 132; the archetypal English heroine's, 132–33; Cinderella stories, 128–29; English novel of education, 130–31; and the Jasmine controversy, 131–36, 185–86; and quest plot, 201 n.18, 210 n.30; supplanting a homosocial plot, 179. See also Interracial romance plots; Marriage plots

Rubin, Gayle, 177

Said, Edward W., 194 n.20, 203 n.3

Sakurai, Patricia Ann, 28, 35

Sansei memoirs. See Mura, David, works by

Sati custom, Hindu, 209 n.25

Sato, Gayle Fujita, 56, 58

"Scar" and "Magpies" stories (in The Joy Luck Club), 153–55, 161

Scripture pilgrimage, 181–84

Secrets: telling family, 179–80, 208 n.21

Sedgwick, Eve Kosofsky, 177

Self: Western and Chinese concepts of, 213 n.14

Self-authoring, literary, 185, 211 n.7

Self-definition: American versus English perspectives on, 185–86; female and Asian American narratives of, 185–86, 199 n.42; intersubjective, 17–18, 68–69, 76–77, 199 n.42; "just say yes" fable of, 155, 158

Self-fathering, 185; in David Mura's memoirs, 79–89; in Frank Chin's plays, 71–79

Self representation: gender and race variations in, 4

Sentimental novel: Chinese American, 185; rise of the, 14–15

Sexual segregation: and contained attraction, 40–41; and exclusion practices, 28–29, 122; and female immigration, 200 n.4; and immigrant bachelor poetry, 21, 93, 123–28, 208 n.24

Shi Nai'an and Luo Guanzhong: *Outlaws of the Marsh* (*Water Margin*), 67, 70, 177

So, Christine, 6

Society, putative feminization of, 54, 61, 69, 75, 76

Sojourners. *See* Bachelors

Sollors, Werner: *Beyond Ethnicity*, 18, 19, 199 n.44

Sons. *See* Father-son relationships

Spence, Jonathan, 212 n.11

Spivak, Gayatri Chakravorty, works by: "Can the Subaltern Speak?" 79, 209 n.25; "The Post-colonial Critic," 204 n.9

Stereotypes: challenging, 174–75

Stereotypes of Asian Americans, 8–9, 187; by American reviewers, 175; as the model minority, 65; racist love, 65, 170–71

Stereotypes of Asians: anti-Chinese, 34, 101, 103–4, 124, 147, 148, 185; by Christians, 65–66; Chinese, 187; as greedy, 124; men, 166, 170–71, 176; Sikh nationalists, 129, 134; women, 5, 36–37, 49, 93, 121, 149–50, 185. *See also* Asian culture

Subaltern negotiation, 79, 179–80, 209 n.25

Subject formation: and abjection, 49–51, 54–60; authorship as central trope of, 19; national and individual narratives of, 10; poststructuralist model of, 10, 13, 195 n.23; unmarked, 14. *See also* Bildungsroman

Subjectivity, Asian American: becoming American, 187; constructed as masculine, 20, 61–63, 90–91, 137; as a dialectic, 6–7; the double problem of, 136–37; Eaton's construction of, 120; female, 21, 136–37; subaltern, 79, 136–37, 209 n.25; the two-worlds problem of, 146–50, 166–67

Success as an author: criticism of female, 94;

popular, 141; and postcolonial politics, 129–30

Success myths: American, 130–31, 132; English domestic novel, 131–33; entrenched contradictions of, 135

Suicides, 31–32, 56; Chinese women's, 154–55, 161, 164–65; Hindu *sati,* 209 n.25

Sumida, Stephen H., 57–58, 202 nn.22, 23

Sundquist, Eric J., 69, 202 n.2

Sun Tzu: *Art of War,* 177. *See also* Chinese classics

Survival, the trope of, 4, 11

Suzuki, Peter, 70

Swan feather image, 144–45, 147

Tan, Amy, work by: *The Joy Luck Club,* 22, 23, 141–68, 186–87, 212 nn.10, 13

Temporal distancing (allochronism), 148, 156, 159

Third World politics: and immigrant novels, 129–30, 134, 148

Traffic in women, 177

Triangular relationships: homosocial brotherhood, 180; romantic, 110–22, 185

Trilling, Lionel, 68

Tripmaster Monkey. See Kingston, Maxine Hong, works by

Trophy paradigm. *See* White women characters

Two-worlds problem, 146–50

Typist, the rival, 175–76, 182

"Ugly duckling" tale, Chinese American, 144–45

Verbal texts as shells, 183

Violence: anti-Asian, 193 n.19; innocence and random, 135–36; and nation founding, 195 n.25

Virtues: Buddhist, 182; martial homosocial, 177; middle-class domesticized, 14–15, 96–97, 123

Voice: Chinese poetry's double, 123–28; domestic novel focuses on, 15–16; Filipino struggles for, 36; membership based on, 2–3

"Waiting between the Trees" (in *The Joy Luck Club*), 158–59

Wald, Priscilla: *Constituting Americans,* 10, 11, 18

Waley, Arthur (trans.), *Monkey. See* Wu Ch'eng-en

Warfare: celebration of, 177; ideological, 171

Warrior, The Woman. See Kingston, Maxine Hong, works by

WASP culture. *See* Middle class

The Water Margin (*Outlaws of the Marsh*). *See* Shi Nai'an and Luo Guanzhong

Weglyn, Michi, 70

Western classics: Asian writers citing, 33–34, 200 n.11

Western culture: as labyrinth, 32; love of, 33

Westernization, 208 n.23

White: passing as, 83, 101, 104–5

White fathers: acceptance by, 83–84, 185

White intervention: criticism of, 119–20, 209 n.25

White men in female Asian American texts, 21, 93, 135–36

White-Parks, Annette (ed.), *Sui Sin Far/Edith Maude Eaton,* 99

White romantic partners: as symbols for America, 20–21, 199 n.44

White stereotypes. *See* Stereotypes of Asians

White women characters: contained sexual interest in, 40–41; fallen angel, 36–37; femme fatale, 36; as literary mentor or muse, 33, 37–39; moral instruction by, 116; as object of quest for America, 34, 62; political desire for, 27–42; stereotyped, 36–37; Western observer, 120

White women in female Asian American texts, 93, 108, 110–20, 209 n.25

White women in male Asian American texts, 20, 36–37; functions of, 42, 62, 91, 185; immigrant romances, 27–42, 185; the trophy paradigm of, 28, 35

Whitman, Walt, 173

Wilderness, the American: as nurturing female, 69

Winant, Howard K., 8, 9

Wolf, Margery, 154

The Woman Warrior. See Kingston, Maxine Hong, works by

Women: courtship as hard work by, 132; disinheritance of, 85; duty and allegiance of, 178–80; escaping the homeland, 151–55, 159; fat, prejudice against, 174–75; left in the homeland, 28–29, 122, 124; as outsiders in patriarchy, 175–76, 179–80; the traffic in, 177

Women, Asian American: as allies in Asian American subject formation, 91–92; emancipated, 126–27; exclusion of, 29, 91–92, 122, 123–28; personifying the homeland, 43, 54–60, 61, 90–91, 92, 100, 112–15; stereotypes of, 5, 36–37, 49, 93, 121, 149–50, 185

Women characters: Chinese American matchmaker, 107–8; domestic, 14–15, 81, 96–97, 117–18, 123, 132; as dramatic victims, 155; escaping the homeland, 151–55, 159; estranged homeland wives, 124–25; Indian immigrant, 128–38; knowledge and education of immigrant, 134, 155–59; lingering illness of, 118; as national or American subjects, 5, 136–37, 187; personal traits of immigrant, 152–53; representing socialization, 54, 61, 123; resisting Americanization, 110–16; self-empowerment by, 78–79, 155, 158; well-married hero, 18–19; writers, 33–35, 74–79, 107–8, 117–18, 146, 163, 169, 175–76. *See also* Asian women characters; Heroines; White women characters

Women's plots, 90–138, 205 nn.1-31; adapting, 17–18; Eaton's fictions of Americanization, 105–23; immigration narratives, 91, 92–93; intersubjectivity versus individualism in, 17–18; linking domestic women with nationalism, 206 n.12; mother figures in, 91; Mukherjee's *Jasmine,* 128–38, 186; revising classic Chinese stories, 177–80; romantic triangles, 110–22. *See also* Bildungsroman; Mother-daughter plot; Romance plot

Women writers: difficulties facing, 93–96; exclusion of, 67–69; as just typists, 175–76, 182

Women writers, Asian American: alternate tradition of, 127–28, 185; art and family responsibilities of, 96–97; authority of, 94–95, 97; as characters, 33–35, 74–79, 107–8, 117–18, 146, 163, 169, 175–76; Chin and "fake," 70–71, 74–75, 173, 181, 186; mediators for, 94–95; narrative strategies of, 5, 69, 70, 96–97, 185

Wong, Jade Snow: *Fifth Chinese Daughter,* 95

Wong, Sau-ling Cynthia, 159, 193 n.16, 204 n.12, 208 n.22

Wong, Shawn, 188–89. *See also* Chin, Frank, et al. (eds.)

Woolf, Virginia, 5

Work, courtship and marriage as hard, 132

Writerly texts, 9–12; versus readerly texts, 171, 184

Writing: as a dialogic process, 175–76, 181, 187; individual subject formation and national, 9–12

Wu Ch'eng-en: *The Journey to the West,* 180, 181–84

Wu San-kuei, 208 n.23

Yamamoto, Hisaye, works by, 95–96

Yamauchi, Wakako: life of, 206 n.10

Yamauchi, Wakako, works by: *Songs My Mother Taught Me,* 96

Yankee, Oriental. See Kang, Younghill

Yeats, William Butler, 34

Yu, Anthony C. (trans.). *See* Wu Ch'eng-en

Patricia Chu is Associate Professor in the Department
of English at George Washington University.

Library of Congress Cataloging-in-Publication Data
Chu, Patricia P.
Assimilating Asians : gendered strategies of authorship in
Asian America / Patricia P. Chu.
p.   cm. — (New Americanists)
Includes bibliographical references and index.
ISBN 0-8223-2430-x (cloth : alk paper).
ISBN 0-8223-2465-2 (paper : alk. paper)
1. American literature—Asian American authors—History and
criticism.   2. American literature—Women authors—History
and criticism.   3. National characteristics, American, in
literature.   4. Assimilation (Sociology) in literature.
5. Women and literature—United States.   6. Asian Americans
in literature.   7. Group identity in literature.   8. Authorship
—Sex differences.   9. Bildungsroman.   I. Title.   II. Series.
PS153.A84C485   2000
810.9'895073—dc21   99-33229   CIP